‖‖ ‖‖‖‖‖‖‖ ‖‖‖‖ ‖ ‖‖‖‖‖‖‖‖‖‖ ‖‖ ‖
W9-CPF-437

Praise for *Criminals of the Bible*

"For anyone who has ever wondered what it was like to live in the biblical world, here is a book that certainly paints the picture. It is a sobering reminder that many of the characteristics of the so-called outlaws of the Bible are often just under the surface of all of us and within our culture as well. But Mark Jones provides lessons of hope that can steer individuals and cultures back on the straight and narrow way ... . It is the kind of book that is not limited just to people of faith. These lessons apply to our world today."

—Dr. Ron Johnson
Professor and Associate Dean
McAfee School of Theology
Mercer University

"As a criminal justice scholar, dedicated churchman, and experienced Bible teacher, Mark Jones has produced a valuable resource in *Criminals of the Bible*. This book will be helpful to pastors, seminary students, Sunday School teachers, and small group leaders seeking to understand, teach, and apply these ancient stories to contemporary life. With sensitivity to the unique historical and cultural setting of the scriptural texts, Jones skillfully uncovers timeless truths that span the centuries between the biblical era and our time. I commend this book to anyone wishing not only to view the Bible from a fresh, new perspective, but also desiring to grow in faith and discipleship."

—Dr. Larry Hovis
Coordinator of the Cooperative
Baptist Fellowship of North Carolina

"This book is uniquely suited for a wide audience of readers interested in the Bible, criminal justice, or both. Biblical students will find it to be a unique exploration of some of the most notorious violent acts and characters in the Bible. Criminal justice students will find the book to be an insightful examination of how crimes played out in ancient literature. In *Criminals of the Bible*, Mark Jones has done a fine job intersecting two different fields that normally have very little overlap."

—Dr. Glenn Jonas
Chair, Dept. of Religion
Campbell University

CRIMINALS
OF THE BIBLE

Twenty-Five Case Studies of Biblical Crimes and Outlaws.

CRIMINALS
OF THE BIBLE

Twenty-Five Case Studies of Biblical Crimes and Outlaws.

MARK JONES

FaithWalk
PUBLISHING
Grand Haven, Michigan

©2006 Mark Jones

Published by FaithWalk Publishing
333 Jackson Street, Grand Haven, Michigan 49417
faithwalkpub.com

All rights reserved. No part of this book may be reproduced or transmitted in any form by any means, electronic or mechanical, including photocopying and record-ing, or by any information storage and retrieval system, except as may be expressly permitted by the 1976 Copyright Act or by the publisher. Requests for permission should be made in writing to: FaithWalk Publishing, 333 Jackson Street, Grand Ha-ven, Michigan, 49417.

Unless otherwise noted, Scriptures in the text contained herein are taken from the HOLY BIBLE, NEW INTERNATIONAL VERSION®. NIV®. Copyright ©1973, 1978, 1984 by International Bible Society. Used by permission of Zondervan. All rights reserved.

Scripture quotations marked NKJV are taken from The New King James Version / Thomas Nelson Publishers, Nashville : Thomas Nelson Publishers., Copyright © 1982. Used by permission. All rights reserved.

Printed in the United States of America

11 10 09 08 07 06   7 6 5 4 3 2 1

Library of Congress Cataloging-in-Publication Data

Jones, Mark (Gerald Mark)
 Criminals of the Bible : twenty-five case studies of biblical crimes and outlaws / Mark Jones.
 p. cm.
Includes bibliographical references.
ISBN-13: 978-1-932902-64-8 (pbk. : alk. paper)
ISBN-10: 1-932902-64-3
1. Crime in the Bible—Case studies. 2. Criminals—Biography. 3. Crime—Religious aspects—Christianity. I. Title.
BS680.C7J66 2006
220.8'364—dc22
2006020082

Dedication

This book is dedicated to five very special people in my life. First, to my parents, Herbert Jones, Jr. and Dorothy Jones, for being such great parents and loving me enough to provide a Christian home for me. This book is also dedicated to my son Sam Jones and my daughter Beth Jones. Thanks for all of the love and laughter you provide. Finally, I dedicate this book to the love of my life, my wife Donna Jones. I love you, too.

Contents

Foreword

Criminals of the Bible is an innovative and interesting bridge between then and now—a bridge that explores the complexity, ambiguity, despair, and triumph that is a part of the Bible's DNA. From Shakespeare to Jung to the likes of Mel Gibson, many have tried to describe and explain the human journey toward Ultimate Reality. The Bible, like no other document, embodies the human quest for experiencing and understanding the great mystery and our relationship to it. The lessons of human history remind us time and again that there can be no heroes without villains—no moral leaders without criminal conspirators. As if such lessons were not paradox enough, we find that today's hero may become tomorrow's villain and vice versa. David, the same person who as a youth stepped out in faith and proved that under God's direction long-shots can literally come in, later succumbed to his lust for Bathsheba by having her husband, Uriah the Hittite, killed. Saul of Tarsus, who served as a kind of Gestapo for the religious establishment of his day in persecuting followers of Jesus, was transformed into Paul, who cajoled, encouraged, and prodded those same followers into the beginnings of what has become known as Christianity.

If *Criminals of the Bible* accomplishes anything, I believe it is in trying to illuminate the timeless truths and lessons that Bible stories written long ago have for us today in contemporary society. The twenty-five case studies to which Mark Jones exposes us are as diverse and eclectic as the Bible itself. From the sibling rivalry of Cain and the brothers of Joseph, to the sexual lust of the men of Sodom and King David, to the greed of Solomon and the obsession with power of Saul, Pharoah and Jezebel, and Ahab, these outlaws both remind and warn us that such characters live on today in pornographers, sexual predators, corporate thieves, and political tyrants throughout our and other cultures. The good news is that the story does not have to end there. There are other kinds of outlaws—the ones who are unjustly labeled "outlaws"—the legal criminals who are, in fact, moral heroes. There was John the Baptist, who spoke against the sin of political tyranny and corruption and lost his head, but not his message. The untouchable and unworthy good Samaritan who crossed over to help the one in need while the religiously pious walked on. Most importantly, Jesus Christ, according to some, a blasphemer who associated with the unsavory characters of his day, was convicted and crucified for love's sake by the prevailing religious establishment. Yet even death and the grave could not silence the truth of his grace and mercy.

The Bible tells us that the Holy Spirit remains with us to guide and help us. The Holy Spirit is also referred to as the "spirit of truth"—one that both comforts and convicts. The outlaws Mark Jones writes about and invites us to explore and reflect upon offer us more than interesting insights and legal/moral considerations. They also offer us a choice: *What kind of outlaw will we choose to be?* Will we be an outlaw in the tradition of Stephen or Paul or will we be an active or passive apologist for those in power? Will we choose the wisdom and promises of the world or the foolishness and humility of the Spirit?

—Michael Braswell
Professor of Criminal Justice and Criminology
East Tennessee State University

Acknowledgments

I would like to extend my thanks to the fine folks at Faithwalk Publishing, especially to Dirk Wierenga for embarking on this project with me, and to Louann Werksma and Ginny McFadden for their meticulous copyediting and support. My thanks also go out to Ian North for lending his talents to promoting this book.

Introduction

"History is indeed little more than the register of the crimes, follies and misfortunes of mankind," said English historian Edward Gibbon.[1] Although the Bible is much more than a history book, it is also a history of the shortcomings and outright evil acts committed by human beings over many centuries. This book contains twenty-five accounts of biblical "crimes" and "outlaws." The meaning of the word "outlaw" has changed over the centuries. It is derived from the Old English word "outlawry," in which a person, as a result of offenses against the government, was deprived of the protections and benefits the law provided, such as the right to own property or the right of inheritance, as in the quasi-historical story of Robin Hood, who was forced to live outside the law after being deprived of the right to own or inherit his family's property. Therefore, using the original definition of outlaw, there are plenty of biblical figures who wore the outlaw label unjustifiably, provided they were accused of crimes they did not commit, or if they violated an unjust law. Today, the term is used to describe a person who intentionally and repeatedly violates the law.

What Is a Crime?

I encountered several challenges writing this book, one of which was deciding what constitutes a "crime." Studying biblical crime invites the same difficulty as studying crime from other eras. What we call a crime today may not have been a crime then. Selling alcohol in most areas of the United States is not a crime now, provided one is properly licensed; but it *was* a crime during the Prohibition-era 1920s. Conversely, a crime in a previous era may not be viewed as a crime today. Witchcraft and adultery, long viewed as crimes throughout history in a number of cultures, are viewed differently in Western culture today; the former is legal, and the latter, while still illegal in some jurisdictions, almost never results in arrest.

The same challenge occurs in studying crime across cultures. Many crimes in the United States are not crimes in other cultures, and vice versa. Polygamy is legal in many African countries, but not in the

United States. Alcohol consumption is legal in most places within the United States, but not in some Islamic countries. I once asked a colleague of mine about crime in his home country, India. He said that it is difficult to compare American crime with Indian crime. For example, if a person were to fire a gun into a crowd in India, there would be no arrest. It would not be unusual for the crowd to simply kill the assailant on the spot, without regard for any legal niceties and without concern for whether the crime was recorded by the government. While we try to keep an accurate account of the prevalence of crime in the United States, it is difficult to tell whether we have more crime now than in previous time periods, let alone in a time period and place as far removed as the biblical era, in cultures radically different from our own.

The Bible is replete with examples of evil acts, some of which were defined as crimes under the laws or customs that existed at that time, and some of which were not. This book contains some examples of behaviors that were treated as crimes in the biblical era, but which would not be viewed as crimes in the Western world of the twenty-first century. The book also includes examples of behaviors that we treat as crimes today, but which were viewed differently during the era in which that person lived. When I showed the list of "criminals" and "outlaws" for this book to other people, one of the first reactions when viewing some of the names was, "But that person did nothing wrong." This is true; some of the people discussed here were falsely accused of committing illegal acts, and others were guilty of breaking the law by their own admission, but they broke the law because they believed they were answerable to an authority higher than that of a civil government—the will of God.

We can learn many lessons from studying famous crimes. The Bible is a collection of many types of literature, one of which is historical. One of the benefits of studying history is the lesson we can learn from those who made it. We can learn from the mistakes made by biblical characters and the governments under which they lived. We learn that, as members of a civilized society, there are certain behaviors by which we must abide so that we can coexist in harmony.

We learn that there is great danger in allowing government officials to have unfettered power. Some of the crimes discussed here were committed under the protection of the existing government, and some were actually committed by government rulers and officials. Most biblical-era government leaders were temperamental, petty tyrants who tolerated little dissent and hated hearing the word "no."

This takes us back to the question about what constitutes a crime. Slavery, which is illegal around the world, is still practiced in many countries, although without the official approval of any government. If we judge slavery by modern moral and legal standards and call it a crime, then practically every society discussed in the Bible, from Pharaoh's Egypt to the Roman Empire, was a rogue regime.

The most important message of this book is that every life contains lessons for others. These cases present examples of astoundingly strong faith in God, of personal courage, of the dangers of taking our eyes off God, of the dangers of legal sins—such as coveting, lust, and jealousy—leading to illegal sins such as robbery, rape, and murder. These cases also remind us that there is no sin that is unforgivable. While intellectual lessons are certainly worth learning, spiritual lessons are even more important.

Which Crimes to Include?

Another challenging task was deciding which cases to include. Anyone else who wrote a book like this might use a different list. The cases I chose are those that struck me as significant. The only conclusion I can make is that there is no perfect set of criteria for selecting cases for a book like this. Of more importance are the lessons we can learn from these case studies. I hope that these cases provide better guidance for us as members of society, as citizens in a democracy, and, most importantly, in our Christian lives.

The Cultural Differences of Biblical Eras

In studying biblical crime, we should be aware of the differences between our culture and the cultures of that era. There are many differences, some of which have a bearing on how reactions to crime were treated. I identify four such cultural differences.

1. Cultural and Ethnic Superiority. Americans, at least officially, subscribe to the premise that all people are created equal. Although racial and ethnic prejudice is not absent from the United States, our legal system no longer formally recognizes the superiority of one ethnic group over another. This was not always true. Prior to the Civil War, many laws relegated slaves and free black citizens to inferior status. Similar laws applied to other ethnic minorities, including Chinese immigrants in the West and Hispanics in the Southwest. Jim Crow Laws enacted after the Civil War perpetuated the second-class status of African-Americans and upheld the order of segregation. Legalized discrimination was applied to women throughout American history, as well.

Given the egalitarian nature of twenty-first-century American culture, it is difficult to imagine ourselves having the same mindset as people in biblical cultures. Prejudice or outright hatred of other ethnic groups was the rule, not the exception. Coexistence and tolerance of other ethnic and religious groups were usually the best that one could hope for in many biblical cultures. Heartfelt acceptance and love of people from other ethnic groups were considered radical. Few people dared bridge ethnic gaps. Witness several instances in both the Old and New Testaments. The Mosaic Law did not recognize all nationalities as equal before the Law. Only fellow Israelites were entitled to certain protections, such as the right not to be held as a slave in perpetuity. During the New Testament era, Jews so despised their "mixed race" Samaritan "cousins" that they would travel hundreds of miles out of the way merely to avoid walking through Samaritan territory, which made the impact of Jesus's befriending the woman at the well much more profound to his contemporaries than it might seem to modern readers. One of the primary battles that the early Christian church faced was centered on this very issue. Many of the early apostles, Simon Peter among them, were reluctant to view other ethnic groups as equals.

If the people of a culture harbor such attitudes in personal dealings, those attitudes will inevitably infect the legal culture. The idea that a white person and a black person who commit similar crimes under similar circumstances should receive different treatment under the law—although we must recognize that the individual discretion utilized by criminal justice officials invariably invites personal prejudices—would offend most Americans and would not withstand legal scrutiny. In other societies, however, including those of biblical times, "color-blind" justice is the exception rather than the rule. Bible-era legal officials did not hesitate to recognize the rights of one group over another, be it the enhanced legal rights of Roman citizens, the rights of free people over slaves, the privileges of men over women, the privileges of native inhabitants over foreign immigrants, and so on.

2. Separation of Church and State. The First Amendment to the United States Constitution states: "Congress shall make no law respecting an establishment of religion, or prohibiting the free exercise thereof; or abridging the freedom of speech, or of the press; or the right of the people to assemble, and to petition the government for a redress of grievance." As a nation, we likely will never agree on how this Amendment should be interpreted and applied, but most of us agree that there should not be a government-operated church.

The modern view of church-state separation is not the same as that of many biblical writers; and when we read the Bible, we take a different view of the church-state separation idea as it is depicted there from how we view it in our modern culture. Because the nation of Israel was a theocracy, Old Testament writers labeled monarchs as either good or evil—based upon their religious practices, not on their political accomplishments. Monarchs that encouraged or coerced Yahweh worship, as did David, were labeled as good. Others—such as Ahab—who allowed other forms of worship were labeled evil. Old Testament Israel was unapologetically theocratic and discouraged religious pluralism.

3. Freedom of Speech. Not only are Americans free to worship as they see fit, they can express an unpopular religious view as well. The Bible and subsequent history are filled with examples of people being persecuted and killed simply for expressing unpopular religious or political views. The New Testament contains numerous examples of persecution simply for advocating a position contrary to the prevailing religious establishment; the stories of Stephen, John the Baptist, and Paul are such examples. Jeremiah is an example from the Old Testament.

4. An Independent Judiciary. The practice of judicial review, established in the early nineteenth century by the United States Supreme Court in *Marbury v. Madison*,[2] allows courts to review laws and render them null and void. Judicial review provides a check against abuse of authority by the legislative and executive branches of government.

When reading some of the accounts in this book, especially ones that involved an immoral action by a ruler or the application of an immoral law, think of what the outcome might have been if that government had had a strong and independent judiciary.

The Bible's Legal Eras

A fourth challenge, both from the standpoint of researching these case studies and understanding the legal and social nuances of them, is identifying and understanding the legal era in which the event took place. There are seven major legal eras in the Bible:

1. The Pre-Israel Era. From the first chapter of Genesis through the Exodus from Egypt, the nation of Israel did not exist. What held the families of the early patriarchs together was a series of informal rules and norms, rather than a codified legal system. Tribal and family custom governed the behavior of most major figures in Genesis, and kinship was the foundation of most ancient communities. This is not to say that there were no rules. Family rules and norms in a small community, though often unwritten, were understood by each member of the family and community. Practically all societies in human history have had some sort of formal rules or informal norms that its citizens are expected to obey, and all societies have enacted sanctions for violations.

Although the prominent figures in the book of Genesis did not live by written legal codes, some of the city-states around them did. The oldest known legal code is traceable to the Sumerians, an extinct people that lived in Mesopotamia. The Sumerian code of Urukagina was written around 2400 BC, several centuries before the Babylonian Code of Hammurabi, long thought to be the oldest legal code, was assembled.[3]

2. The Mosaic Era. This was the second major legal era in Bible history. The Mosaic Law, found in the books of Exodus, Leviticus, Numbers, and Deuteronomy, is thought to have been written around 1300 B.C. The foundation of the Mosaic Law is the Ten Commandments. The significance of the Ten Commandments cannot be overestimated. The Ten Commandments form the basis for the legal systems of three of the world's major religions: Judaism, Christianity, and Islam. The Ten

Commandments also form the basis of the rest of the Mosaic Law. It governed the Jews for thousands of years, but was alternately ignored and reinterpreted throughout the Old and New Testament periods.

3. The Judges Era. The period of the judges is the third major legal era of the Old Testament. This period, which lasted from around 1300-1100 B.C., was characterized by a lack of centralized leadership. The modern definition of judge does not apply to the judges of this period. The judges led primarily in times of crisis and were part prophet, part military commander, and part government dictator. The judges ruled by right of "divine inspiration." Once the crisis was past, the judge would often step down.[4] Mosaic Law continued to govern the Israelites, but, under the period of the judges, the Israelites were living a settled existence, in contrast to the nomadic lifestyle they were living at the time the Mosaic Law was written.

4. The Kings Era. The fourth era was the era of the kings. Responding to the cries of the people, Samuel, the spiritual and political leader of the Israelites during the last days of the judges, selected a king to rule over them. The cry from the people resulted from threats from hostile neighbors, all of whom were governed by kings. Being ruled by a king, the Israelites thought, would make them strong. Samuel followed the will of the people, despite his own warnings that appointing a king would be a mistake. It did not take long for Samuel's prediction to be fulfilled. Saul, the first king of Israel and one of the subjects of this book, acted very much in the manner of the tyrants that ruled other kingdoms in the Middle East. His reign was distinguished more by his own criminality, mental instability, and poor spiritual example than by any accomplishment that brought honor and glory to God or the Israelites.

The era of the kings was characterized by alternating periods of allegiance to Yahweh and worship of the pagan deities that were popular with Israel's neighbors. Some of the kings were fair and just; but arbitrary, cruel, and oppressive rulers—Saul and Ahab prominent among them—also characterized the period. While the Mosaic Law still ruled the Israelites, it too was alternately ignored, interpreted, and misapplied to suit the needs of those in authority.

This era also witnessed the division of Israel. Solomon, the son of David, was the last king of a united Israel. Following Solomon's death, the foolish actions of his son, Rehoboam, led to a rebellion among the ten northern tribes of Israel. The ten northern tribes formed the kingdom of Israel, governed by an equally foolish king named Jeroboam, while the remaining two southern tribes, governed by Rehoboam, formed the kingdom of Judah.

5. The Exile Era. The fifth major legal era was the exile period. After many generations of repeated admonitions to worship Yahweh, and after repeated warnings by a succession of prophets—including Jeremiah, the subject of one the forthcoming chapters—of dire consequences for not worshipping Yahweh, the Jews were attacked and carried into exile by the Babylonians around 600 B.C. The kingdom of Israel had fallen to the Assyrian empire over a century earlier.

Most Jews lived in captivity in Babylon for several decades and were subject to the laws of the Babylonians, which sometimes conflicted with the Mosaic Law. This era presents the issue of civil disobedience and whether it is ever right to intentionally ignore or violate a law that violates one's beliefs. Stories of great courage and faith emerge from the Babylonian captivity, such as the story of Daniel. The Jewish exile came to a gradual halt, culminating in a return to Jerusalem by most of the exiles in the fifth century B.C., thanks to the benevolence of the Persians, who had overthrown the Babylonian kingdom in the sixth century B.C. The reestablishment of Jerusalem ushered in the end of the Old Testament.

6. Between the Testaments. The 400-year period between the Old and New Testaments was characterized by a decline in Persian influence and a rise in the influence of first the Greeks—due in great measure to the efforts of Alexander the Great, who defeated the Persians around 331 B.C.—and then the Romans. Greek culture influenced the Jews, many of whom learned to speak Greek and read the works of the great Greek thinkers. Roman political and military rule eventually supplanted the Greeks. By the time of Jesus's birth, Jews in Palestine, along with most of the Middle East, North Africa, and southern Europe were under the dominion of the Romans.

The period between the Old and New Testaments was an eventful one for the Jews. It witnessed the Maccabean revolt around the second century B.C. and the formation of strident and militant Jewish nationalist groups dedicated to ridding Palestine of Roman influence.[5] Prominent among them were the Zealots, one of whom—Simon, a subject of this book—became one of Jesus's twelve disciples.

7. The Roman Era. The early Roman Republic was characterized by bold experiments in democracy and due-process rights for criminal defendants. By the time of Jesus's birth many of these due-process rights were gone. Roman citizens, including the apostle Paul, still enjoyed some due process and appellate rights. However, Jesus Christ and many early Christians were unjustly persecuted and killed by the Roman government. This period was also marked by tension between Roman officials and Jewish religious authorities. Jewish religious authorities wielded a considerable degree of power over their fellow Jews, and abuses of power occurred in that realm as well, including the persecutions of Jesus Christ, Stephen, and Paul. The Herodians were puppet Jewish kings who ruled at the pleasure of the Romans. They walked the fine line between maintaining control over their fellow Jews and keeping Jewish religious authorities and political radicals, such as Barabbas, from inciting rebellion. Many New Testament believers, including John the Baptist, suffered unjustly at the hands of these kings.

General Chapter Outline

Most of the chapters cover these points:

1. The scriptural reference for the crime;
2. A short biography of the principle character or characters;
3. The legal, social, and political definition and context of the crime for that era;
4. The same crime viewed through a modern legal, social, and political lens;
5. The lessons that can be learned from the crime, on a societal or individual level.

1

Cain | Murder

Genesis 4:1–15

1 Adam lay with his wife Eve, and she became pregnant and gave birth to Cain. She said, "With the help of the Lord I have brought forth a man." 2 Later she gave birth to his brother Abel.

Now Abel kept flocks, and Cain worked the soil. 3 In the course of time Cain brought some of the fruits of the soil as an offering to the Lord. 4 But Abel brought fat portions from some of the firstborn of his flock. The Lord looked with favor on Abel and his offering, 5 but on Cain and his offering he did not look with favor. So Cain was very angry, and his face was downcast.

6 Then the Lord said to Cain, "Why are you angry? Why is your face downcast? 7 If you do what is right, will you not be accepted? But if you do not do what is right, sin is crouching at your door; it desires to have you, but you must master it."

8 Now Cain said to his brother Abel, "Let's go out to the field." And while they were in the field, Cain attacked his brother Abel and killed him.

9 Then the Lord said to Cain, "Where is your brother Abel?"

"I don't know," he replied. "Am I my brother's keeper?"

10 The Lord said, "What have you done? Listen! Your brother's blood cries out to me from the ground. 11 Now you are under a curse and driven from the ground, which opened its mouth to receive your brother's blood from your hand. 12 When you work the ground, it will no longer yield its crops for you. You will be a restless wanderer on the earth."

13 Cain said to the Lord, "My punishment is more than I can bear. 14 Today you are driving me from the land, and I will be hidden from your presence; I will be a restless wanderer on the earth, and whoever finds me will kill me."

15 But the Lord said to him, "Not so; if anyone kills Cain, he will suffer vengeance seven times over." Then the Lord put a mark on Cain so that no one who found him would kill him.

THE PRINCIPAL CHARACTERS

Cain, the name given to the oldest son of Adam and Eve, means "spear" or "smith." He was a farmer, and his brother Abel tended flocks. The question of whether Cain, Abel, Adam, and Eve were real people—and whether Cain's story is literally true—has been debated ad infinitum in schoolrooms, courtrooms, and churches for centuries. Some readers treat the story as literal historical fact; some view the characters as symbolic; and others view the story as part of an ancient Hebrew creation story, noting that all ancient Middle Eastern societies passed down to succeeding generations a story of how civilization began. Such stories usually affirmed their religious beliefs or basic worldview, or their view toward a rival ethnic group. Clyde Francisco views Adam, Eve, Cain, and Abel as representative of humankind and our basic nature.[1]

Whether one views the Genesis account of Cain's life as a literal historical event, thus becoming entwined in unanswerable questions such as where Cain found his wife (Genesis 4:17),—or whether one views the story of Cain as a literary device—is beside the point for this book, which is to examine the lessons learned from this story. It is no coincidence that the writer of Genesis tells us that the first person to be born of man and woman was a remorseless murderer. The story of Cain is an insightful yet distressing tale of our inhumanity to each other, of man's basic predisposition toward evil, and a window on God's merciful response to the evil acts of human beings, even those who have no love for him. Cain embodies the Old Testament view of humankind's basic nature: selfish, jealous, petty, and violent.

THE CRIME AND PUNISHMENT

The seed of Cain's crime lay in his angry reaction to God's disapproval of his offering and God's approval of Abel's offering. The reason for God's disapproval of Cain's offering is not clearly provided, but a clue is found in verses 3 and 4, in which Cain merely brought "some" of his crop, probably some of his poorer crops, whereas Abel brought the "fat," or best, or "firstling" portions of his flock. When rebuked by

God, Cain exacerbates his sinful attitude by becoming sullen, angry, and jealous of Abel. God offered Cain a chance to repent and warned him of the dire consequences of sin, that sin was crouching at his door and seeking to devour him, which it did. Cain spurned God's warning.

Unlike the other crimes discussed in this book, Cain's crime was committed during an era in which there was no formal legal system to govern human behavior. The story of Cain is set prior to the adoption of any earthly legal framework such as the Ten Commandments, or any of its Middle Eastern antecedents. In instances where no legal code exists, tribal or familial customs usually govern behavior. Those who hold to a literal interpretation of Cain's story suggest that the people he feared (verse 14) were unmentioned relatives who, in accordance with family custom, would take revenge on anyone who harmed a member of the family. Subsequent passages in Genesis tell of other children born to Adam and Eve.

The story of Cain also introduces a common theme in Genesis and the Old Testament—sibling rivalry, an especially significant occurrence given that family and kinship—not the government or the church—was the strongest institution in ancient Middle Eastern society. This rivalry ends violently, and with the clear message from God that violence is an undesirable means of settling human differences.[2]

Cain's punishment may seem light to modern readers. If a person was exiled from his home today, it would not be extremely difficult to simply begin anew somewhere else, but Cain's punishment was not as light as it may appear. Exile has been a common punishment for lawbreakers since the beginning of human civilization. In many cultures, leaving one's home was (and is) a traumatic and risky proposition, as many societies throughout human history have a practice of being hostile to strangers or people of a different ethnic group, including those who stumble into their midst. Banishment is still imposed as a punishment in some communities today, especially in developing countries where many people live in small close-knit villages and are surrounded by unfriendly neighbors.

It is not unusual for a court to ban an offender from its jurisdiction, or for parole boards to ban offenders from the state in which they were convicted as a condition of release. Given the highly mobile nature of American society, with easy access to fast means of transportation, and given that it is much easier for an offender to live in obscurity, even in a small town, than it was in small communities where everyone knew their neighbors very well, such a punishment is very difficult to enforce. The legality of such punishments is suspect in the United States. In 1958, the United States Supreme Court ruled in *Trop v. Dulles* that stripping someone of his or her citizenship for wartime desertion from the military constituted cruel and unusual punishment.[3]

Cain's punishment involved more than exile. His livelihood suffered. The earth that had fed him would no longer yield crops. His life as a settled farmer was over. In the Septuagint, verse 12 reads, "Thou shalt be groaning and trembling upon the earth—the horror of thy crime shall ever haunt thee, and thou shalt never have any well-grounded hope that God will forgive the punishment thou deservest."[4] Worst of all, Cain not only had to endure physical separation from his roots, he lived the rest of his life apart from God, but that was Cain's choice, not God's. God essentially allowed Cain to choose his own punishment. In short, Cain, rather than choosing to be reconciled with God in spite of his crime, chose a lifetime of misery.

Cain was never confronted by another human being for the murder of his brother. He was confronted by God and expressed no remorse. His only concern was for himself. Apparently, even God cannot, or at least will not, force a person to feel remorse for his or her wrong deeds. John Braithwaite, an Australian criminologist, writes, "Remorse that is demanded is remorse that is destroyed. Demanding, coercing, or even expecting remorse or apology may be a bad objective."[5] God punished Cain by denying him the fruits of his labor and by turning him out of his home. Genesis 4:16 states that Cain settled in the land of Nod and started a family, though whether he actually lived a settled life is in doubt, as Nod means "wandering," suggesting that Cain lived the rest of his life as a nomad.[6]

THE CRIME NOW

Murder is the most serious crime in contemporary times, and the only one that carries a possible death sentence in some (thirty-nine) states and in federal courts. Modern legal systems recognize several categories of murder, and the definitions vary by jurisdiction. There are three generic definitions of murder:

1. Murder: Intentionally causing the death of another without reasonable provocation or legal justification, or causing the death of another while committing or attempting to commit another crime;

2. Murder in the First Degree: A killing done with premeditation and deliberation or, by statute, in the presence of other aggravating circumstances;

3. Murder in the Second Degree: A killing done with intent to cause death but without premeditation and deliberation.[7]

Based on two factors, we can conclude that Cain's crime was premeditated. First, his sullenness at God's rebuke indicated he developed a seething hostility toward God and Abel that eventually would boil over. Second, Cain lured his brother to a secluded spot, away from the rest of the family, no doubt with premeditation of killing him. No details of the slaying are given.

 In the Old Testament and throughout much of human history, the prescribed punishment for murder in many legal systems has been the death penalty. In the books of Exodus, Leviticus, and Deuteronomy, God's Law, as given to Moses, commands capital punishment for more than thirty offenses, including murder. But the Mosaic Law was written long after the story of Cain and Abel.

MODERN DAY IMPLICATIONS

Many death penalty advocates argue that God approves of, or even commands, capital punishment in cases of premeditated murder. In the case of Cain, God, rather than any human intermediary, was the direct arbiter of Cain's crime, and God alone meted out the punishment. Since God imposed Cain's punishment directly, the case should tell us in clear terms how God thinks a murderer should be punished. If God commands capital punishment for murder, and if his will and nature are eternal and unchanging, why did he not strike Cain dead for his crime, especially given Cain's lack of remorse? God not only spared Cain's life, he protected Cain from anyone seeking vengeance or seeking to harm him, much like contemporary law enforcement does to protect convicted and suspected criminals from vigilante justice. Blood feuds have been an integral part of most societies throughout human history, especially in communities without a strong government to formally administer justice. Based on this passage, it seems that God took an equally or more disdainful view of blood feuds and vigilantism as murder.

D.R. Biddy states, "That the motivation for this murder had its origins in a worship environment, in the shadow of the altar, can only be described as ironic."[8] Cain's crime laid the foundation for murder in the name of religion, which persists to this day and pervades all major religions, including Judaism, Christianity, and Islam, all of which trace their beginnings to the book of Genesis. From the bloody religious battles of the Middle Ages to the unceasing violence between Protestants and Catholics in Northern Ireland to the tragic events of September 11, 2001 and the uproar in some parts of Islam in 2006 over the publication in Denmark of cartoons mocking Mohammed, religion continues to be the motivation for all sorts of violent behavior.

Lessons for Individual Christians

One course that I have taught for many years is Criminal Justice Ethics, and I have led numerous ethics workshops for police and probation officers over the years. Very often, when people suggest that criminal justice professionals need ethics training, they think of behaviors such as the brutal beating of Rodney King at the hands of Los Angeles police officers in 1991. Whenever I lead a workshop or teach a course on criminal justice ethics, I focus on legal behaviors instead of illegal behaviors. By the time someone commits a serious crime, it is too late for ethics. Ethics is the study of right and wrong, not legal and illegal. The seeds of illegal behaviors are legal behaviors. It is not against the law to hate someone or to have a selfish or jealous attitude; it sometimes becomes illegal when we act on those attitudes.

J.S. Exell states that the murder of Abel is a lesson in

1. The power of envy;
2. The ambition of selfishness, and
3. The quick development of passion.[9]

Murder was Cain's crime, but it was the end result of other sins. Cain's initial sin was not giving his best to God. When confronted by

God about his crime, Cain initially lied and asked sarcastically if he was his brother's keeper. Matthew Henry's Commentary states that Cain "flies in the face of God himself," and should have humbly stated, "Am I not my brother's murderer?"[10] God did not answer Cain directly, but his response suggests that we are indeed our brother's keepers. It was at that point that God presented Cain with the gravity of his sin and pronounced sentence. Despite Cain's unrepentant attitude, God still showed mercy on him. The unknown "mark" placed on Cain was not a curse, but protection.[11]

The Hope

One question that cannot be answered is what God's response would have been had Cain repented of his sin. We do not know whether God would have spared Cain any punishment had he repented. Like many people today, Cain's pride and stubbornness knew no end. Also, as with many criminal offenders today, Cain complained about his punishment, even though the punishment was lenient and resulted mostly from his own intransigence.

What lesson can be learned from Cain? He certainly does not serve as any sort of role model. All sinful acts, including many crimes that people commit today, are the end product of sinful attitudes that they carry with them. Hate, greed, envy, and jealousy are not illegal, but they can easily lead to behaviors that are. When we harbor such sinful attitudes and thoughts, we are confronted by God and given the chance to repent. God confronts us in a different manner than he did Cain, who did not have access to biblical Scripture, Christian leaders, and friends. Very often, modern Christians, like Cain, choose to hold on to their sinful attitudes, ignoring God's command to repent.

Clyde Francisco also states that Cain's reply to God's sentence was, "My iniquity is more than I can bear," followed by a lament about the gravity of his punishment.[12] All human beings are like Cain, in that we cannot bear our iniquity on our own. Fortunately we do not have to. We know from the story of Cain that God offers the opportunity for repentance and for a close walk with him, and that sin cannot overtake us if we walk closely with God.

2

The Men of Sodom | Attempted Rape

Genesis 18: 16–33 & 19:1–25

16 When the men got up to leave, they looked down toward Sodom, and Abraham walked along with them to see them on their way. 17 Then the Lord said, "Shall I hide from Abraham what I am about to do? 18 Abraham will surely become a great and powerful nation, and all nations on earth will be blessed through him. 19 For I have chosen him, so that he will direct his children and his household after him to keep the way of the Lord by doing what is right and just, so that the Lord will bring about for Abraham what he has promised him."

20 Then the Lord said, "The outcry against Sodom and Gomorrah is so great and their sin so grievous 21 that I will go down and see if what they have done is as bad as the outcry that has reached me. If not, I will know."

22 The men turned away and went toward Sodom, but Abraham remained standing before the Lord. 23 Then Abraham approached him and said: "Will you sweep away the righteous with the wicked? 24 What if there are fifty righteous people in the city? Will you really sweep it away and not spare the place for the sake of the fifty righteous people in it? 25 Far be it from you to do such a thing—to kill the righteous with the wicked, treating the righteous and the wicked alike. Far be it from you! Will not the Judge of all the earth do right?"

26 The Lord said, "If I find fifty righteous people in the city of Sodom, I will spare the whole place for their sake."

27 Then Abraham spoke up again: "Now that I have been so bold as to speak to the Lord, though I am nothing but dust and ashes, 28 what if the number of the righteous is five less than fifty? Will you destroy the whole city because of five people?"

"If I find forty-five there," he said, "I will not destroy it."

29 Once again he spoke to him, "What if only forty are found there?"

He said, "For the sake of forty, I will not do it."

30 Then he said, "May the Lord not be angry, but let me speak. What if only thirty can be found there?"

He answered, "I will not do it if I find thirty there."

31 Abraham said, "Now that I have been so bold as to speak to the Lord, what if only twenty can be found there?"

He said, "For the sake of twenty, I will not destroy it."

32 Then he said, "May the Lord not be angry, but let me speak just once more. What if only ten can be found there?"

He answered, "For the sake of ten, I will not destroy it."

33 When the Lord had finished speaking with Abraham, he left, and Abraham returned home.

19:1 The two angels arrived at Sodom in the evening, and Lot was sitting in the gateway of the city. When he saw them, he got up to meet them and bowed down with his face to the ground. 2 "My lords," he said, "please turn aside to your servant's house. You can wash your feet and spend the night and then go on your way early in the morning."

"No," they answered, "we will spend the night in the square."

3 But he insisted so strongly that they did go with him and entered his house. He prepared a meal for them, baking bread without yeast, and they ate. 4 Before they had gone to bed, all the men from every part of the city of Sodom—both young and old—surrounded the house. 5 They called to Lot, "Where are the men who came to you tonight? Bring them out to us so that we can have sex with them."

6 Lot went outside to meet them and shut the door behind him 7 and said, "No, my friends. Don't do this wicked thing. 8 Look, I have two daughters who have never slept with a man. Let me bring them out to you, and you can do what you like with them. But don't do anything to these men, for they have come under the protection of my roof."

9 "Get out of our way," they replied. And they said, "This fellow came here as an alien, and now he wants to play the judge! We'll treat you worse than them." They kept bringing pressure on Lot and moved forward to break down the door.

10 But the men inside reached out and pulled Lot back into the house and shut the door. 11 Then they struck the men who were at

the door of the house, young and old, with blindness so that they could not find the door.

12 The two men said to Lot, "Do you have anyone else here—sons-in-law, sons or daughters, or anyone else in the city who belongs to you? Get them out of here, 13 because we are going to destroy this place. The outcry to the Lord against its people is so great that he has sent us to destroy it."

14 So Lot went out and spoke to his sons-in-law, who were pledged to marry his daughters. He said, "Hurry and get out of this place, because the Lord is about to destroy the city!" But his sons-in-law thought he was joking.

15 With the coming of dawn, the angels urged Lot, saying, "Hurry! Take your wife and your two daughters who are here, or you will be swept away when the city is punished."

16 When he hesitated, the men grasped his hand and the hands of his wife and of his two daughters and led them safely out of the city, for the Lord was merciful to them. 17 As soon as they had brought them out, one of them said, "Flee for your lives! Don't look back, and don't stop anywhere in the plain! Flee to the mountains or you will be swept away!"

18 But Lot said to them, "No, my lords, please! 19 Your servant has found favor in your eyes, and you have shown great kindness to me in sparing my life. But I can't flee to the mountains; this disaster will overtake me, and I'll die. 20 Look, here is a town near enough to run to, and it is small. Let me flee to it—it is very small, isn't it? Then my life will be spared."

21 He said to him, "Very well, I will grant this request too; I will not overthrow the town you speak of. 22 But flee there quickly, because I cannot do anything until you reach it." (That is why the town was called Zoar.)

23 By the time Lot reached Zoar, the sun had risen over the land. 24 Then the Lord rained down burning sulfur on Sodom and Gomorrah—from the Lord out of the heavens. 25 Thus he overthrew those cities and the entire plain, including all those living in the cities—and also the vegetation in the land.

THE PRINCIPAL CHARACTERS

None of the Sodomite men, except Lot, are mentioned by name. We only know that they were extremely depraved, not only as evidenced by their actions in Genesis 19, but because they had been condemned in the previous chapter for unspecified sins.

There were other principal characters involved in this story, spread over Chapters 18 and 19. One was Abraham, the Old Testament patriarch who pleaded with God to spare the city for the sake of ten righteous men. Abraham is reduced to the role of observer in Genesis 19. Another was Lot, the nephew of Abraham, who had settled in Sodom sometime earlier. Lot is one of the most tragic figures in Genesis, his gradual physical, economic, and moral decline presented throughout the book. In fact, some Bible scholars see Lot as the central figure in Genesis 19, viewing the men of Sodom as mere ancillary figures in his terrible life story.[1] Genesis 13 states that Lot settled near Sodom because of its fertile landscape. By Chapter 19, Lot had become a prominent citizen in Sodom, evidenced by the fact that he was found sitting at the city gates, which indicated that Lot served as a magistrate who resolved disputes.[2] Lot's wife, whose name is not mentioned, is remembered only because of the fate she suffered for looking back at the doomed city. Lot's daughters reappear later in Genesis 19, when they purposely get their father drunk and have him impregnate them.

A great deal of debate about this passage centers on what made the men of Sodom evil. Was it because they were homosexual, or was it because they were homosexual rapists? Neither of those acts was actually committed in this passage, but it is clear that the homosexual population in Sodom was very powerful. Unlike many societies where homosexuality is driven underground, Sodom's men were open about their homosexuality. Note in Chapter 19 that when the angels told Lot they would sleep in the public square, Lot urged them not to, believing justifiably that they would not be safe from his fellow Sodomites. It is also clear that they plotted to gang rape Lot's two male "visitors." Not even Lot's offer of his two daughters placated their urge to rape the two men.

Contemporary sensitivities notwithstanding, the Bible clearly condemns homosexuality in both the Old and New Testaments. The Mosaic Law (Leviticus 18:22) calls sexual relations between men a detestable offense punishable by death.[3] The term "sodomite" (Hebrew *qadhesh*) was used in subsequent passages of the Old Testament to describe a male temple prostitute who was used in heathen worship rituals.[4] The

Sodomites served as symbols of debauchery in the Old Testament. Paul condemns homosexuality in two of his New Testament letters, calling it wicked (1 Corinthians 6:9) and a perversion (Romans 1:27).

 The word "sodomy" is derived from this passage. Sodomy involves placing one's mouth on a man's sex organ or placing the male sex organ in the anus. Throughout American history, sodomy has been criminalized in many jurisdictions. Although some anti-sodomy statutes have included both heterosexual and homosexual relationships, the primary targets of these laws have been homosexuals. Another rationale for some anti-sodomy statutes has been a prohibition against sex for non-procreative purposes. In some instances, sodomy is synonymous with the term "crime against nature" or "deviant sexual intercourse."

Throughout most of American history, consensual sodomy was not prohibited by criminal law, even though it was considered a social taboo. It was not until the middle portion of the twentieth century that states singled out homosexuals for criminal prosecution.[5] As recently as 1986, the constitutionality of an anti-sodomy law in Georgia was upheld by the United States Supreme Court in *Bowers v. Hardwick*.[6] In 2003, the United States Supreme Court effectively struck down anti-sodomy laws in *Lawrence v. Texas*, overturning the 1986 Bowers ruling.[7] The *Lawrence* case makes it unconstitutional for states or localities to ban homosexual relations between consenting adults.

Forced sodomy involving a man and a woman is practically synonymous with rape. Homosexual rape is another matter. Not only is this behavior a perennial scourge of prison life, it is one of the great hidden crimes in modern society. Many cases of homosexual rape go unreported to authorities, both in correctional institutions and in the community. To admit being raped still carries stigmas for females, but the stigma is even greater for males. Many males see such victimization as a sign of weakness, and they perceive, sometimes justifiably, that their allegations will not be taken seriously. In one self-report study, 12 percent of a sample of gay men reported that they had been the victim of forced sodomy. A German study reported a 16-percent rate and a group of British researchers reported that 28 percent of their sample had been victims of homosexual rape. Virtually none of the cases (in any of these countries) were reported to authorities. Some were raped by acquaintances or dating partners while others reported being raped by strangers, usually as a result of frequenting homosexual pick-up areas.[8]

THE PUNISHMENT

All of the inhabitants of Sodom were killed, not just for the attempted rape of the two visitors, but because they had, in God's eyes, become so depraved and evil that they had to be destroyed. In Genesis 18, the "men" who visited Abraham said that God was going to destroy the city, but they offered one last chance at repentance. Abraham pleads with God to spare the city if ten righteous people are found, no doubt considering the welfare of Lot. This does not happen, and everyone in the city dies, except for Lot, his wife, and their two daughters. Actually, God destroyed at least four cities—Sodom, Gomorrah, Admah, and Zeboiim (Genesis 13:10, Deuteronomy 29:23, Jeremiah 49:18). The NIV states that God destroyed the cities by raining down fire and sulfur on them. The RSV uses the phrase "brimstone" and fire. Clyde Francisco ventures that the brimstone and fire may have been petroleum gases ignited by subterranean fires.[9]

Lessons for Today

This story is often used as a justification for criminalizing homosexual relations, or at least as strong evidence that the Bible condemns homosexuality. While the Bible condemns homosexuality, it is not clear whether homosexuality should be equated with other serious crimes such as rape or murder, or whether it is homosexual rape that should be criminalized.

One of the great dangers of studying this story is that we may believe that every tragic act that befalls any community, city, state, or country is a sign of God's vengeance. For instance, there were some murmurs that Hurricane Katrina of 2005 was God's judgment on the city of New Orleans, because of New Orleans' long history of tolerating vice crimes and other unsavory activities in its French Quarter. In the eyes of some, every earthquake that strikes the California bay area is God's judgment on San Francisco's tolerance of the gay lifestyle.

Bible history shows that God does visit divine retribution on entire communities that flagrantly flout his will, but Christians should be careful when they try to attach divine motives for every natural disaster that befalls a population they do not like. If a Christian ascribes divine judgment as the reason for natural disasters that strike New Orleans or San Francisco, how does one explain a natural disaster that occurs in other areas, where the general population may be more devoted to traditional Christian ideals? The area in which I live, eastern North Carolina, has been struck by several hurricanes and floods. In 1999, more than fifty people in our area died as a result of Hurricanes Floyd and Dennis. Was God visiting his wrath on eastern North Carolina, a politically and religiously conservative part of the Bible belt, just as some claimed he did in 2005 with New Orleans and the Gulf Coast? The truth is that, while we can gain a clear idea of what is right or wrong on many moral issues by studying the Bible, we tread in dangerous waters when we try to ascertain God's motives for all the tragedies that befall individuals or communities.

The Hope

The hope from this story can be found in Genesis 18. Even though the men of Sodom had been engaged in a depraved lifestyle for some time (their depravity was first mentioned in Genesis 13), God still offered to save the lives of all of the inhabitants, even if only a few repented, but they would not. We do not know what other evil acts occurred in Sodom and the other cities of the plain, but threats of public rape give us some idea of how depraved they had become. While we never know exactly why God allows tragedies to befall us, we know from the story of Sodom that God can impose his divine punishment on us for our misdeeds, but he also stands ever ready to offer forgiveness for our sins.

3

Shechem, Dinah, Simeon, and Levi | Fornication and Murder

Genesis 34:1–31

1 Now Dinah, the daughter Leah had borne to Jacob, went out to visit the women of the land. 2 When Shechem son of Hamor the Hivite, the ruler of that area, saw her, he took her and violated her. 3 His heart was drawn to Dinah daughter of Jacob, and he loved the girl and spoke tenderly to her. 4 And Shechem said to his father Hamor, "Get me this girl as my wife."

5 When Jacob heard that his daughter Dinah had been defiled, his sons were in the fields with his livestock; so he kept quiet about it until they came home.

6 Then Shechem's father Hamor went out to talk with Jacob. 7 Now Jacob's sons had come in from the fields as soon as they heard what had happened. They were filled with grief and fury, because Shechem had done a disgraceful thing in Israel by lying with Jacob's daughter—a thing that should not be done.

8 But Hamor said to them, "My son Shechem has his heart set on your daughter. Please give her to him as his wife. 9 Intermarry with us; give us your daughters and take our daughters for yourselves. 10 You can settle among us; the land is open to you. Live in it, trade in it, and acquire property in it."

11 Then Shechem said to Dinah's father and brothers, "Let me find favor in your eyes, and I will give you whatever you ask. 12 Make the price for the bride and the gift I am to bring as great as you like, and I'll pay whatever you ask me. Only give me the girl as my wife."

13 Because their sister Dinah had been defiled, Jacob's sons replied deceitfully as they spoke to Shechem and his father Hamor. 14 They said to them, "We can't do such a thing; we can't give our sister to a man who is not circumcised. That would be a disgrace to us. 15 We will give our consent to you on one condition only: that you become like us by circumcising all your males. 16 Then we will give

you our daughters and take your daughters for ourselves. We'll settle among you and become one people with you. 17 But if you will not agree to be circumcised, we'll take our sister and go."

18 Their proposal seemed good to Hamor and his son Shechem. 19 The young man, who was the most honored of all his father's household, lost no time in doing what they said, because he was delighted with Jacob's daughter. 20 So Hamor and his son Shechem went to the gate of their city to speak to their fellow townsmen. 21 "These men are friendly toward us," they said. "Let them live in our land and trade in it; the land has plenty of room for them. We can marry their daughters and they can marry ours. 22 But the men will consent to live with us as one people only on the condition that our males be circumcised, as they themselves are. 23 Won't their livestock, their property and all their other animals become ours? So let us give our consent to them, and they will settle among us."

24 All the men who went out of the city gate agreed with Hamor and his son Shechem, and every male in the city was circumcised.

25 Three days later, while all of them were still in pain, two of Jacob's sons, Simeon and Levi, Dinah's brothers, took their swords and attacked the unsuspecting city, killing every male. 26 They put Hamor and his son Shechem to the sword and took Dinah from Shechem's house and left. 27 The sons of Jacob came upon the dead bodies and looted the city where their sister had been defiled. 28 They seized their flocks and herds and donkeys and everything else of theirs in the city and out in the fields. 29 They carried off all their wealth and all their women and children, taking as plunder everything in the houses.

30 Then Jacob said to Simeon and Levi, "You have brought trouble on me by making me a stench to the Canaanites and Perizzites, the people living in this land. We are few in number, and if they join forces against me and attack me, I and my household will be destroyed."

31 But they replied, "Should he have treated our sister like a prostitute?"

THE PRINCIPAL CHARACTERS

Shechem was the son of Hamor, the leader of the region where Jacob had settled. The story implies that he was accustomed to getting whatever he wanted, no matter the cost to others. This passage contains the only mention of Jacob's daughter. Given that the ancient Near East was such a male-centered society, it is not surprising that the female offspring of a prominent man like Jacob would receive scant mention; and here Dinah is portrayed almost as a subordinate child, subject to the control of the men in her life—her brothers, her father, sexual partner, and his father. Such was the life of women in that culture.

Jacob, whose name was changed by God to Israel in Genesis 32:28, was one of the great patriarchs of the Old Testament. The son of Isaac and the grandson of Abraham, his name alone makes him one of the most important figures in world history. Given the natural improbability of any man fathering thirteen children, and only one being a female, it is likely that Jacob had more daughters who are never mentioned, especially given that verse 21 contains reference to other daughters that Jacob may have had. Dinah's mother was Leah, Jacob's (unloved) first wife whom he married because of a deception hatched by Leah's father (Genesis 29: 16–35).

Like Dinah, Simeon and Levi were two of Leah's six sons, which explains their anger toward Shechem. Apparently Simeon and Levi saw the need to avenge their sister's honor when they realized that their father would not. Simeon and Levi reappear several times in the Joseph narratives.

Was Dinah raped? Biblical translations differ on this question. Some translations (*New American Standard, New Living Translation, The Living Bible*) use the word rape, or state that Shechem forced Dinah to have intercourse with him. Other translations suggest that Dinah consented. Bruce Waltke states that the Hebrew wording for "saw" and "took" is the same as that describing the actions of unrestrained tyrants in Genesis 6:2. The Hebrew word *halot*, used to describe the nature of their intercourse, means "to do violence … to rape a woman."[1] Whether Dinah was raped or consented to have intercourse with Shechem, which means the two committed fornication, is not answered definitively. Although her exact age at the time of this occurrence cannot be exactly determined, she was probably somewhere between thirteen and sixteen years old, old enough to marry in ancient Near East society.

Verse 1 states that Dinah "went out to visit the women of the land," which suggests that she was actively pursuing a social life with the Hivites. It also suggests that Dinah was heading for trouble. For a young woman to venture unaccompanied into the domain of heathen foreigners was foolhardy. In the course of seeking these inadvisable social ties, she developed a relationship with Shechem, the son of the Hivite ruler.

Even if Shechem and Dinah's sexual encounter was consensual, Dinah had violated the customs and mores of her family; and her brothers felt that their younger sister's honor had been defiled by a wealthy, manipulative, heathen outsider. After their sexual encounter, Shechem took the honorable route (albeit too late) of asking Dinah's male relatives for her hand in marriage. Jacob's mild reaction suggests that he thought the sexual relationship was consensual, or that he feared making enemies of Shechem and his family. Shechem may have been dealing with Jacob and his sons in a dishonest way, keeping Dinah, perhaps without her consent, in his house, in effect negotiating with her family as she was being kept captive.[2] Even though avenging the honor of a young sister was considered noble or at least understandable in that culture, the brothers went far beyond merely evening the score for their sister's dishonor. Rather than honestly confront Shechem, perhaps realizing that they could not win a man-to-man battle with Shechem and his father's subjects, the brothers tricked Shechem and all of the men in the region and went to the savage length of murdering all of them, taking advantage of their weakened condition; thus going way beyond the bounds of acceptable behavior even for that setting, and compounding their crime by looting their murder victims' possessions and kidnapping the women in the territory.

What makes the brothers' behavior even more egregious is that that they used circumcision as a tool in their deception. Circumcision, first commanded by God to Abraham in Genesis 17, was more than a physical act; it served as the symbol of a sacred covenant between God and Abraham's descendants, including the sons of Jacob. Here, Jacob's sons used this holy covenant to further their own bloody vendetta. Only Simeon and Levi (and probably their servants) participated in the massacre, but the other eight brothers compounded the crime by partaking in the looting. Jacob did not forget this incident. On his deathbed, he cursed Simeon and Levi for their violence and impetuosity (Genesis 49:5–7).

THE CRIME TODAY

Doing what the brothers did in this passage would certainly be illegal and socially unacceptable in today's society. However, a few Jewish extremists use this story to justify murderous atrocities, despite Jacob's rebuke. Alan Dershowitz points to Baruch Goldstein, who supposedly used this story to justify the February 25, 1994 murder of twenty-nine Muslims praying in Hebron.[3] There is a story common to criminal justice textbooks about an early twentieth-century immigrant to the United States who found himself in a position similar to Jacob's. The immigrant's teenaged daughter had been "seduced" by a local boy of about the same age. The girl's father—upon finding that his daughter's virginity had been lost, thus making her "damaged goods" in the marriage "market"—killed the young man. The assumption in this immigrant's culture was that young women did not have the maturity to make such a decision on their own, and that any man who did such a thing would know that such an action would merit deadly vengeance. The immigrant was shocked when the police arrested him for murder. In this immigrant's native culture, killing the young man was not only legal and socially acceptable, it was expected. Not killing the young man further dishonored the family and suggested that the father was unwilling or unable to protect his family.

Voluntary fornication, defined as sexual relations outside of marriage, is still illegal in some states, but the prohibition is seldom enforced. However, a personal "war story" is in order here. When I worked as a probation officer in the 1980s for the Georgia Department of Corrections, one of my probationers was arrested for fornication. This unmarried young man had been caught having sexual relations with a married woman, and the woman's husband had taken warrants, one charging my probationer with fornication, the other charging his wife with adultery. The charges were dropped before the case went to trial, but I was surprised to discover that laws prohibiting fornication and adultery were still in place, and even more surprised to find a magistrate who would issue a warrant for these crimes.

The Lesson

This story gives a lesson in the consequences of taking justice into one's own hands. Of course Levi and Simeon had no legal recourse at that time, but their actions could hardly be justified under any legal or social code. First, their sister may have been a willing participant in this encounter, in which case they had no real call for vengeance, at least by modern standards. Second, if Dinah was raped, justice, at least by modern standards, would have called for Shechem to be punished, but not murdered. Third, even if the killing of Shechem could be justified, the murder of his fellow tribesmen cannot, especially given Simeon and Levi's use of the circumcision rite to carry out the plan. Fourth, the subsequent looting of the town, including kidnapping the city's female inhabitants, cannot be justified, or connected in any moral sense to the brothers' desire for avenging their sister.

The doctrine of "an eye for an eye" or *lex talionis*, was adopted under Mosaic Law in part to avert the sort of behavior exhibited by Simeon and Levi. The eye-for-an-eye doctrine was meant to control vengeful behavior and limit the punishment. It would not have called for the killing of all the inhabitants, let alone for the looting that occurred afterwards. Therefore, this story tells us that the meting out of justice should be left to a neutral governing body, because private parties have such an emotional investment in crimes like this that it is difficult to be fair and objective, and private parties may take their vengeance to an extreme, choosing to somehow profit from their actions, which were originally taken to insure justice.

There is another lesson in this story. Dinah's irresponsible actions set this tragedy in motion. Naturally she could not foresee the ramifications of merely enjoying a precocious lifestyle that she craved. Very often we do not understand the limits that our earthly authority figures impose on us, be they parental or governmental. We also fail to understand why God imposes limits on our behavior. Christians are not unlike Simeon and Levi as well, in that we often think we know what is best, giving little thought to the consequences of our actions. No matter how tempting it may be, or how morally justified we may feel, the Christian should not take matters of vengeance into their own hands, or impose our own view of justice while simultaneously ignoring the law that we think others should obey.

The Hope

No matter how imperfect the human vessel meant to carry it out, God's will will be done. The name of Levi is not associated with his crime here, but instead it is associated with the Old Testament priesthood, because the tribe of Levi was the one from which the Old Testament priesthood would be drawn. Simeon and Levi are like us in that they could not foresee the consequences of their actions. Also, as is often the case with us, they did not know how they would be used for God's ultimate purpose, but God uses us all.

4

Joseph's Brothers | Human Trafficking

Genesis 37:12-36

12 Now his brothers had gone to graze their father's flocks near Shechem, 13 and Israel said to Joseph, "As you know, your brothers are grazing the flocks near Shechem. Come, I am going to send you to them."

"Very well," he replied.

14 So he said to him, "Go and see if all is well with your brothers and with the flocks, and bring word back to me." Then he sent him off from the Valley of Hebron.

When Joseph arrived at Shechem, 15 a man found him wandering around in the fields and asked him, "What are you looking for?"

16 He replied, "I'm looking for my brothers. Can you tell me where they are grazing their flocks?"

17 "They have moved on from here," the man answered. "I heard them say, 'Let's go to Dothan.'"

So Joseph went after his brothers and found them near Dothan. 18 But they saw him in the distance, and before he reached them, they plotted to kill him.

19 "Here comes that dreamer!" they said to each other. 20 "Come now, let's kill him and throw him into one of these cisterns and say that a ferocious animal devoured him. Then we'll see what comes of his dreams."

21 When Reuben heard this, he tried to rescue him from their hands. "Let's not take his life," he said. 22 "Don't shed any blood. Throw him into this cistern here in the desert, but don't lay a hand on him." Reuben said this to rescue him from them and take him back to his father.

23 So when Joseph came to his brothers, they stripped him of his robe—the richly ornamented robe he was wearing—24 and they

took him and threw him into the cistern. Now the cistern was empty; there was no water in it.

25 As they sat down to eat their meal, they looked up and saw a caravan of Ishmaelites coming from Gilead. Their camels were loaded with spices, balm and myrrh, and they were on their way to take them down to Egypt.

26 Judah said to his brothers, "What will we gain if we kill our brother and cover up his blood? 27 Come, let's sell him to the Ishmaelites and not lay our hands on him; after all, he is our brother, our own flesh and blood." His brothers agreed.

28 So when the Midianite merchants came by, his brothers pulled Joseph up out of the cistern and sold him for twenty shekels of silver to the Ishmaelites, who took him to Egypt.

29 When Reuben returned to the cistern and saw that Joseph was not there, he tore his clothes. 30 He went back to his brothers and said, "The boy isn't there! Where can I turn now?"

31 Then they got Joseph's robe, slaughtered a goat and dipped the robe in the blood. 32 They took the ornamented robe back to their father and said, "We found this. Examine it to see whether it is your son's robe."

33 He recognized it and said, "It is my son's robe! Some ferocious animal has devoured him. Joseph has surely been torn to pieces."

34 Then Jacob tore his clothes, put on sackcloth and mourned for his son many days. 35 All his sons and daughters came to comfort him, but he refused to be comforted. "No," he said, "in mourning will I go down to the grave to my son." So his father wept for him.

36 Meanwhile, the Midianites sold Joseph in Egypt to Potiphar, one of Pharaoh's officials, the captain of the guard.

THE PRINCIPAL CHARACTERS There are seven principal characters or sets of characters in this passage: Joseph, Israel (Jacob), Reuben, Judah, Joseph's eight other half brothers, the Midianites, and Potiphar. Joseph was one of the greatest figures in the Old Testament. He was honest, smart, persistent, and faithful to God. His only flaw was his propensity to brag and lord his favored status, bestowed by his wealthy father, over his ten half-brothers. Subsequent chapters in Genesis show Joseph's noble and brave character against overwhelming misfortune. They demonstrate a remarkable faith in God despite his misfortune and despite the fact that he lived much of his life in a culture that knew or cared little for his type of faith. Like his father, Joseph is listed in Hebrews 11 and its "hall of faith," a list of people that the writer saw as embodiments of true faith in God.

His major accomplishments notwithstanding, Israel (Jacob) also possessed some considerable flaws. The one that stands out most clearly in this passage was that he favored two of his sons over his other ten. Joseph and Benjamin were the only sons bore to him by his favorite wife and his only true love, Rachel; the other sons were borne by his other wife and his concubines. Joseph's brothers were jealous of that favoritism, which was demonstrated on at least two occasions. First, Genesis 37:3–4 states that Jacob loved Joseph more than the other sons, and he showed this love by giving him a richly ornamented coat. This is comparable to a modern father buying a 16-year-old son a brand new Humvee, but buying a cheap used car, or no car at all, for his other, older sons. Second, Genesis 33 provides the account of Jacob's confrontation with his sibling rival, Esau. Fearing a battle with his brother (that did not materialize), Jacob placed his concubines and their children in the front, Leah (his less favored wife) and her sons behind them, and Rachel and Joseph in the rear, hoping that if fighting ensued, Rachel and Joseph would be the least vulnerable.

Reuben was Jacob's oldest son, born to Leah, his first wife. Reuben was held in low regard by his father, in part because he was the offspring of a wife Jacob did not want, but also because Reuben had a sexual relationship with one of Jacob's concubines. In Genesis 37, Reuben exhibits leadership, albeit weak, by saving Joseph's life, but allowing his brothers to imprison him in a cistern. In his defense, Reuben may have feared for his own safety or he may have thought a cooling-off period was what the situation required. Reuben intended to free Joseph; maybe he thought he could return and reason with his brothers once they had calmed down.

Judah, the subject of a later chapter in this book, devised the scheme of selling his brother into slavery, perhaps because he was at a loss as to what to do after Joseph was thrown into a cistern. Reuben stopped Judah and the others from killing Joseph, which left them in a dilemma. They could leave him to die, or they could free him, in which case Joseph would have reported their misdeed to Jacob. The appearance of the Midianites solved their dilemma. Whether Judah's statements in verses 26 and 27 should be interpreted as irony or sarcasm is not clear.

Besides Reuben and Judah, Joseph had eight other half-brothers: Simeon, Levi, Issachar, Zebulun, Dan, Naphtali, Gad and Asher. All of these half-brothers participated in selling Joseph into slavery. The latter six men never speak in Genesis. The only insights into their characters are given in the Joseph stories and in Genesis 49, when Jacob summarizes his vision of their lives and futures. None of the eight half-brothers are mentioned by name in this passage, but their collective guilt is implied.

The people who purchased Joseph are referred to in verse 25 as Ishmaelites and in verse 28 as Midianites. The Midianites were a nomadic people and perennial enemies of the Israelites throughout the Old Testament. Their patriarch, Midian, was Abraham's son via a concubine named Keturah. Midian was banished from his home by Abraham, which began a history of enmity between the Midianites and the Israelites. Ironically, Moses, who led Joseph's descendants out of Egyptian slavery several centuries later, married into a Midianite family. The Midianites sometimes traveled with the Ishmaelites, or the descendants of Ishmael, another outcast son of Abraham. Modern Arabs claim Ishmael as their ancestor. However, the term Ishmaelites was not always used to literally describe descendants of Ishmael. The word was sometimes used to refer to all Arabian merchants. Also, many wild and war-like desert inhabitants claimed Ishmaelite ancestry.[1]

Potiphar can be viewed with ambivalence or with outright disdain. The fact that he engaged in the buying and selling of human beings makes him appear wicked by modern Western standards. However, modern readers should bear in mind that buying slaves was common in the ancient Middle East, so he was no different from most of his contemporaries. It appears that Potiphar treated Joseph well, but this came to an end when Potiphar's wife falsely accused Joseph of sexual misconduct (Genesis 39). However, even in that scenario, Potiphar acted with greater compassion than many other slave masters would have. Instead of killing Joseph, which probably would have been legal and acceptable, he had him imprisoned, perhaps doubting the veracity of his wife's story.

THE CRIME

Joseph's brothers committed the crime of human trafficking, although this behavior was not a crime during Joseph's lifetime. Many Americans see slavery as something confined to the pre-Civil War American South. Slave trading has never been confined to the trafficking of Africans to the Western hemisphere. In fact, very few societies throughout human history have not engaged in some form of legalized slavery or human trafficking. Modern Western culture is somewhat of an anomaly, being one of the few cultures that does not allow slavery.

The Bible does not explicitly condemn slavery. The only condemnation is found in the Mosaic Law, where Israelites are forbidden to permanently enslave each other (Leviticus 25). The Mosaic Law does not condemn the enslavement of non-Israelites; it merely prescribes fair treatment of slaves and honest dealing in the acquisition and selling of slaves. Slavery is not condemned in the New Testament, either. In Ephesians 6:5, Paul instructs slaves not to rebel, but to obey their masters. In his letter to Philemon, Paul makes a plea on behalf of Philemon's runaway slave, Onesimus, but he merely pleads that Philemon treat Onesimus kindly. Paul does not ask for the slave's freedom, let alone pronounce a categorical condemnation of slavery.

Discussions about the complexities of slavery notwithstanding, Joseph's brothers committed a dastardly act by selling him to the Midianites. They compounded their crime by telling Jacob that Joseph had been killed, and living that lie for many years, not caring that their father's heart was broken.

THE CRIME TODAY

Slavery and trafficking of human beings are illegal in the United States. They are illegal in every country in the world, yet they are rampant. Trafficking in human beings is a worldwide enterprise. It is a lucrative business for criminal organizations, both large and small, which operate in the Middle East and North Africa, the setting of the Joseph story. The greatest growth in human trafficking is occurring in Eastern Europe and countries of the former Soviet Union.[2] Human trafficking generates over $9 billion annually for organized crime, trailing only weapons and drug trafficking in generated revenue.[3]

There is a difference between trafficking and smuggling. Smuggling involves the voluntary transport of human beings, through illegal means, into another country. People being smuggled often pay to be smuggled, but they are often subjected to very inhumane treatment and dangerous conditions. Human smuggling is a lucrative business in Mexico and Central America. Those who smuggle people from Mexico and Central America into the United States are called "coyotes." They charge over $1,500 per person to smuggle illegal immigrants across U.S. borders.[4] Sometimes the smuggling leads to far worse crimes. In May 2003, nineteen Mexican nationals died while being illegally transported through Texas, the result of being loaded with more than fifty other illegal immigrants into an airtight tractor trailer where temperatures reached over 170 degrees.[5]

As for the crime in Genesis 38, the United Nations defines trafficking in persons as, "The recruitment, transportation, transfer, harboring or receipt of persons, by means of threat or use of force or other forms of coercion, of abduction, of fraud, of deception, of the abuse of power or of a position of vulnerability or of the giving or receiving of payments or benefits to achieve the consent of a person having control over another person, for the purpose of exploitation. Exploitation shall include, at a minimum, the exploitation of the prostitution of others or other forms of sexual exploitation, forced labor or services, slavery or practices similar to slavery, servitude or the removal of organs."[6]

As strange as it may seem, criminalizing human trafficking has probably compounded the cruelty imposed on those who are caught in its clutches. Because of the consequences of getting caught, people who sell or buy people often go to great lengths to cover up their activity, including isolating the victims from the public, often in extremely cruel ways. In ancient Egypt, Joseph and those like him did not have to be hidden from public view, because trafficking in persons was legal and socially acceptable.

Even worse, many modern human traffickers will not hesitate to kill their victims to avoid getting caught. On one occasion, human traffickers in the Mediterranean Sea off the coast of North Africa threw dozens of victims overboard when they realized that law enforcement authorities were in pursuit. Trafficking victims are sometimes murdered, and many of these murders are never reported to authorities.

The United Nations estimates that more than 12 million people are enslaved, with 600,000 to 800,000 people trafficked each year. Approximately 80 percent of these victims are women, and over 50 percent, like Joseph, are minors.[7] Human beings are sold into slavery for numerous reasons, including:

1. Labor exploitation, being forced to work in factories under deplorable conditions;

2. Domestic servitude, being forced to work as a domestic servant, also under deplorable conditions;

3. Sexual exploitation, be it prostitution, performing in strip shows, pornography, or being used as a sex slave by the owner;

4. To be used as soldiers and forced to fight; and

5. Illegal adoption. Children trafficked to Arab countries are sometimes used as jockeys in camel races. Many children are sold by their own families, sometimes in the naïve belief, instilled in them by the trafficker, that the child will learn a trade, work for wages, and send the money back to the family. Sometimes a child or woman is sold simply for money.

Once caught in the trafficking web, most victims are constantly monitored or totally deprived of their liberty. Their identification documents are confiscated and they are reminded that they are in their country of residence illegally, giving them no recourse; they are afraid to contact local law enforcement or their own diplomatic officials. Many of these victims do not trust police officers or government officials in their home country, and that distrust of authority comes with them to the country where they are transported. The victims also know that they may be deported if they are discovered by law enforcement or diplomatic officials. Worse, they fear that the traffickers will harm their family in their native country.

Each spring, the United States Department of State is required by law (the Victims of Trafficking and Violence Protection Act of 2000) to issue a report on worldwide human trafficking. This report details the efforts that countries are taking to prevent trafficking and the actions they are taking to prosecute those who engage in trafficking. The State Department places all countries in one of three tiers, with tier 3 being the worst. Tier 3 countries are subject to the withholding of non-humanitarian and non-trade-related assistance from the United States.

The 2005 Trafficking in Persons (TIP) report listed fourteen countries as Tier 3, meaning that these countries, according to the State Department, had the worst record in preventing human trafficking and prosecuting human traffickers. The countries are Bolivia, Burma, Cambodia, Cuba, Ecuador, Jamaica, Kuwait, North Korea, Qatar, Saudi Arabia, Sudan, Togo, United Arab Emirates, and Venezuela.[8] This categorization is tinged with politics. Given the overall poor relations with some of these countries (Cuba, North Korea), it is not surprising to find them on this list, along with other undesirable designations, such as support for terrorism and drug trafficking. However, the list also includes important trade partners and strategic allies in the United States' war on terror, such as Qatar and Saudi Arabia. Other countries are not included in the State Department report because they are in such turmoil that adequate information cannot be obtained. Human trafficking in some of these countries (Liberia, Somalia) is probably worse than in the Tier 3 countries.

Far more poignant and heart wrenching than the political discussions and aggregated statistics are the stories of individuals victimized by human trafficking. Like Joseph, each person who falls victim to human trafficking is a potential human tragedy and the victim of a degrading injustice. Most human trafficking stories do not lead to happy endings like Joseph's. Presented below are three case studies taken from the U.S. Department of State Internet Web Site:[9]

Singapore: Karin, a young mother of two, was looking for a job in Sri Lanka when a man befriended her and convinced her that she could land a better job in Singapore as a waitress. He arranged and paid for her travel. A Sri Lankan woman met Karin upon arrival in Singapore, confiscated her passport, and took her to a hotel. The woman made it clear that Karin had to submit to prostitution to pay back the money it cost for her to be flown into Singapore. Karin was taken to an open space for sale in the sex market where she joined women from Indonesia, Thailand, India, and China to be inspected and purchased by men from Pakistan, India, China, Indonesia, and Africa. The men would take the women to nearby hotels and rape them. Karin was forced to have sex with an average of fifteen men a day or night. She developed a serious illness, and three months after her arrival was arrested by the

Singaporean police during a raid on the brothel. She was deported to Sri Lanka.

Cambodia: Neary grew up in rural Cambodia. Her parents died when she was a child, and, in an effort to give her a better life, her sister married her off when she was seventeen. Three months later Neary and her husband visited a fishing village. Her husband rented a room in what Neary thought was a guest house, but when she woke the next morning her husband was gone. The owner of the house told her she had been sold by her husband for $300 and that she was actually in a brothel. For five years, Neary was raped by five to seven men every day. In addition to brutal physical abuse, Neary was infected with HIV and contracted AIDS. The brothel threw her out when she became sick, and she eventually found her way to a local shelter. She died of HIV/AIDS at the age of twenty-three.

Lebanon: Silvia was a young, single, Sri Lankan mother seeking a better life for herself and her three-year-old son when she answered an advertisement for a housekeeping job in Lebanon. In the Beirut job agency, her passport was taken and she was hired by a Lebanese woman who subsequently confined her and restricted her access to food and communications. Treated like a prisoner and beaten daily, Silvia was determined to escape. She jumped from a window to the street below, landing with such force that she is permanently paralyzed. She is now back in Sri Lanka. Today, she travels around the country telling her story so that others do not suffer a similar fate.

The Lesson

In Genesis 45, Joseph tells his brothers that it was not they who led him to Egypt, but God. Joseph would not have traveled to Egypt or have become governor if his brothers had not sold him into slavery. He would not have delivered the Egyptians, or his own family from famine, had he not been sold into slavery. The miracle of the Exodus and the parting of the Red Sea, which occurred several centuries later, would not have occurred had Joseph not been sold into slavery.

God had a purpose for Joseph, which neither he nor his brothers understood when he was sold into slavery. The life of Joseph after being sold into slavery was filled with peaks and valleys but, through it all, he never lost his faith in God, and he always gave God the glory for his accomplishments. It would have been very easy for Joseph to abandon his faith in God or to have exacted vengeance on his brothers when he had the chance. Joseph persevered, never losing faith and never taking his eyes off God, a lesson for anyone who finds himself or herself in dire circumstances, even those who suffer the indignity and cruelty of slavery.

5

Judah and Tamar | Prostitution

Genesis 38

38:1 At that time, Judah left his brothers and went down to stay with a man of Adullam named Hirah. 2 There Judah met the daughter of a Canaanite man named Shua. He married her and lay with her; 3 she became pregnant and gave birth to a son, who was named Er. 4 She conceived again and gave birth to a son and named him Onan. 5 She gave birth to still another son and named him Shelah. It was at Kezib that she gave birth to him.

6 Judah got a wife for Er, his firstborn, and her name was Tamar. 7 But Er, Judah's firstborn, was wicked in the Lord's sight; so the Lord put him to death.

8 Then Judah said to Onan, "Lie with your brother's wife and fulfill your duty to her as a brother-in-law to produce offspring for your brother." 9 But Onan knew that the offspring would not be his; so whenever he lay with his brother's wife, he spilled his semen on the ground to keep from producing offspring for his brother. 10 What he did was wicked in the Lord's sight; so he put him to death also.

11 Judah then said to his daughter-in-law Tamar, "Live as a widow in your father's house until my son Shelah grows up." For he thought, "He may die too, just like his brothers." So Tamar went to live in her father's house.

12 After a long time Judah's wife, the daughter of Shua, died. When Judah had recovered from his grief, he went up to Timnah, to the men who were shearing his sheep, and his friend Hirah the Adullamite went with him.

13 When Tamar was told, "Your father-in-law is on his way to Timnah to shear his sheep," 14 she took off her widow's clothes, covered herself with a veil to disguise herself, and then sat down at the entrance to Enaim, which is on the road to Timnah. For she saw

that, though Shelah had now grown up, she had not been given to him as his wife.

15 When Judah saw her, he thought she was a prostitute, for she had covered her face. 16 Not realizing that she was his daughter-in-law, he went over to her by the roadside and said, "Come now, let me sleep with you."

"And what will you give me to sleep with you?" she asked.

17 "I'll send you a young goat from my flock," he said.

"Will you give me something as a pledge until you send it?" she asked.

18 He said, "What pledge should I give you?"

"Your seal and its cord, and the staff in your hand," she answered. So he gave them to her and slept with her, and she became pregnant by him. 19 After she left, she took off her veil and put on her widow's clothes again.

20 Meanwhile Judah sent the young goat by his friend the Adullamite in order to get his pledge back from the woman, but he did not find her. 21 He asked the men who lived there, "Where is the shrine prostitute who was beside the road at Enaim?"

"There hasn't been any shrine prostitute here," they said.

22 So he went back to Judah and said, "I didn't find her. Besides, the men who lived there said, 'There hasn't been any shrine prostitute here.'"

23 Then Judah said, "Let her keep what she has, or we will become a laughingstock. After all, I did send her this young goat, but you didn't find her."

24 About three months later Judah was told, "Your daughter-in-law Tamar is guilty of prostitution, and as a result she is now pregnant."

Judah said, "Bring her out and have her burned to death!"

25 As she was being brought out, she sent a message to her father-in-law. "I am pregnant by the man who owns these," she said. And she added, "See if you recognize whose seal and cord and staff these are."

26 Judah recognized them and said, "She is more righteous than I, since I wouldn't give her to my son Shelah." And he did not sleep with her again.

27 When the time came for her to give birth, there were twin boys in her womb. 28 As she was giving birth, one of them put out his hand; so the midwife took a scarlet thread and tied it on his wrist

and said, "This one came out first." 29 But when he drew back his hand, his brother came out, and she said, "So this is how you have broken out!" And he was named Perez. 30 Then his brother, who had the scarlet thread on his wrist, came out and he was given the name Zerah.

THE PRINCIPAL CHARACTERS

Judah, whose name means "praise," was Jacob's fourth son. Judah's mother was Leah, Jacob's first and least favorite wife. Judah was the patriarch of one of the largest of Israel's twelve tribes. Many centuries after Judah's death, following the death of King Solomon, the nation of Israel split. The ten northern tribes formed the kingdom of Israel and the two southern tribes formed the kingdom of Judah. The northern kingdom of Israel disappeared to history when it was overrun by the Assyrian Empire in the seventh century B.C., but the kingdom of Judah remained. Its inhabitants survived the Babylonian conquest and returned to rebuild their nation. These returning exiles called themselves Jews, or *yehudi*, descendants of Judah.

His legacy and great name aside, Judah was a very flawed man. Both Judah's weaknesses and strengths come across in this passage, namely, his tendency to engage in illicit sex, but also his forthrightness in admitting his sin. He suggested selling his brother Joseph into slavery in Genesis 37. While Joseph resisted the allure of improper sexual relations (Genesis 39), Judah, in direct contrast, solicited sex from someone he believed to be a prostitute. Judah eventually acquired the traits of bravery and compassion, which one may assume were acquired through time, maturity, and experiences like this one. His bravery and compassion are demonstrated in Genesis 44. Out of love for his father and half-brother, he offered to take his half-brother Benjamin's place as prisoner in Egypt.

THE CRIME

Tamar committed the act of prostitution, which is performing, offering, or agreeing to perform a sexual act for hire. Judah, who would be labeled a "John" today, was guilty of pandering, the solicitation of prostitution. Prostitution has a very complicated history, both in biblical and other cultures. This is the earliest example of prostitution in the Bible, but some form of prostitution existed in all ancient Middle Eastern cultures.

Tamar posed as a shrine prostitute, or *qedesha*, which means "to consecrate." Prostitutes were common in ancient Canaanite worship.[1] Not only was Judah partaking in the immoral act of prostitution, he was indirectly engaging in pagan worship. Although the motives for involving prostitutes in worship have varied, one common motive in ancient Canaanite worship centered on the deification of reproductive organs and consequently the reproductive act. Far from being shielded from public view, or existing as a society's dirty little open secret, as is the case in many cities today, many pagan cultures openly consecrated prostitutes for worship ceremonies. Many Canaanite temples were little more than giant brothels, some employing both male and female prostitutes.[2]

Throughout the Old Testament, and in the book of Revelation, the term "harlot" is used figuratively. It usually is used to symbolize abandonment of Godly principles, or to engage in immoral worship practices. However, in this case, the term is used in its literal sense.

There is at least one noticeable difference between the prostitution of Genesis 38 and modern prostitution in Western culture. Today, most prostitutes can be identified by the suggestive or scant amount of clothing they wear. Scant or revealing clothing is an advertisement for modern prostitutes, but in Judah and Tamar's time, a prostitute was identified by the way her face was covered. She did not reveal her face, let alone her body, to the public. Sometimes the prostitute concealed her face to hide a deformity or an unattractive facial feature. In any case, Judah recognized Tamar as a prostitute by her appearance. Unlike most modern prostitutes, prostitutes like Tamar used the temple as their brothel, and did not solicit business by walking the street alone or in small groups.

THE CRIME TODAY

The question of whether it is right to engage in prostitution has a simple answer. Sex outside of marriage is condemned in the Old and New Testaments, regardless of whether money or material possessions are exchanged. The question of how a government or a society should deal with prostitution is more complex. Prostitution is inevitable. It exists in every country in the world, past and present. No matter how many laws are passed, no matter how vigilant the enforcement, prostitution will exist. Even the Mosaic Law, while condemning prostitution (Leviticus 19:29), implicitly acknowledges its existence (Deuteronomy 23:18).

Not only does prostitution have a complicated history in other countries, it also has a complex history in the United States. In eras when prostitution has been legal, or where there were no laws specifically outlawing the practice, as in the early American West, many prostitutes plied their trade in brothels that operated openly. House madams often operated these brothels, frequently under the protection of the local government. Today, prostitution is illegal in most jurisdictions in the United States. As happens when any vice is outlawed, unintended consequences of prostitution have resulted. Lawrence Friedman writes that the outlawing of brothels pushed prostitution into the streets. Instead of house madams or brothel owners, brutal pimps control street prostitution.[3] Pushing prostitution into the streets has made it more dangerous, for both the prostitute and the customer.

Nevada presents an exception to other prostitution laws in the United States. Nevada has adopted a "local option" approach to prostitution, meaning that counties (with populations of less than 400,000) may allow prostitution subject to strict government regulation.[4] There are approximately thirty legal brothels in Nevada. Brothels are subject to rigorous health standards and inspections. As a result, sexually transmitted disease is practically nonexistent in these brothels. In fact, brothel management can be held liable if a customer is infected with HIV, if the prostitute has previously tested positive.[5]

This is not meant to sound like an endorsement of legalized prostitution, but it presents a dilemma, the same dilemma a society faces when it criminalizes "immoral"deeds, such as adult prostitution, drug use, and gambling. By criminalizing these behaviors, we make participation in them, which is inevitable, more dangerous. The danger is created because these behaviors are driven underground, away from the protective eye of public scrutiny and government regulation. The people willing to assume the risk of engaging in illegal vice behaviors are unsavory and often violent as well.

On the other hand, by legalizing vice behaviors, a society sends the message, to young and old alike, that the behaviors are morally acceptable. A society that legalizes vice behaviors such as prostitution, drug use, and gambling also must accept the fact that legalization will lead to increased occurrence of these behaviors. For example, although the Prohibition experiment of the 1920s was a failure, alcohol consumption and alcohol-related deaths decreased. The city of Amsterdam, Holland, decriminalized marijuana possession in 1976, making possession of marijuana an offense punishable by a small fine. As a result, marijuana, though technically still illegal, is smoked openly in "coffee houses," and the patrons need not worry about being ticketed by police. Critics charge that these liberal drug laws have made Amsterdam a giant skid row.

Even with the availability of legal prostitution, illegal prostitution has not gone away. It still exists in Nevada, both in the counties where it is illegal, such as Clark (Las Vegas) County, and in counties where it is legal. Some prostitutes cannot get jobs at legalized houses of prostitution or as call girls. Some men are unwilling to pay the price of legal prostitution, or they are unwilling to submit to the required health or behavioral regulations. Others will not be satisfied with relatively conventional forms of sex between consenting adults. Some patrons insist on sexual behaviors that are physically harmful. Many patrons insist on having sex with underage girls or boys. Therefore, moral arguments aside, legalizing prostitution will not spell an end to illegal prostitution.

Although prostitution has changed in many ways over the centuries, one thing that Genesis 38 has in common with prostitution in many other eras and cultures is the double standard, that is, it is wrong for a woman to be a prostitute, but it is acceptable for a man to pay a prostitute. Judah was quick to condemn his daughter-in-law, and many cultures have been quick to condemn the prostitute, but take a less judgmental attitude toward the man who pays for sex. To his credit, or perhaps realizing he had little choice, Judah quickly admitted his own hypocrisy, even saying that his daughter-in-law was more righteous than he.

The Lesson

Should a child be disparaged because of a parent's sin in conceiving the child? Should a child or descendant of a prostitute suffer the stigma of prostitution? If the answer is yes, consider the fact that Jesus was a direct descendant of Tamar, a woman who became pregnant as a result of an act of prostitution with her father-in-law, Judah, the patriarch of the Jewish people (Matthew 1:3). T.H. Leale states that the greatest and most shameful sinners are found in Jesus's birth register.[6] In reality, there is no such thing as a pure blood line, because no human being is pure. We are all the descendants and future ancestors of sinners, no better than Judah and Tamar. Sometimes, like Judah, we have to be caught redhanded and in public before we are fully aware of the gravity of our sins. Like Judah, we all can be forgiven of our sins, and we can learn and grow from them.

6

Pharaoh | Genocide

Exodus 1:1–22

1:1 These are the names of the sons of Israel who went to Egypt with Jacob, each with his family: 2 Reuben, Simeon, Levi and Judah; 3 Issachar, Zebulun and Benjamin; 4 Dan and Naphtali; Gad and Asher. 5 The descendants of Jacob numbered seventy in all; Joseph was already in Egypt.

6 Now Joseph and all his brothers and all that generation died, 7 but the Israelites were fruitful and multiplied greatly and became exceedingly numerous, so that the land was filled with them.

8 Then a new king, who did not know about Joseph, came to power in Egypt. 9 "Look," he said to his people, "the Israelites have become much too numerous for us. 10 Come, we must deal shrewdly with them or they will become even more numerous and, if war breaks out, will join our enemies, fight against us and leave the country."

11 So they put slave masters over them to oppress them with forced labor, and they built Pithom and Rameses as store cities for Pharaoh. 12 But the more they were oppressed, the more they multiplied and spread; so the Egyptians came to dread the Israelites 13 and worked them ruthlessly. 14 They made their lives bitter with hard labor in brick and mortar and with all kinds of work in the fields; in all their hard labor the Egyptians used them ruthlessly.

15 The king of Egypt said to the Hebrew midwives, whose names were Shiphrah and Puah, 16 "When you help the Hebrew women in childbirth and observe them on the delivery stool, if it is a boy, kill him; but if it is a girl, let her live." 17 The midwives, however, feared God and did not do what the king of Egypt had told them to do; they let the boys live. 18 Then the king of Egypt summoned the midwives and asked them, "Why have you done this? Why have you let the boys live?"

19 The midwives answered Pharaoh, "Hebrew women are not like Egyptian women; they are vigorous and give birth before the midwives arrive."

20 So God was kind to the midwives and the people increased and became even more numerous. 21 And because the midwives feared God, he gave them families of their own.

22 Then Pharaoh gave this order to all his people: "Every boy that is born you must throw into the Nile, but let every girl live."

 **THE PRINCIPAL CHARACTERS** The principal character in this passage is identified as a Pharaoh. Pharaoh, which means "the great house," was a title bestowed on the monarchs who ruled the Egyptian empire for more than 1,200 years. The Pharaoh in Exodus 1 may have been named Aahmes or Amosis, but some sources identify this "Pharoah of the Oppression" as Thutmose III or Seti I.[1] Egyptians believed that ruling Pharaohs were the children of the sun god Ra, and the incarnation of the god Horus. When a Pharaoh died, he became the Osiris, the god of the underworld. During their lifetime, the Pharaohs were in charge of governmental and military affairs. They were also seen as intermediaries with the gods, and they ruled by divine right, making their dictums the absolute and unquestioned law of the land.[2]

The Pharaoh in Exodus 1 was motivated partly by jealousy. The Israelites were living in Goshen, a fertile, desirable habitat, thanks to the kindness showed to Jacob's and Joseph's families 300 years earlier. Pharaoh thought the Israelites possessed a disproportionate amount of the country's wealth, much as Adolph Hitler and his Nazi minions thought of the Jews in 1930s Europe. Pharaoh wanted Goshen for the Egyptians.

Exodus 1:10 states that the Pharaoh feared Israelite collaboration with Egypt's enemies in the event of war. He was afraid that the Israelites would side with a group of people called the Shasous, who lived near Goshen, or with other groups from western Asia. These groups, who frequently made war with Egypt, were similar to the Israelites in language, culture and appearance.[3]

THE
CRIME

The unspeakably evil act described in Exodus 1 was not a crime at the time because the ruler who ordered the killings was not legally accountable for his actions. As the unquestioned ruler by divine right, Pharaoh was not subject to the laws of his country, like a President or Prime Minister would be in a modern democracy.

The modern concept of international law did not exist in the ancient Middle East. The actions in Exodus 1 would constitute a crime under international law today. That crime is genocide, which is derived from the Greek word *genos* (race) and the Latin word *cide* (killing). The word genocide was coined in 1944 by a Polish lawyer named Raphael Lemkin to describe the Nazi-led Holocaust of the 1930s and 1940s.[4] Genocide is often tied to a broader category of offense called "crimes against humanity." Enacted in 1948, shortly after the end of World War II, Article II of the Genocide Convention defines genocide as "an intent to destroy, in whole or in part, a national, ethnical, racial or religious group through one or more of the following means: (1) killing members of the group, (2) causing serious bodily or mental harm to members of the group, (3) deliberately inflicting on the group conditions of life calculated to bring about its physical destruction in whole or in part, (4) imposing measures intended to prevent births within the group, or (5) forcibly transferring children of the group to another group."[5]

Throughout the 1930s, Adolph Hitler and his supporters in Germany and elsewhere in Europe propagated hatred against several ethnic groups, including Gypsies, people of Slavic origin, and Jews. The hatred toward these groups had been festering in Europe for centuries. A number of Germans, and many other Europeans eventually convinced themselves that these people, especially the Jews, were less than human, and that they were responsible for whatever social and economic problems that befell everyone else.

For centuries, Jews had suffered persecution throughout Europe. The most infamous persecution of European Jewry in the Middle Ages occurred during the Spanish Inquisition of the fifteenth and sixteenth centuries. With the blessing of the Roman Catholic hierarchy, thousands of Spaniards who did not conform to official Church teachings were imprisoned, tortured, and killed under the guise of stamping out heresy. The Inquisition affected numerous non-Catholic groups, Protestants and Muslims prominent among them, but the group that probably suffered the harshest persecution was the Jews. While many people in these religious groups escaped persecution by renouncing their "heretical" beliefs, many others did not, and Jews, by virtue of being born into a Jewish household, were heretics from birth. The exact number of Jews and other religious minorities killed in Spain and other European countries is not known, but it is believed to number in the thousands.

 As repellent as the Inquisition and other outbreaks of Jewish persecution were, nothing compared to the magnitude of the European Holocaust of the 1930s and 1940s. During those two decades, an estimated 6 million European Jews were murdered by Germany's Nazi regime and their collaborators throughout Europe. The first true test of genocide laws occurred as a result of the European Holocaust. From 1945–1946, shortly after the end of World War II, a series of trials was conducted in Nuremberg (or Nurnberg), Germany, in which leaders of Germany's Nazi regime were tried by an international military tribunal for crimes stemming from Germany's involvement in World War II. One set of crimes was "crimes against humanity," which included the systematic extermination of European Jews. After more than 200 court sessions which stretched out for one year, nineteen of the twenty-four indicted Nazi officials were convicted of one or more crimes. Some were sentenced to lengthy prison terms and others were put to death.[6]

The Nazi-led Holocaust is not the only example of twentieth-century genocide. There are others:

1. In the early 1930s, millions of peasants in the Ukraine were intentionally starved to death by Joseph Stalin and his Communist regime in the U.S.S.R.;

2. During the early 1940s, the Croatian Ustashi killed more than 650,000 Serbs, Jews, and Gypsies;

3. During the late 1930s, the Japanese Army, during the "Rape of Nanking," murdered more than 200,000 Chinese;

4. During the early 1970s, the Burundi Tutsi murdered 150,000 ethnic Hutus;

5. Between 1975–1987, the Indonesian Army massacred 150,000 Timorese.[7]

Another related term that has entered the vocabulary in recent years is "democide," a word coined by political scientist R. J. Rummel. Democide describes all forms of mass killings, including mass murders of people that may be based on factors other than race or ethnicity. Here is a partial list:

1. From 1949–1953, China, led by Communist tyrant Mao Tse-tung, murdered more than 4 million wealthy citizens and landlords under the guise of land reform;

2. Between 1964–1975, the same Chinese regime murdered more than 1.6 million of its intellectuals and government officials in the name of cultural revolution;

3. Between 1971–1979, Uganda, led by its maniacal dictator Idi Amin, murdered 300,000 political opponents and government critics.[8]

Yugoslavia. Lest anyone think that genocide and democide are relics of the past, witness two events that occurred in the 1990s. A new term, "ethnic cleansing," came into use during the 1990s, the result of a genocide campaign in the countries of the former Yugoslavia, especially in Bosnia. Ethnic hatred between Yugoslavia's diverse ethnic and religious groups, which had been ongoing for centuries, lay dormant during the post-World War II rule of Communist dictator Josip Tito. Several years after Tito's death ended his iron-clad reign of Yugoslavia, these ethnic rivalries reignited.

Atrocities were committed by all sides of this conflict, but the greatest atrocities were perpetrated by Bosnian Serbs against their Bosnian Muslim neighbors. The details of the conflict are complex, but hundreds of thousands of Bosnian Muslims were massacred over a period of several years. Systematic rape, torture, and murder characterized this genocide campaign, led largely by Yugoslavian President Slobodan Milosevic, who was put on trial in 2002 by an international court in the Netherlands for war crimes and genocide (and died in his cell in March, 2006, while the trial was still in progress), and a self-proclaimed Bosnian Serb President named Radovan Karadzic, who is still at large and whose capture is being impeded because of the loyalty of his fellow Bosnian Serb protectors. Before this organized mass murder masquerading as a military operation got under way in the early

1990s, Milosevic, his stately demeanor and deportment notwithstanding, was little more than an unsophisticated former Communist Party hack. Karodzic, on the other hand, was a university professor, a poet, and a psychiatrist. Many of the Serbs who joined in the slaughter of Bosnian Muslims had been law-abiding, well behaved model citizens. Some were police officers. Many of those that were killed or persecuted were turned in by their neighbors with whom they had lived peaceably for many years.

Criminal atrocities are committed every day, but it seems that genocide campaigns, which are basically organized mass murder, bring out the most odious side of human nature. A passage from Franklin Graham's *Rebel with a Cause*, in my view, provides an example of the type of behavior that simply cannot be explained by any secular explanation or by the greatest criminological mind. More than anything else, this story from Graham's book provides the greatest proof possible that evil does indeed exist.

Graham's missionary work took him to Mostar, Bosnia in 1992, at the height of the murderous ethnic cleansing campaign led by Milosevic and Karodzic. This is not an exposé on foreign policy, and it is not an attack on all Serbs, and it does not mean that similar atrocities were not inflicted against the Serbs. I included this repulsive passage to simply raise the same question asked of Franklin Graham by a Pentecostal minister he met there, "Why do men do these things?" The minister, whom Graham met in Mostar, insisted on showing him a videotape that had been captured from Bosnian Serb "soldiers." Because they were in a very dangerous spot at a dangerous moment—shells were exploding nearby—Graham cared little about seeing the tape or sticking around long enough to hear a narrative. However, the minister was persistent, and Graham relented. Presented below are excerpts from Graham's recollections of the event:

> "You see, Mr. Graham, we captured some enemy soldiers and found this videotape in their possession. They had taped themselves raping a nine-year-old girl. Would you like to see the tape?"
>
> "No, sir," I said, thinking, *I'd like to be able to sleep tonight.*

"They brought the girl's father into the room and told him to rape his own daughter. He refused. So they put a gun into his mouth and blew his brains out the back of his head in front of his daughter. Then they brought her older brother into the room. They told him to rape his sister. The boy saw his dead father and probably thought the only way to save his life was to obey them. So he did. Afterward, they blew out his brains. Then they laughed.

What I don't understand is that after the soldiers killed the girl's father and brother, why did they have to saw off her legs, causing her to bleed to death?

Mr. Graham, why do men do these things?"[9]

The answer, Yugoslavian President Slobodan Milosevic told *Time* magazine essayist Lance Morrow, was "protection." Milosevic once stated, "There is no Serb aggression ... We are merely protecting ourselves."[10] The Egyptian Pharaoh of Exodus 1 convinced himself and his minions that the murders of Hebrew babies were acts of protection. This is very often the case with genocidal campaigns. One side convinces itself that the only means of protecting itself is the extermination of the group that is the "cause" of their problems or may be a threat to them in the near future. With Egypt it was the Israelites; in Yugoslavia it was the Muslims or anyone of a different ethnic group.

Rwanda. The other great genocide of the 1990s occurred in the central African nation of Rwanda. This story, which was dramatized (and sanitized) in the film *Hotel Rwanda*, resulted from another centuries-old feud, this one between two rival ethnic groups, the Hutus and the Tutsis. The Tutsis make up approximately 10 percent of the Rwandan population, but they have long enjoyed wealth and power disproportionate to their numbers. The Tutsi have lived in Rwanda since the fifteenth century and dominated the majority Hutus almost since their arrival. The Tutsis acted as feudal lords over the Hutus for centuries, but the two groups lived together somewhat peacefully, even though the seeds of antagonism were present. When Rwanda came under Belgian colonial rule, the antagonism between the rural, agrarian Hutus and Tutsis intensified, largely because of the favoritism shown by the Belgians to the more affluent, urbane and (typically) taller, lighter skinned Tutsis. Rwanda's early post-colonial governments were Tutsi-dominated monarchies.

Atrocities had been perpetrated by both sides off and on for several centuries, mostly because of back-and-forth attempts to claim and/or reclaim political power. In the early 1970s, more than 100,000 Hutu were killed in a military insurrection in neighboring Burundi. The 1990s genocide erupted after the suspicious death of Rwanda's Hutu President Juvenal Habyarimana, a death many Hutus blamed on the Tutsis, although there was some evidence that Hutus were responsible. Almost overnight, or at least it seemed that way to the rest of the world, the Hutus went on a rampage. In less than one year, approximately 500,000 people, mostly Tutsis, were murdered.[11] Just as had happened in Bosnia, many Tutsis were betrayed by their neighbors and acquaintances.

Internment of Japanese-Americans. The Exodus story presents another common historical occurrence, how an ethnic minority comes under suspicion by the majority, with the majority fearing that the minority will side with an enemy in wartime. This happened in the United States during the 1940s. President Franklin Roosevelt and California Governor Earl Warren were among those who distrusted Japanese-Americans on the west coast. This resulted in the internment of many Japanese-Americans in relocation camps for the duration of World War II. Many of these people lost not only their freedom, but their property in the process. It should be noted that the Japanese-Americans of World War II may have been victims of mass racial discrimination, but not genocide.

Armenia. While most Americans now acknowledge that Japanese-Americans were treated unfairly during World War II, those actions pale in comparison to what happened to another ethnic minority believed to be in collaboration with foreign invaders. During World War I, an estimated 1 million Armenians were slaughtered by Muslim Turks. Armenians, most of whom were aligned with Christian denominations, had lived under Turkish rule, with diminished rights, rather peacefully for centuries, but Turkey's (which controlled the Ottoman

Empire) entry into World War I changed all of that. The Ottoman Turks fought and lost battles against Russia, which had been encouraging an Armenian uprising against the Turks. Some Turkish rulers blamed its Armenian minority for these battlefield defeats. The Ottoman Turks responded by initiating a campaign of genocide against its Armenian population.[12] This type of feared collaboration with a foreign enemy was similar to what the ancient Egyptians felt toward its Israelite population.

Another irony we confront with genocide is that, many times, differing religious beliefs spark the animosity between rival groups. This was the case in ancient Egypt with the Israelites. One of the pretexts for division between the Turks and Armenians was that the former are predominantly Muslim and the latter are predominantly Christian. In Yugoslavia the fact that the Serbs come from a Christian tradition and their adversaries are Muslim is a blight on Christianity, especially given the fact that modern Serbs are proud of their Christian ancestry. After all, Serbia is credited with stopping Turkish-Muslim aggression in Europe during the Middle Ages.

The Lesson

Joycelyn Pollock is a criminologist and author of one of the leading textbooks on criminal justice ethics. She writes, "Even with all these scientific and philosophical attempts to explain human action, we are still left with troubling questions when we read or hear about people who kill, steal, or otherwise offend our sense of morality. Evil is still one of the great mysteries of life."[13]

Pollock's statement is true. Some types of evil behavior are beyond human explanation. As Exodus 1 demonstrates, genocide is nothing new. As the current situation in Sudan demonstrates, genocide is not extinct. Darfur, a region in Western Sudan, has been the subject of intense scrutiny and concern among governments throughout the world. The majority of Darfur's population are Arab Muslims with ties to Sudan's central government. Ethnic Furs, the dark-skinned, sedentary, agricultural people for whom the region is named, have long been at odds with the region's Arab Muslim majority. In 2003, this long-simmering tension mushroomed, and tens of thousands of Furs have been killed with the backing of the Sudanese government. Diplomatic and economic pressure from other countries has not stopped the genocidal campaign against the Furs. The terrible irony when discussing the Darfur story along with the story of Exodus 1 lies in the distinct probability that the Darfur region was under the control of the Egyptian empire during the time of Pharaoh's genocide campaign against the Hebrews.[14]

The Hope

All any human being can do is have faith that God can work through even the most heinous conduct imaginable, which is what he did in the story of Exodus 1. The people who lived through that terrible ordeal could not see God's redemptive hand at work, as they witnessed the mass murder of infant boys, but, thanks to the gift of the Bible and the lessons of history, we can. This event in Exodus, tragic and evil though it was, set in motion the subsequent events of the book of Exodus and the entire Old Testament, and the rest of human history. If the Israelites had not been subjected to this persecution, they would have remained in Egypt and lived lives of quiet contentment, but they also may have disappeared into history. They would not have fulfilled God's plan that they be a people set apart to do his will and reclaim their ancestral homeland, the same land in which Jesus was born centuries later. The history of the Jews as a people and, by extension, the life of Christ and the founding of the Christian faith, owes itself in part to the murderous tragedy of Exodus 1.

7

Moses | Homicide, Concealing a Homicide,
| and Being a Fugitive from Justice

Exodus 2:11-15

11 One day, after Moses had grown up, he went out to where his own people were and watched them at their hard labor. He saw an Egyptian beating a Hebrew, one of his own people. 12 Glancing this way and that and seeing no one, he killed the Egyptian and hid him in the sand. 13 The next day he went out and saw two Hebrews fighting. He asked the one in the wrong, "Why are you hitting your fellow Hebrew?"

14 The man said, "Who made you ruler and judge over us? Are you thinking of killing me as you killed the Egyptian?" Then Moses was afraid and thought, "What I did must have become known."

15 When Pharaoh heard of this, he tried to kill Moses, but Moses fled from Pharaoh and went to live in Midian, where he sat down by a well.

 Moses is one of the most important figures in world history. Even the most casual Bible reader is acquainted with his name. He led the Israelites out of Egyptian slavery to the Promised Land; he had a visual encounter with God; his name is tied to the Bible's most prominent system of law and justice; he was the original recipient of the Ten Commandments, the foundation for moral life and legal systems for Jews, Christians, and Muslims even today.

THE PRINCIPAL CHARACTERS

The life of Moses is even more complex and fascinating than is revealed in the passage just mentioned. As an infant he narrowly escaped death at the hands of the man who would become his step-grandfather. He grew up as a child of the royal family in the most powerful empire in the Near East, only to abandon and rebel against his royal upbringing to attend to the welfare of his fellow Hebrews, who were living under the cruel domination of the Egyptian government, headed by a succession of Pharaohs, some of whom were probably his close family, though not by blood.

 Moses committed two or maybe three crimes in Exodus 2. The first crime was homicide. Exodus tells us that Moses killed the Egyptian because the Egyptian was beating a fellow Hebrew. We do not know anything more about the killing—what, if any, type of weapon was used, whether there was a struggle, and so forth.

THE CRIMES

Several scenarios are possible. One, Moses may have killed the Egyptian to save the Hebrew's life. If this was the case, the killing could be deemed "excusable" by today's standards. Murder in defense of an innocent life, provided this can be proved, constitutes excusable homicide.[1] However, this presupposes that the innocent life is of equal value to the life of the person killed. Modern American law does not make any formal distinction between homicide victims based on social status. Since the Hebrew was a slave, and the man Moses killed was an Egyptian, the life of the Hebrew had diminished value under Egyptian law. It would be a greater crime to intervene on the Hebrew's behalf than it would be for the Egyptian to kill the slave. Similar laws existed in the United States during the days of slavery. For example, a South Carolina law forbade a slave from intervening to save his master in a fight with another white man, unless the slave was ordered to intervene by the master. If the slave intervened without permission, the slave could be punished.[2]

There is a second scenario. "Felonious" homicide is the killing of a human being without justification.[3] One type of felonious homicide is manslaughter, the intentional killing of a human being without deliberation, premeditation, or malice. Moses may have intervened to save the Hebrew, with no intention of killing the Egyptian. Under this scenario, the Egyptian offered resistance, and Moses killed him during the altercation. The modern equivalent in this scenario is involuntary manslaughter, in which a person kills another but does so while committing an act not designed to inflict bodily harm.[4] For example, an automobile was not invented for the purpose of killing anyone, but if used recklessly, it can kill. Therefore, in instances where a person is killed in an automobile accident, it is not unusual for the driver to be charged with involuntary manslaughter, provided the driver operated the vehicle in a reckless manner.

The third and most likely scenario is that Moses killed the Egyptian in anger, or in the heat of passion. Verse 12 states that Moses glanced "this way and that," indicating that he saw a chance to take out some of his pent-up anger against the Egyptians by avenging the beating of his fellow Hebrew. Even so, the killing might fit the modern definition of voluntary manslaughter. Voluntary manslaughter is the unlawful taking of a human life but without premeditation.[5]

Such legal distinctions meant nothing to the Pharaoh. Moses was his familial rival, and the Pharaoh probably viewed him as a traitor to the monarchy that had reared him in the royal household. Moses became a political criminal. Because of his status and background, Moses's crime was viewed as more egregious than if it had been committed by an ordinary inhabitant. In the Pharaoh's eyes, Moses was not only a killer, but a traitor to his family and his people.

Moses compounded the crime of homicide by committing a second crime, concealing the body. Concealing any death, especially a homicide, was probably against Egyptian law or contrary to custom at the time, and it is against the law today. Concealing a nonhomicidal death is against the law, but it is not a very serious crime. For example, Nebraska law states, "Any person who conceals the death of another person and thereby prevents a determination of the cause or circumstances of death commits a Class I misdemeanor," which carries a maximum penalty of one year imprisonment and a $1,000 fine.[6]

Concealing a homicide is a more serious matter, even if subsequent investigation shows that the homicide may have been excusable. The crime is especially serious if the concealment hinders investigation of the offense or prevents discovery of the body, which is what happened in Exodus 2. For example, Georgia law states, "A person who, by concealing the death of any other person, hinders a discovery of whether or not such person was unlawfully killed is guilty of a felony and upon conviction shall be punished by imprisonment for not less than one nor more than ten years, a fine of not less than $1,000.00 nor more than $5,000.00, or both."[7]

Moses's third offense was being a fugitive from justice. A fugitive from justice is a person who flees a state or country in which he or she is accused of a crime in order to avoid punishment, or to avoid testifying in a criminal proceeding, even if the person is innocent of the crime of which accused. [8] In the 1993 movie, *The Fugitive*, Harrison Ford portrays Richard Kimble, a doctor convicted of murdering his wife. Kimble is innocent of the crime but is convicted nonetheless, a common Hollywood scenario. Kimble escapes from custody and is pursued by Samuel Gerard, a Deputy U.S. Marshal portrayed by Tommy Lee Jones. At one point, the two men confront each other, but from a distance. Kimble shouts to Gerard, "I didn't kill my wife." Gerard responds, "I don't care." To the Deputy Marshal, the facts of the original crime are immaterial. All he cares about is that Richard Kimble is a fugitive from justice, and it is his job to return him to custody. It is up to the courts to determine innocence or guilt. Being a fugitive from justice is a crime itself.

Modern legal complexities notwithstanding, Moses knew he was in trouble for killing the Egyptian. He knew that either his killing the Egyptian could not be justified under Egyptian law, or that no one would accept his word that the killing was justified nor sympathize with any mitigating circumstances that may have been present. Knowing that he was in trouble, Moses, rather than admitting and taking accountability for his actions, ran away to Midian, where he lived for many years. Ironically, Moses lived among the people whose ancestors took Joseph to Egypt and sold him into slavery several hundred years earlier. We do not know how far away from Egypt Moses ran. The land called Midian could have been anywhere from the Sinai Peninsula to the Arabian Desert. So it could have been several hundred miles away.

THE CRIME TODAY

Running from the law is common today, as well. Accused criminals often hide from the law by trying to go beyond the reach of those who seek them. Today, the process of extradition might apply to cases like that of Moses. There are two types of extradition, interstate and international. Within the United States, it is not unusual for an accused offender to flee from the state in which he or she is accused. The state charging the offender may seek extradition of the offender. Article

IV Section 2. (2) of the United States Constitution states, "A Person charged in any State with Treason, Felony, or other Crime, who shall flee from Justice, and be found in another State, shall on demand of the executive Authority of the State from which he fled, be delivered up, to be removed to the State having Jurisdiction of the Crime." This Article of the Constitution is enforced by the Uniform Criminal Extradition Act, which most states have adopted.[9]

International extradition is more complicated. Extradition treaties provide for the holding or transportation of fugitives to the country where they face charges. Countries with poor relationships, such as the United States and Cuba, seldom cooperate with each other in extradition proceedings. Even countries that enjoy otherwise friendly relationships encounter problems with extradition matters. Three cases provide illustrations.

First, there is the case of Charles Ng. Ng, along with Leonard Lake, was accused of raping, torturing, and killing more than twenty people, two of them baby boys, in California during the 1980s. After he was arrested, Ng escaped custody and fled to Canada, where he was arrested for shoplifting and shooting a police officer. California requested Ng's extradition. Canada, which does not allow capital punishment, wrestled with the question of whether its law allowed extradition when the accused might face the death penalty in the jurisdiction to which he was being extradited. After some tense legal and diplomatic wrangling, Ng was finally extradited to California, where he was convicted of eleven murders and sentenced to death.

During the 1990s, relations between the United States and Israel were slightly strained because of a case involving a Maryland teenager named Samuel Sheinbein. In 1997, Sheinbein murdered his roommate in Maryland and fled to Israel a few days after the killing. Israeli law prohibits the extradition of its citizens to other countries. Given the history of persecution against Jews, Israel's law is understandable, and some other countries have similar laws. Actually Sheinbein had never lived in Israel; his father was born in Palestine before the founding of the nation of Israel, which legally entitled Sheinbein to the benefits of Israeli citizenship. The United States was outraged when Israel refused to extradite Sheinbein. Rather than usurp its own laws or set a dangerous precedent, the Israeli government sentenced Sheinbein to twenty-four years in prison.[10]

Another modern example that illustrates the complexities of extradition is that of Roman Polanski. Polanski is a French-born film director of Polish extraction, whose credits include the 1968 horror classic *Rosemary's Baby*, the 1974 Academy-Award-winning film *Chinatown*, and the critically acclaimed 2002 film *The Pianist*. In 1977, Polanski was arrested and charged by California authorities with the statutory rape of a 13-year-old girl. Polanski pleaded guilty in 1978, but fled the United States for France before his sentencing date. French policy and its treaty with the United States forbid extradition of French citizens, and the United States, realizing a request to extradite Polanski would be futile, has never pushed for his return, although American authorities have made it known that it may seek extradition if Polanski travels to other countries that are amenable to its extradition requests. Most fugitive stories are not as high profile, and most fugitives are not as wealthy or successful in evading prosecution as Polanski.

The Lesson

In 1973, Harry Chapin released a song called "W.O.L.D," in which he sang, "Sometimes I get this crazy dream, that I just take off in my car, but you can travel on 10,000 miles, and still stay where you are."[11] Moses could run from the Pharaoh, but not from God; and yet God's will was carried out through Moses, despite, or perhaps because of, the complicated twists and turns that comprised the life of Moses. When he went to Midian, Moses hoped to live in obscurity, escaping his past life as an Egyptian and not wanting to return to Egypt to face the future as a Hebrew. It was in Midian, where Moses was trying to hide, that Moses received the call from God that would lead to his placement in the pantheon of Old Testament figures, and more importantly, his role in the fulfilling of God's will. No one can hide from God. Like Moses, God confronts us. He does not force us to follow his will, but he does force us to make a choice. Either we will live for God or we will not. Those who, like Moses, follow God's plan for their life will reap rewards both in the current life and the one to follow.

8

The Israelite Spies and Rahab | Espionage

Joshua 2: 1-22

2:1 Then Joshua son of Nun secretly sent two spies from Shittim. "Go, look over the land," he said, "especially Jericho." So they went and entered the house of a prostitute named Rahab and stayed there.

2 The king of Jericho was told, "Look! Some of the Israelites have come here tonight to spy out the land." 3 So the king of Jericho sent this message to Rahab: "Bring out the men who came to you and entered your house, because they have come to spy out the whole land."

4 But the woman had taken the two men and hidden them. She said, "Yes, the men came to me, but I did not know where they had come from. 5 At dusk, when it was time to close the city gate, the men left. I don't know which way they went. Go after them quickly. You may catch up with them." 6 (But she had taken them up to the roof and hidden them under the stalks of flax she had laid out on the roof.) 7 So the men set out in pursuit of the spies on the road that leads to the fords of the Jordan, and as soon as the pursuers had gone out, the gate was shut.

8 Before the spies lay down for the night, she went up on the roof 9 and said to them, "I know that the Lord has given this land to you and that a great fear of you has fallen on us, so that all who live in this country are melting in fear because of you. 10 We have heard how the Lord dried up the water of the Red Sea for you when you came out of Egypt, and what you did to Sihon and Og, the two kings of the Amorites east of the Jordan, whom you completely destroyed. 11 When we heard of it, our hearts melted and everyone's courage failed because of you, for the Lord your God is God in heaven above and on the earth below. 12 Now then, please swear to me by the Lord that you will show kindness to my family, because I have shown kindness to you. Give me a sure sign 13 that you will spare the lives

of my father and mother, my brothers and sisters, and all who belong to them, and that you will save us from death."

14 "Our lives for your lives!" the men assured her. "If you don't tell what we are doing, we will treat you kindly and faithfully when the Lord gives us the land."

15 So she let them down by a rope through the window, for the house she lived in was part of the city wall. 16 Now she had said to them, "Go to the hills so the pursuers will not find you. Hide yourselves there three days until they return, and then go on your way."

17 The men said to her, "This oath you made us swear will not be binding on us 18 unless, when we enter the land, you have tied this scarlet cord in the window through which you let us down, and unless you have brought your father and mother, your brothers and all your family into your house. 19 If anyone goes outside your house into the street, his blood will be on his own head; we will not be responsible. As for anyone who is in the house with you, his blood will be on our head if a hand is laid on him. 20 But if you tell what we are doing, we will be released from the oath you made us swear."

21 "Agreed," she replied. "Let it be as you say." So she sent them away and they departed. And she tied the scarlet cord in the window.

22 When they left, they went into the hills and stayed there three days, until the pursuers had searched all along the road and returned without finding them. 23 Then the two men started back. They went down out of the hills, forded the river and came to Joshua son of Nun and told him everything that had happened to them. 24 They said to Joshua, "The Lord has surely given the whole land into our hands; all the people are melting in fear because of us."

THE PRINCIPAL CHARACTERS We know nothing about the spies other than what is contained in this passage. Their names are never revealed. This is the second recorded mission of Israelite spying. The first mission is recorded in Numbers 13. Moses sent twelve spies, one from each tribe, to spy out the land of Canaan and report back. Ten of the spies reported that the Canaanites were too fearsome for the Israelites to take on. The people believed the spies' account, doubting God, which led to the forty years (the approximate length of a generation) of wandering the wilderness. Only two of the spies, Caleb and Joshua, encouraged their fellow Israelites to invade Canaan.

Because of his faith, Joshua was selected to succeed Moses as Israel's leader. Whereas Moses sent twelve spies in Numbers, Joshua sent only two. Perhaps only two were sent on this assignment because only two spies returned a favorable report a generation earlier, but that possibility is not mentioned. Secrecy was also paramount. It is likely that very few of the Israelites knew of this mission. When Moses sent the twelve spies out forty years earlier, they spied the entire land of Canaan. In this case the two spies were assigned to focus on the city of Jericho.

Another principal character in this story is Rahab. Rahab was a *zonah*, or a common harlot.[1] She may have been an innkeeper, which, given the culture, was the near equivalent of a brothel operator. The two Israelite spies, coming from a nation that was set apart from their neighbors as the chosen people that worshipped the one true God, had to make a deal with a prostitute to accomplish their mission. The intermingling that God warned the Israelites to avoid began even before they launched their foray into the promised land.[2] However, a more charitable view of Rahab can also be offered, or a window into the true forgiving and accepting nature that God wanted to inspire in the Israelites. She married into the Israelite nation and was held in high esteem by subsequent generations of Israelites.[3] Rahab is listed in the book of Hebrews' "hall of faith," as one of the Old Testament heroes whose faith in God was their salvation (Hebrews 11:31).

THE CRIME

The crime the spies committed was espionage. Espionage is the act of covertly obtaining a military secret for a foreign government in time of war or peace.[4] In this case the spies were scouting out Jericho to lay plans for a military invasion. Spying and espionage have been a part of government, especially military campaigns, throughout human history. The first mention of spying in the Bible even predates Numbers 13. In Genesis 42, Joseph accuses his half-brothers of spying the land of Egypt to assess its weaknesses. Of course Joseph was knowingly making a false accusation, but this passage indicates that espionage was a concern even in that era.

Historically, the primary method of gathering intelligence has simply involved observation and interpersonal communication, one person sharing secrets with the enemy. Technological advances have changed intelligence gathering to some degree. Many espionage missions rely on satellite technology and various forms of eavesdropping devices. The same can be said of undercover police work. Electronic eavesdropping and video surveillance are valuable tools in some undercover operations. The Israelite spies in Joshua had no such technology. Also, even though technology has changed espionage and undercover work, good intelligence-gathering still depends on human interaction. Despite technological advances, often the best way to infiltrate an enemy organization—be it an organized crime group, a terrorist organization, or a country's military—is person-to-person communication.

What one country calls espionage or spying, another country calls gathering intelligence. In other words, one country's "spy" is another country's "intelligence agent." The United States' primary spy agencies are the Central Intelligence Agency (CIA), which was created in 1947, primarily because of the fear of the Soviet Union and communism. The second is the National Security Agency (NSA) which was created by a secret Presidential order in 1952. Even though these agencies are less than sixty years old, espionage is as old as American history itself.

During the Civil War, the Union's chief spymaster was Allan Pinkerton, the founder of the Pinkerton Detective Agency. Pinkerton and his agents spied in the South, reporting troop movements, strengths, and vulnerabilities, probably much the same as the two spies in Joshua did, to the Union. Pinkerton also conducted counter-espionage activity in the North, looking for Confederate sympathizers.

While the book of Joshua had its Rahab, the Civil War had its own famous or infamous spy, Rose Greenbow. Greenbow, also called the "wild rose of the Confederacy," was a prominent Washington DC socialite who, in the course of wining and dining important government officials, would elicit secret information, which she would pass along to the Confederacy. Greenbow was arrested by Pinkerton and eventually imprisoned, but she continued to spy for the Confederacy.[5] Greenbow illustrates the moral ambiguity of espionage. In the North she was vilified as a spy but in the South she was treated as a heroine.

Because of the nature of spying, the identities of the most successful spies are lost to history. Even the two spies in Joshua are anonymous. Most famous spies—Joshua and Caleb representing notable exceptions—are the ones who get caught. Along those lines, the most famous spy in American history is Nathan Hale. Hale was a 21-year-old Yale College graduate and school teacher who, after infiltrating a British unit, was caught trying to obtain secret information to pass along to his American regiment in New York. Shortly before he was hanged, Hale was reported to have stated that his only regret was that he had but one life to lose for his country.[6]

The story in Joshua 2 brings to mind one of the unsavory realities of espionage and undercover police work. When doing it, one must get one's hands dirty by partnering with unsavory characters. Espionage is a key weapon in the current war against terror, and it has long been a part of anti-terrorism efforts waged by governments around the world.

One country with a long history of engaging in antiterrorism efforts is Great Britain. The British have long been engaged in a battle with the Irish Republican Army (IRA), a group of radical Irish Catholics dedicated to ridding Northern Ireland of British rule. The British campaign against the IRA has come to be known as the Dirty War. Wars against terrorist organizations are fought by covert means, which necessitates spying. The key, according to *Atlantic Monthly* correspondent Matthew Teague, "is to not mind killing, and to expect dying."[7] Teague also quoted a British agent who infiltrated the IRA and killed many people while conducting his assignment, including people whom he knew to be innocent civilians or who also worked for the British government. The agent said, "You cannot pretend to be a terrorist. I had to be able to do the same thing as the IRA man next to me (including committing murder). Otherwise I wouldn't be there."[8]

The work done by spies is very often dirty work, but the only dirty work that seemed required of the two spies in Joshua 2 was that they deceive the leaders of Jericho. Nevertheless, we can assume that if the spies would have been required to kill to fulfill their mission, they would have. In fact, the espionage mission they were on was a prelude to a full-scale battle between the inhabitants of Jericho and the Israelites, part of the Holy War the Israelites were waging to reclaim the land of their ancestors.

It is ironic that the Israelites are depicted in Joshua 2 as skilled spies, because even today, Israel is widely admired (and detested by its enemies) for its espionage work. Like all other developed countries,

Israel relies on technology to assist in its intelligence and espionage work, but Israel still places great emphasis on human intelligence. Even though Israel is surrounded by avuncular allies (Egypt and Jordan) or outright hostile neighbors (Syria and the Palestinians), it still excels at gathering intelligence and engaging in espionage the old fashioned way, personal communication with informants. Like the spies in Joshua, modern Israeli spies are adept at infiltrating hostile territory. The two agencies that bear the greatest responsibility for intelligence gathering and espionage in Israel are the Mossad and Shin Bet. The Mossad is largely responsible for espionage and intelligence operations outside Israel, and Shin Bet is responsible for similar operations within or close to Israel.

The Lesson

Christians very often like to live the Christian life by enjoying a comfortable, middle-class lifestyle, holding down good jobs, attending and giving to their church, avoiding immoral vices, and sometimes doing good works. Christians pay their taxes and usually expect others to do the dirty work that keeps them safe. We expect police officers to do the dirty work it takes to keep the community safe from criminals, which might include living undercover as a drug dealer, gang member, or organized crime soldier. Two examples of the ethical dilemmas inherent in undercover police work are provided in *Donnie Brasco* and *Under and Alone*. *Donnie Brasco* tells the story of FBI agent Joseph Pistone, who spent two years undercover with a New York organized crime "family." Agent Pistone was required to live the life of a mafia soldier.[9] *Under and Alone* is the story of William Queen, an Alcohol, Tobacco, and Firearms agent who lived undercover as a member of the Mongols, an outlaw motorcycle club in Southern California.[10] Pistone and Queen had to shed the traditional coat-and-tie trappings of typical federal law enforcement work and act like the criminal population they were investigating. While most Christian law enforcement officers can perform their normal duties without compromising their beliefs, officers who work undercover do not have such an option. They are forced to live a sinful lifestyle and a lie.

We expect corrections officers to do the dirty work of containing criminals in prisons and jails, or to administer the death penalty in rare cases. We expect the military to do the dirty work of killing others to defend our national interests. We expect spies to do the dirty work of espionage, living double lives, engaging in deception, dealing with rogue characters to perform their jobs, and to kill when their mission calls for it.

Christians often voice blanket moral support for the people who do these jobs for us, but we do not like to be bothered with gory details. Referring to police work, but using an analogy that cuts across professions that occasionally require unpleasant duties, criminologist Joycelyn Pollock states it this way: "Police, in effect, become our 'sin eaters' of early folklore; they are the shady characters on the fringe of society who absorb evil so that the rest of us may remain pure—shunned and avoided, these persons and their value are taken for granted."[11]

Another unsavory reality of espionage is that by its very nature, espionage involves lying and deception. When, if ever, is it right to lie or deceive someone? This is a question that is not clearly addressed in the Bible. Many point to the Ninth Commandment forbidding false witness as a direct command from God that all lying is bad. However, such an interpretation broadens the Commandment beyond its intended purpose. In Exodus 1:18–21, God rewards the midwives who lied to the Pharaoh and did not obey his orders to kill Hebrew babies. The Ninth Commandment was not meant to categorically prohibit any deception. The NIV states that no one may give false testimony against a neighbor, which is more narrow than saying that all lies are prohibited. The Christian church has wrestled with the question of whether there is such a thing as a good lie. St. Augustine stated that all lies are bad and that liars endanger their mortal souls. He later modified his view, stating that all lies are sins, but they are easily pardoned.[12]

When, if ever is it ethical for government officials to engage in deception? No one likes being deceived by a politician, but the same people that detest dishonesty in politics have no moral reservations about two blatantly deceptive activities engaged in by government, namely espionage, and on a far more common level, undercover police work.

I authored a book in 2004 entitled *Criminal Justice Pioneers in U.S. History*.[13] It is a book of short biographies of important figures in the history of American criminal justice. In a telephone interview with one of the subjects of the book, we had a discussion about whether it is ever right to lie. This person—a devout Roman Catholic, philosopher, and law school professor—took the position that all lies are bad, no matter what the context in which the lie is told or the intent of the liar. Suppose, I said, you were living in Nazi-occupied Holland, and you were aware that there were Jews being hid in an attic. When confronted with a direct question from a Nazi official about whether any Jews were hiding in the house in question, should you lie and save the lives of the Jews, or would you tell the truth, leaving whatever evil acts that would follow to the conscience of those committing them? According to the absolutist view, held by this man, the proper course is to tell the truth, and if those who heard your words chose to commit an evil act as a result, they were the evildoers, not you, and your conscience was clear. (Bear in mind that this was merely an intellectual exchange between two professors. I have little doubt that if presented with such a situation in real life, the person with whom I spoke, a kind and decent man, would opt for saving lives.)

Sisela Bok, author of *Lying*, states that there are four rules one should consult when contemplating the telling of a lie:

1. First seek truthful alternatives;
2. If a lie and truth achieve same result, tell the truth;
3. Lie only as a matter of last resort; and
4. The lie must result in a higher moral value.[14]

Hugo Grotius, a seventeenth-century Dutch Christian philosopher, stated that lying to liars should not be considered lying, which could be interpreted to mean that lying to someone who is basically dishonest is not really lying.[15] This is the position that spies and undercover police officers basically assume. When dealing with dishonesty or evil, the lie that is being told is far less objectionable than the evil or the wrong that the person being deceived may do if left alone.

A more appropriate ending for this chapter might be "the questions" instead of "the lesson." That is because the story in Joshua 2 leaves us with some questions that are difficult to answer. Does the end justify the means? Is it morally acceptable to lie to achieve a higher purpose, especially if the higher purpose is what we believe to be the will of God? Is it morally acceptable to do what might be labeled "dirty work"

76

in the name of God? Are Christians justified in lying in the name of God? What about Christians who assisted in helping African-American slaves escape through the "underground railroad" when the United States practiced slavery? People employed in the fields of criminal justice, the military, and some other professions are forced to wrestle with these questions. The decision to enter a profession that requires unpleasant duties is one that any Christian should make prayerfully and with some idea of what moral boundaries should govern them, and with a clear focus on what the will of God should be for their life.

9

Achan | Looting and Vicarious Punishment

Joshua 7

7:1 But the Israelites acted unfaithfully in regard to the devoted things; Achan son of Carmi, the son of Zimri, the son of Zerah, of the tribe of Judah, took some of them. So the Lord's anger burned against Israel.

2 Now Joshua sent men from Jericho to Ai, which is near Beth Aven to the east of Bethel, and told them, "Go up and spy out the region." So the men went up and spied out Ai.

3 When they returned to Joshua, they said, "Not all the people will have to go up against Ai. Send two or three thousand men to take it and do not weary all the people, for only a few men are there." 4 So about three thousand men went up; but they were routed by the men of Ai, 5 who killed about thirty-six of them. They chased the Israelites from the city gate as far as the stone quarries and struck them down on the slopes. At this the hearts of the people melted and became like water.

6 Then Joshua tore his clothes and fell facedown to the ground before the ark of the Lord, remaining there till evening. The elders of Israel did the same, and sprinkled dust on their heads. 7 And Joshua said, "Ah, Sovereign Lord, why did you ever bring this people across the Jordan to deliver us into the hands of the Amorites to destroy us? If only we had been content to stay on the other side of the Jordan! 8 O Lord, what can I say, now that Israel has been routed by its enemies? 9 The Canaanites and the other people of the country will hear about this and they will surround us and wipe out our name from the earth. What then will you do for your own great name?"

10 The Lord said to Joshua, "Stand up! What are you doing down on your face? 11 Israel has sinned; they have violated my covenant, which I commanded them to keep. They have taken some of the devoted things; they have stolen, they have lied, they have put them with their own possessions. 12 That is why the Israelites

cannot stand against their enemies; they turn their backs and run because they have been made liable to destruction. I will not be with you anymore unless you destroy whatever among you is devoted to destruction.

13 "Go, consecrate the people. Tell them, 'Consecrate yourselves in preparation for tomorrow; for this is what the Lord, the God of Israel, says: That which is devoted is among you, O Israel. You cannot stand against your enemies until you remove it.

14 "'In the morning, present yourselves tribe by tribe. The tribe that the Lord takes shall come forward clan by clan; the clan that the Lord takes shall come forward family by family; and the family that the Lord takes shall come forward man by man. 15 He who is caught with the devoted things shall be destroyed by fire, along with all that belongs to him. He has violated the covenant of the Lord and has done a disgraceful thing in Israel!'"

16 Early the next morning Joshua had Israel come forward by tribes, and Judah was taken. 17 The clans of Judah came forward, and he took the Zerahites. He had the clan of the Zerahites come forward by families, and Zimri was taken. 18 Joshua had his family come forward man by man, and Achan son of Carmi, the son of Zimri, the son of Zerah, of the tribe of Judah, was taken.

19 Then Joshua said to Achan, "My son, give glory to the Lord, the God of Israel, and give him the praise. Tell me what you have done; do not hide it from me."

20 Achan replied, "It is true! I have sinned against the Lord, the God of Israel. This is what I have done: 21 When I saw in the plunder a beautiful robe from Babylonia, two hundred shekels of silver and a wedge of gold weighing fifty shekels, I coveted them and took them. They are hidden in the ground inside my tent, with the silver underneath."

22 So Joshua sent messengers, and they ran to the tent, and there it was, hidden in his tent, with the silver underneath. 23 They took the things from the tent, brought them to Joshua and all the Israelites and spread them out before the Lord.

24 Then Joshua, together with all Israel, took Achan son of Zerah, the silver, the robe, the gold wedge, his sons and daughters, his cattle, donkeys and sheep, his tent and all that he had, to the Valley of Achor. 25 Joshua said, "Why have you brought this trouble on us? The Lord will bring trouble on you today."

Then all Israel stoned him, and after they had stoned the rest, they burned them. 26 Over Achan they heaped up a large pile of rocks, which remains to this day. Then the Lord turned from his fierce anger. Therefore that place has been called the Valley of Achor ever since.

Achan, or Achar as he is called in 1 Chronicles 2:7, is only mentioned in the context of this story. Nothing else is known about him. The name Achan means "troubler," so this may have been a name ascribed to him retrospectively, rather than being his given name, or he may have been prophetically named, as some Old Testament figures were said to be. Joshua, the other character in this passage, ranks as one of Old Testament Israel's greatest military leaders, exceeded only by David in military accomplishments.

THE PRINCIPAL CHARACTERS

Achan's crime was fairly straightforward and uncomplicated. He looted some of the items he came across during a battle, a common action in war, but something that was forbidden in this instance. In some Old Testament battles, the Israelites were permitted to take the spoils of the battle, meaning material possessions, animals, and human captives. In other cases they were instructed to destroy all, the thinking being that any possession, human or not, would taint the Israelites with the morally corrupt culture from which the spoils were obtained; or if they obtained certain possessions, especially precious metals, they were to offer them to God rather than enrich themselves.

THE CRIME

The point of interest in this story is not Achan's crime, but the punishment. This story raises the question posed by Alan Dershowitz, "Can God's justice be judged by human beings according to standards of human justice?"[1] Dershowitz posed the question about the innocents who may have been killed when God destroyed Sodom, but it also can be raised here. It should be noted that whether Achan alone suffered the death penalty or whether his family was killed as well is the subject of debate. Some translations of verse 25 leave room for doubt, but the evidence seems to favor the interpretation that his wife and children were executed as well.

THE PUNISHMENT

This passage is very difficult for modern sensitivities. Vicarious punishment toward family members is outlawed in Deuteronomy 24:16, which makes this story especially puzzling. In the United States, the focus of a criminal inquiry is on the individual. In a criminal proceeding, individual rights trump the will of the community. No matter how unpopular an accused might be, the government is obligated by law to protect the rights of that person. The idea of vicarious punishment or punishing someone for the crimes of another is foreign to us, as well, assuming that the person had no part or knowledge of the crime being committed. *Barnes' Notes* state that it is highly unlikely that Achan's family was unaware of his crime, that it would seem unlikely he could conceal these items in a small living space. [2]

But the Middle East during the time of Joshua was nothing like our modern democratic society. Even some modern legal systems in the Middle East recognize the well-being of the community as more important than that of an individual. In the modern U.S. legal system, the guiding assumption is that it is better that twenty guilty people go free rather than one innocent person be convicted. Again, this pattern of thinking was not prevalent in ancient Middle Eastern culture, and it is not predominant in some contemporary Middle Eastern cultures. For example, there is no Arabic word for freedom; hence the welfare of the entire community is assigned greater importance than the welfare of the individual.

A little mental exercise that some professors like to have with students goes roughly like this: A small group of people are aboard a raft in the ocean, but the raft is too small and the rations too meager to support everyone on the raft. A decision must be made about whether to throw someone off the raft for the good of those who remain. The professor provides a description of each person on the raft, and students argue about who should be sacrificed for the well-being of the others. Inevitably someone will say that it is wrong to sacrifice anyone. No person's life is less important than anyone else's. They should stay together no matter what and pray for a miracle. Under Sharia (Islamic law), the thinking would be that one person should be sacrificed if it means the survival of the rest of the community. Preference would be given to Muslims, provided that any non-Muslim is unwilling to convert to Islam.

Given the different worldview of ancient Israelite culture, the story in Joshua 7 is easier to understand, even if it is hard to digest and accept. Furthermore, the laws of some cultures provide that sacrificing an innocent life is justified if it will result in the saving of other lives down the road. This thinking also would endorse the idea that, in order to deter others from committing crimes, it is acceptable to make an example of offenders. Morton calls the events in Joshua 7 an example of the ancient social concept of community solidarity, in which a group could be held responsible for the sins of one of its members.[3]

Something else worth considering is that the nation of Israel may have become complacent or, even worse, arrogant, forgetting how dependent they were on God. Throughout the Old Testament, God punished Israel whenever they turned away from him, and it is possible that a sense of independence from God was beginning to settle in at the time of this story. Consider the fact that they had just conquered Jericho, a major military victory. In reading the first several verses of Chapter 7, one gets the sense that they were taking their mission into Ai too lightly, almost as an afterthought. The bitter experiences of Joshua 7 may have been a hard but necessary lesson that they were not to assume an attitude of superiority if they acted outside of God's commands, and that they must assume responsibility for the actions of their fellow Israelites, rather than proceed under the mistaken notion that whatever someone else does is "none of my affair."[4]

VICARIOUS PUNISHMENT AMERICAN STYLE

The American legal system recognizes the concept of vicarious liability in civil lawsuits. Vicarious liability is "the imposition of liability on one person for the actionable conduct of another, based solely on the relationship between the two persons."[5] An example would be an employer being found civilly liable for the actions of an employee. For example, if an employer failed to train an employee adequately and the employee committed an act which led to some assignment of liability, or if an employer was aware or clearly should have been aware of the actions of an employee that resulted in a finding of liability, the employer could be held responsible for the employee's actions. But these two scenarios differ greatly from that of Joshua 7. First, vicarious liability pertains to civil actions only, not crimes. Second, vicarious liability assumes that the third parties were complicit in the action, which clearly could not be the case with a child who is not old enough to fully comprehend the actions of a guilty parent.

Assuming that Achan's family was aware of his crime and that they were old enough to understand his actions, both of which are far from certain, they were guilty of the crime of accessory after the fact. An accessory is one who "is not the chief actor in the offense, or present at its performance, but in some way ... aids, abets, commands, or counsels another in the commission of a crime."[6] There are three categories of accessory: before the fact, during the fact, and after the fact. An accessory after the fact either "receives, relieves, comforts or assists the offender, in order to enable the person to escape from punishment, or the like."[7]

Another criminal law that applies to this discussion is RICO. An acronym for Racketeer Influenced and Corrupt Organization, RICO laws target criminal groups or organizations. The original RICO statute, written by Robert Blakey, a Department of Justice lawyer who served under President John Kennedy, was enacted by Congress in 1968. Most states have enacted their own RICO statutes. The primary target of RICO prosecutions have been organized crime groups, and RICO prosecutions have been successful in crippling criminal organizations in many large cities, especially high-profile mafia crime families in New York City. RICO has also been used to prosecute other organizations large and small, including street gangs and the Ku Klux Klan. Under RICO, if a prosecutor can prove that a person belongs to an "enterprise" that engages in a "pattern" of criminal or racketeering activity, any person which belongs to that enterprise is subject to severe criminal and civil penalties.[8] When RICO was first enacted, critics called it a form of vicarious punishment, arguing that the American legal system should not be used to criminalize membership in an organization. Nevertheless, RICO laws have stood the test of time and are frequently used by state and federal prosecutors.

Modern readers have difficulty perceiving Achan's family as the ancient equivalent to a RICO organization, however. His family, or at least the young sons and daughters, could not be fully complicit members of a criminal enterprise, even if this one instance constituted a pattern of criminal activity, which it did not.

Although a scenario like this one is all but impossible in today's modern legal climate, we should remember that, whenever a criminal offender is punished, others suffer as well. When a man or woman is sent to prison, the family may suffer. Even though an offender is imprisoned to protect the public, the public suffers nonetheless because it loses a potentially productive member of the community, who becomes someone for whom the community must now provide basic care, shelter, and sustenance.

When someone is placed under probation or parole supervision, everyone in the offender's household usually deals with a probation or parole officer. As a former probation officer myself, I can attest to that, but the best illustration I heard came from a panel presentation at an academic conference. A professor told us about some probation officers with whom he had worked. The officers had related to him how, when they were assigned a new probationer, they would often explain the rules of the program to the entire family so that the family would have an idea of what to expect and also so that relatives could assist probationers in abiding by the terms of supervision. This program entailed very strict, intensive rules of supervision.

On Friday of the week that a young man was placed under the officers' supervision, the young man's father telephoned one of the probation officers to ask if going to a movie was okay. The officer carefully explained to the father that going to a movie was against the rules of supervision; the father said okay, and they hung up. A question arose in the officer's mind as to who he was talking about when he asked. He called the father back, and the father said that he was asking if it would be okay if the father and his wife went to a movie.[9] Sometimes the criminal justice system unwittingly punishes innocent third parties.

When a criminal offender is fined, very often someone else suffers, either the family member who pays the fine for the offender, or the family that is deprived of the money that goes toward the fine. So, in a sense, vicarious punishment is still very much a part of the American legal and correctional system. The difference is that the vicarious punishment is hidden today, and is much less severe than what is recorded in Joshua, whereas in other cultures the punishment suffered by others is more obvious.

85

The Lesson

It is hard to place a positive spin on, or find a silver lining in, the story of Achan. This incident served as an extremely hard and brutal lesson for the Israelites. The lesson is that they were "not merely as a number of individuals living together for their own purposes under common institutions, but a divinely-constituted organic whole."[10] It also reminded the Israelites that they should watch out for each other and act as their brother's keeper and overseer.[11] The actions of others affect us, and our own actions affect others, in ways that we often never realize. This is one of the lessons that can be learned, even today, from the tragic story of Joshua 7.

10

Saul and David | War Crimes

6 Now Saul heard that David and his men had been discovered. And Saul, spear in hand, was seated under the tamarisk tree on the hill at Gibeah, with all his officials standing around him. 7 Saul said to them, "Listen, men of Benjamin! Will the son of Jesse give all of you fields and vineyards? Will he make all of you commanders of thousands and commanders of hundreds? 8 Is that why you have all conspired against me? No one tells me when my son makes a covenant with the son of Jesse. None of you is concerned about me or tells me that my son has incited my servant to lie in wait for me, as he does today."

9 But Doeg the Edomite, who was standing with Saul's officials, said, "I saw the son of Jesse come to Ahimelech son of Ahitub at Nob. 10 Ahimelech inquired of the Lord for him; he also gave him provisions and the sword of Goliath the Philistine."

11 Then the king sent for the priest Ahimelech son of Ahitub and his father's whole family, who were the priests at Nob, and they all came to the king. 12 Saul said, "Listen now, son of Ahitub."

"Yes, my lord," he answered.

13 Saul said to him, "Why have you conspired against me, you and the son of Jesse, giving him bread and a sword and inquiring of God for him, so that he has rebelled against me and lies in wait for me, as he does today?"

14 Ahimelech answered the king, "Who of all your servants is as loyal as David, the king's son-in-law, captain of your bodyguard and highly respected in your household? 15 Was that day the first time I inquired of God for him? Of course not! Let not the king accuse your servant or any of his father's family, for your servant knows nothing at all about this whole affair."

16 But the king said, "You will surely die, Ahimelech, you and your father's whole family."

17 Then the king (Saul) ordered the guards at his side: "Turn and kill the priests of the Lord, because they too have sided with David. They knew he was fleeing, yet they did not tell me."

But the king's officials were not willing to raise a hand to strike the priests of the Lord.

18 The king then ordered Doeg, "You turn and strike down the priests." So Doeg the Edomite turned and struck them down. That day he killed eighty-five men who wore the linen ephod. 19 He also put to the sword Nob, the town of the priests, with its men and women, its children and infants, and its cattle, donkeys and sheep.

1 Samuel 27:1-12

27:1 But David thought to himself, "one of these days I will be destroyed by the hand of Saul. The best thing I can do is to escape to the land of the Philistines. Then Saul will give up searching for me anywhere in Israel, and I will slip out of his hand."

2 So David and the six hundred men with him left and went over to Achish son of Maoch king of Gath. 3 David and his men settled in Gath with Achish. Each man had his family with him, and David had his two wives: Ahinoam of Jezreel and Abigail of Carmel, the widow of Nabal. 4 When Saul was told that David had fled to Gath, he no longer searched for him.

5 Then David said to Achish, "If I have found favor in your eyes, let a place be assigned to me in one of the country towns, that I may live there. Why should your servant live in the royal city with you?"

6 So on that day Achish gave him Ziklag, and it has belonged to the kings of Judah ever since. 7 David lived in Philistine territory a year and four months.

8 Now David and his men went up and raided the Geshurites, the Girzites and the Amalekites. (From ancient times these peoples had lived in the land extending to Shur and Egypt.) 9 Whenever David attacked an area, he did not leave a man or woman alive, but took sheep and cattle, donkeys and camels, and clothes. Then he returned to Achish.

10 When Achish asked, "Where did you go raiding today?" David would say, "Against the Negev of Judah" or "Against the Negev of Jerahmeel" or "Against the Negev of the Kenites." 11 He did not leave a man or woman alive to be brought to Gath, for he thought, "They might inform on us and say, 'This is what David did.'" And

such was his practice as long as he lived in Philistine territory. 12 Achish trusted David and said to himself, "He has become so odious to his people, the Israelites, that he will be my servant forever."

THE PRINCIPAL CHARACTERS

"Only the dead have seen the end to war." This quote, alternately attributed to Plato and to Spanish-American philosopher George Santayana, is sad but true. As long as there is life on earth, there is war. As long as there has been war, there has been heroism, but there has also been brutality. Brutal actions in war were common to the Old Testament. In fact one might view the Old Testament as a story of one war after another, with God's will working through or in some cases in spite of some of these wars. Wartime atrocities were not confined to the enemies of Israel and Judah. Some were perpetrated by great figures of the Bible. This chapter examines the battle atrocities of two of those great figures, Saul and David.

Saul

Saul was Israel's first king, and one of the Old Testament's great tragedies and disappointments. He became king, handpicked through divine direction by the prophet Samuel, but only because the people of Israel cried to God for a king so that they could be like the nations and city-states around them. Having a king, they mistakenly thought, would make them stronger than they had been in trusting only God for guidance. Despite the warnings from Samuel that having a king would lead to problems, the Israelites persisted, and Saul was anointed king.

Saul experienced some political and military successes, but his reign was also beset by military failures, one of which brought about his own death (1 Samuel 31). Saul was echoed by William Shakespeare's Macbeth. His insecurity gave way to paranoia, severe mental instability, and an abandonment of his faith, as reflected by the unconscionable act of murdering the priests and their families in 1 Samuel 22, and consulting a witch for guidance in 1 Samuel 28, where his own tragic fate was revealed to him.

Like many dictators, Saul lost touch with reality. This can happen to anyone who surrounds himself only with people who will bow to his every whim. Dictators often surround themselves with people who are afraid of them, and they often do their best to instill fear in those closest to them. In news footage of former Iraqi dictator Saddam Hussein meeting with his top military advisers, the body language of the other men in the room indicates that they were frightened of Hussein. While he usually seemed relaxed, the other men wore forced smiles and sat very stiffly. Based on their knowledge of Hussein's prior behavior, they had reason to be frightened. Throughout his reign Hussein proved he was brutal and unpredictable. One of his most public demonstrations of his brutality came soon after he ascended to power in Iraq. In July of 1979, six days after he assumed power, Hussein convened his party leaders and announced that he had discovered that there were spies and conspirators among them. One by one, Hussein read the names of those he thought were disloyal to him, and one by one they were led away to be executed. Hussein videotaped this ghastly meeting, and he clearly relished the anguish and fear he engendered among his party members. At the conclusion of the meeting, Hussein thanked those who remained, and the message was clear as to the fate of anyone who dared to oppose him. Saul was equally paranoid, suspicious, and ruthless.

Saul's paranoia about David was not totally without foundation. David established himself as a military hero with the slaying of Goliath, and it was evident from that point forward that he was better suited to be king than Saul, and Saul knew it. So did Saul's son Jonathan, who protected David from Saul. Saul's hatred extended to Jonathan, whom he cursed with a wish for his untimely death (1 Samuel 14:44). Even though David respected Saul's position as God's anointed to the point where he spared his life (1 Samuel 24) while Saul was in pursuit of him, and in spite of the fact that David was Saul's son-in-law, Saul's hatred of David was unrelenting. No matter what David did to prove his loyalty, Saul still sought to kill him.

The events of 1 Samuel 22 did not come about suddenly. It took many years for Saul to reach this low point. His kingdom started with great promise. He had good intentions and great potential, but gradually Saul became more dependent on his own wisdom than on God's. He disregarded the instructions given to him by the prophet Samuel, the only man who would stand up to him. After Samuel died, there was no one left who would dare utter a cross word to Saul. The slaughter at Nob was the nadir of Saul's reign.

David

David's most famous military accomplishment, killing Goliath (1 Samuel 17), happened before he became a soldier. Saul was king at the time. How ironic that David fled to Goliath's home city to elude the king he once served. David, in addition to being a great leader and a person described as a man "after God's own heart," was also a ruthless warrior, but the Bible is silent on the morality of David's actions. While Saul is remembered as one of the Old Testament's great disappointments, David has gone down in history as one of the Old Testament's greatest heroes, despite his murderous affair with Bathsheba and his actions in 1 Samuel 27. Whereas Saul killed because of paranoia and jealousy, David and his men slaughtered an entire town to cover up other misdeeds. Unlike many other encounters David had with the Philistines, this was not a military battle; it was a slaughter. The people he killed were not giants like Goliath, or even soldiers. If contemporary standards applied, David would be labeled a war criminal.

The term "war crime" seems nonsensical on the surface. How can a person be charged with a crime in an organized killing campaign? In the 1979 Vietnam War film *Apocalypse Now*, Martin Sheen's character states, "Charging a man with murder in this place was like handing out speeding tickets at the Indy 500."[1] Nevertheless, many governments, over time, have agreed that even war has rules and boundaries. A war crime is an act committed by countries, a group, or an individual that violates the international laws governing war.[2] The term is often associated with Nazi and Japanese officials who were tried for war crimes after World War II. Throughout most of human history, there have been no war crimes trials like those held after World War II. Instead, defeated military leaders and/or the people they led into battle were customarily killed or sent into exile.

If the idea of charging someone with a war crime seems strange today, it seemed even more remote to the Old Testament culture. There was no such thing as a war crime in the Old Testament. Old Testament war was often total war, meaning that anyone was fair game. There was no distinction between innocent civilians and soldiers.

The modern Western concept of war differs from that of the ancient Middle East. Modern thinking about war in the United States is based largely on the Clausewitzian paradigm. This concept of war, named for Carl von Clausewitz, a nineteenth-century Prussian soldier, views a nation as either being at war or at peace, with no state between. War is regarded as an aberration, and peace is assumed to be the natural order. This is the idea that has been conveyed to students in American history classes for several generations. We were told, and were required to memorize, the dates when our wars began and ended. For example, most history textbooks state that American involvement in World War II had a definite beginning, December 7, 1941, and a definite end, September 2, 1945, the day the Japanese surrendered. The Civil War began on April 12, 1861, when Confederate forces fired on Fort Sumter, and ended on April 9, 1865, when Robert E. Lee surrendered to Ulysses S. Grant. Under such a paradigm, wars have a beginning and an end. There is peacetime and there is time of war. Under such a paradigm, the two time periods are distinct and mutually exclusive.

There are other paradigms of war, namely, that wars do not necessarily have a distinct beginning or a clear end. That was the case in the ancient Middle East, where there was no distinction between times of war and times of peace. War was assumed to be ongoing, the natural order, rather than an aberration. War never stopped, it merely experienced occasional slowdowns and interruptions.[3] This concept of war is not entirely confined to the ancient Middle East. For example, World War I and World War II, often taught as having clear beginnings and conclusions, and usually regarded as two distinct and separate events, are referred to by some as one long continuous war, with only brief interludes of ceasefire.[4] This paradigm also applies to the nation of Israel today. Although Israel has had wars with definite beginnings and ends, it also lives in a constant state of conflict or near-conflict with its neighbors, and with significant elements of the population under its control. The modern war on terror seems to be following the same line. There will never be a total end to the war on terror as long as terrorism looms as a threat, which it always will. The nations of the Middle East were constantly at war with one another during the Old Testament era. This partly explains the mindset that there was no distinction between soldiers and civilians, between military and nonmilitary targets, between times of peace and times of war.

Nonetheless, Saul's actions in 1 Samuel 22 were odious, even to his battle-hardened troops. While the killing of soldiers or even civilians was accepted; slaughtering priests and their families was not. Even some of Saul's soldiers, who no doubt feared the retribution of their violent and petulant king, refused to partake in this action, which clearly crossed a moral and religious boundary.

The Modern Response to War Crimes

The idea of putting people on trial for misdeeds committed during war is fairly new. It slowly took shape in the United States and in other countries beginning in the nineteenth century. After the American Civil War, several confederate soldiers and government leaders were charged with crimes stemming from their involvement in the war. Most of the charges were dropped upon the order of President Andrew Johnson, but there was one notable exception. Henry Wirz, the Confederate commander of Camp Sumter—the Andersonville, Georgia prison camp where more than 13,000 Union war prisoners perished—was tried by a military tribunal and hanged in 1865 for "wanton cruelty" inflicted on the Union prisoners in Andersonville.[5]

The British considered the idea of trying war criminals after the Boer War in South Africa, as did the victorious Allied Powers after World War I. War crimes trials were held in earnest after World War II, and a few other trials have been held since. The laws of war are part of the Geneva Conventions, which address acceptable wartime conduct with respect to, among other issues, relations of neutral parties and the treatment of war prisoners.[6] It is worth noting that those defeated in a battle are typically branded war criminals. However, there have been plenty of exceptions in recent years. Some countries have punished their own for wartime misconduct and atrocities. During the Vietnam War, the United States punished some of its own soldiers for crimes committed in combat situations. The most prominent example was that of Willam Calley, an Army Lieutenant who was sentenced to prison for murdering twenty-two Vietnamese villagers in 1968. In 2005, several U.S. soldiers were convicted and sentenced to prison for their role in the Abu Ghraib prison scandal, in which Iraqi prisoners were mistreated.

Another recent case is that of Charles Taylor, the President of Liberia from 1997 to 2003. Taylor fomented and encouraged one of the worst wars in the history of modern Africa. Taylor's warmongering involved his fellow Liberians and the neighboring country of Sierra Leone. Incredible brutalities occurred: rape, torture, and deliberate limb amputation were the hallmarks of Taylor's "armies." One of the worst abuses was Taylor's approval of recruiting children to serve in combat, an all-too-common occurrence throughout Africa. Sierra Leone indicted Taylor on war crimes charges. He fled to Nigeria after being forced from office, partly in response to a specific call from President George W. Bush for Taylor's removal. In March of 2006, Nigeria, after being pressured by the West and the United Nations, handed Taylor over to U.N. authorities to face war crimes charges.

The Lesson

The stories of Saul and David leave lessons for us about the timeless horrors of war and about our inhumanity to each other, about the dangers of unchecked power in the hands of military and political leaders, about how Americans should be thankful for the democracy under which they live, but they also serve as lessons about divine forgiveness. David, with all of his faults, still has an honored place in history as a man after God's own heart. Can God forgive even the vilest sinner? Can God forgive a war criminal? The answer is yes.

If the story of David does not resonate with us about the extent of God's forgiving nature, consider the story of an eighteenth-century Englishman named John Newton. Newton was not a war criminal; he was not even a soldier. He was something that to the modern mind was just as bad, a slave trader. In fact, for two years, Newton was a slave himself, to an African woman in West Africa. As a crewman aboard a slave trading vessel, Newton saw and partook of the most despicable actions imaginable: chaining men, women, and children like animals aboard slave ships, abusing and degrading the slaves for his amusement, physically mistreating the slaves and giving no thought to whether they lived or died, save for the money that might be lost, let alone for their psychological or spiritual welfare. Newton possessed this incredibly callous attitude toward his fellow human beings in spite of the fact that he was born to a Christian mother, who prayed that her son would one day become a minister.

During one particularly perilous storm in March of 1748, Newton, fearing for his life, cried to God for mercy, something he had not done in years. Reflecting on his sudden and uncharacteristic plea for divine mercy, Newton realized that there had never been a more wretched sinner than he. What right did he, a brutal slave trader, have to expect mercy? Newton eventually embraced the Christian faith, quit the slave trade, and fulfilled his deceased mother's dream; he became a minister in the Church of England. He also became an ardent advocate for the abolition of English involvement in the African slave trade. Perhaps even more significant, Newton wrote the words to a hymn that clutches at the heart of all who have sung and heard it:

> Amazing grace, how sweet the sound,
> That saved a wretch like me.
> I once was lost, but now am found
> Was blind but now I see.[7]

If God can grant mercy to a former slave trader like John Newton, or to a person who commits the worst wartime atrocities, he can forgive anyone who seeks him.

11

David and Bathsheba | Adultery and Conspiracy to Commit Murder

2 Samuel 11:1–17, 26–27

11:1 In the spring, at the time when kings go off to war, David sent Joab out with the king's men and the whole Israelite army. They destroyed the Ammonites and besieged Rabbah. But David remained in Jerusalem.

2 One evening David got up from his bed and walked around on the roof of the palace. From the roof he saw a woman bathing. The woman was very beautiful, 3 and David sent someone to find out about her. The man said, "Isn't this Bathsheba, the daughter of Eliam and the wife of Uriah the Hittite?" 4 Then David sent messengers to get her. She came to him, and he slept with her. (She had purified herself from her uncleanness.) Then she went back home. 5 The woman conceived and sent word to David, saying, "I am pregnant."

6 So David sent this word to Joab: "Send me Uriah the Hittite." And Joab sent him to David. 7 When Uriah came to him, David asked him how Joab was, how the soldiers were and how the war was going. 8 Then David said to Uriah, "Go down to your house and wash your feet." So Uriah left the palace, and a gift from the king was sent after him. 9 But Uriah slept at the entrance to the palace with all his master's servants and did not go down to his house.

10 When David was told, "Uriah did not go home," he asked him, "Haven't you just come from a distance? Why didn't you go home?"

11 Uriah said to David, "The ark and Israel and Judah are staying in tents, and my master Joab and my lord's men are camped in the open fields. How could I go to my house to eat and drink and lie with my wife? As surely as you live, I will not do such a thing!"

12 Then David said to him, "Stay here one more day, and tomorrow I will send you back." So Uriah remained in Jerusalem that day and the next. 13 At David's invitation, he ate and drank with him,

and David made him drunk. But in the evening Uriah went out to sleep on his mat among his master's servants; he did not go home.

14 In the morning David wrote a letter to Joab and sent it with Uriah. 15 In it he wrote, "Put Uriah in the front line where the fighting is fiercest. Then withdraw from him so he will be struck down and die."

16 So while Joab had the city under siege, he put Uriah at a place where he knew the strongest defenders were. 17 When the men of the city came out and fought against Joab, some of the men in David's army fell; moreover, Uriah the Hittite died.

26 When Uriah's wife heard that her husband was dead, she mourned for him. 27 After the time of mourning was over, David had her brought to his house, and she became his wife and bore him a son. But the thing David had done displeased the Lord.

2 Samuel 12:1–10

12:1 The Lord sent Nathan to David. When he came to him, he said, "There were two men in a certain town, one rich and the other poor. 2 The rich man had a very large number of sheep and cattle, 3 but the poor man had nothing except one little ewe lamb he had bought. He raised it, and it grew up with him and his children. It shared his food, drank from his cup and even slept in his arms. It was like a daughter to him.

4 "Now a traveler came to the rich man, but the rich man refrained from taking one of his own sheep or cattle to prepare a meal for the traveler who had come to him. Instead, he took the ewe lamb that belonged to the poor man and prepared it for the one who had come to him."

5 David burned with anger against the man and said to Nathan, "As surely as the Lord lives, the man who did this deserves to die! 6 He must pay for that lamb four times over, because he did such a thing and had no pity."

7 Then Nathan said to David, "You are the man! This is what the Lord, the God of Israel, says: 'I anointed you king over Israel, and I delivered you from the hand of Saul. 8 I gave your master's house to you, and your master's wives into your arms. I gave you the house of Israel and Judah. And if all this had been too little, I would have given you even more. 9 Why did you despise the word of the Lord by

doing what is evil in his eyes? You struck down Uriah the Hittite with the sword and took his wife to be your own. You killed him with the sword of the Ammonites. 10 Now, therefore, the sword will never depart from your house, because you despised me and took the wife of Uriah the Hittite to be your own.'

THE PRINCIPAL CHARACTERS

Essayist Lance Morrow wrote, "Evil seeks its opportunities and settles in like a parasite where it finds conditions welcoming."[1] Like many middle aged men today, David's life was at point where evil found welcoming conditions. He had accomplished much in his life and had become very powerful. He was probably bored, complacent, and looking for new adventures. Unfortunately, also like some middle-aged men today, he found his new adventure in a young woman.

Bathsheba was the daughter of Ammiel (also called Eliam), one of David's officers. Her degree of complicity in this affair is a matter of debate. Did she entice David? The fact that she was bathing openly in an area where she may have known she would be in David's line of vision suggests that she did, much like a woman undressing in front of an open window or sunbathing nude within sight of a neighbor.

There is no indication that Bathsheba voiced any reservations about David's advances; but, after all, she would have been powerless to resist. After Uriah's death, Bathsheba mourned, but the Bible does not indicate that she was especially grief-stricken. There is no indication that she was resentful of David either. Some insight into Bathsheba's personality can be found in 1 Kings 1–2. These passages reveal that, far from being a shrinking violet, Bathsheba actively promoted the ascension of her son Solomon to the throne, politicking with skill and subtlety on his behalf.

Uriah, the helpless victim of this crime, was no an ordinary foot soldier. He was one of Israel's most dedicated and able warriors. It is apparent from 1 Samuel 11:11 that Uriah was very loyal to his country and to his king, making David's betrayal and murderous plot all the more odious. In 1 Chronicles 11:41 he is listed as one of David's thirty "mighty men," another indication of his long history with, and undying loyalty to, David.

Nathan, like Samuel before him and Elijah after him, was one of the few true prophets of the Old Testament. Unlike most of the self-proclaimed prophets of his day, who were more concerned with holding on to their positions than speaking the truth, Nathan feared no one, not even the king. The Bible does not reveal how David's plot was revealed to Nathan. We do not know if Nathan received this information through divine means. It is likely that what David and Bathsheba had done was an "open secret." Many people knew about it. Such a salacious story would have been hard to keep secret in the palace, around the town, and through the ranks of the army, but no one dared confront the king except Nathan, who put his life at risk by confronting David.

Lois McMaster Bujold, an American science fiction author, wrote, "The dead cannot cry out for justice; it is a duty of the living to do so for them."[2] Nathan undertook this duty, not only for the sake of Uriah's memory, but because David had abused the authority and power with which God had endowed him.

THE CRIMES

David was guilty of two crimes in this passage. The first, adultery, had been a crime ever since the Ten Commandments were given to the Israelites. During the Old Testament era, the crime of adultery often fell hardest on the female. Given that polygamy was common among many men in the Old Testament, this would figure. If a man took a woman as a concubine, or if a man had more than one wife, that would not have been considered adultery as it would under modern laws.

However, the Mosaic Law was very clear about a man being culpable when the woman he slept with was already married, as was the case with Bathsheba. Leviticus 20:10 reads, "If a man commits adultery with another man's wife—with the wife of his neighbor—both the adulterer and the adulteress must be put to death." Under the Mosaic Law, David would probably not have been subjected to the death penalty—assuming that anyone would dare presume to tell the king that he should die for his behavior anyway—because he was not caught in the act. Nathan did not call for David's death, but he spoke words that cut David to the heart, and which proved to be true. Bathsheba may have been subject to the death penalty according to Mosaic Law, because her guilt was confirmed by her pregnancy while her husband was away. Given that scientific paternity testing that is available today was not available then, a man could successfully deny being the father.

It is clear from the Old Testament that adultery was regarded as a very serious offense. It has remained a criminal offense throughout the history of Western Civilization, until recently. Many jurisdictions have either abolished laws prohibiting adultery, or, as is more common, simply stopped enforcing them. The same is true of illicit cohabitation, that is, living together and having a sexual relationship, and illicit relations, or the act of fornication.

As of 2005, however, the Georgia Code still read, "A married person commits the offense of adultery when he voluntarily has sexual intercourse with a person other than his spouse and, upon conviction thereof, shall be punished as for a misdemeanor."[3] Some states have repealed adultery statutes, but it may still be used as evidence in a divorce. In other states, Rhode Island for example, adultery statutes are still part of the criminal code, but they are tied to bigamy statutes.

Illicit cohabitation is still against the law in some states as well, but it is seldom enforced. It was not until recently that living together out of wedlock became "de-radicalized" or socially tolerated. The social changes of the 1960s and 1970s and the increased access to birth control made living together much more commonplace than it once had been. Again, there are rare instances where laws against illicit cohabitation are enforced or are relevant.

A female sheriff's deputy in North Carolina recently discovered this in a very unpleasant way. In Pender County, North Carolina, Sheriff Carson Smith, knowing that the deputy was living with a man that was not her husband, pointed to a 200-year-old North Carolina law that prohibits illicit cohabitation. Violation of the law carries a maximum penalty of sixty days in jail and a $1,000 fine. Sheriff Smith ordered the deputy to marry the man, move out, or resign. She resigned and the American Civil Liberties Union (ACLU) took on her case. A local judge ruled the law unconstitutional, but the ruling did not apply to other cases in North Carolina. According to the ACLU, thirty-six people have been prosecuted under this law since 1997.[4]

The second crime that David committed was conspiracy to commit murder. A conspiracy is "a combination or confederacy between two or more persons formed for the purpose of committing, by their joint efforts, some unlawful or criminal act."[5] The crime of conspiracy is often difficult to prove in the modern legal system, especially if the act that was being plotted was not actually carried out. The person or persons can claim that they were not serious about committing the crime. In cases where the crime is committed, it is easier to prove.

David seemed determined to remove himself from Uriah's death to the greatest degree possible. He did not kill Uriah himself; he did not order one of his men to actually kill Uriah either. He made arrangements for his nation's enemies to do his dirty work. As Nathan says to him in 2 Samuel 12:9, "You killed him with the sword of the Ammonites." Nathan makes it clear to David that every nuance of his scheme had been uncovered.

Put this type of crime in a modern context. If the President of the United States were to order a military official to intentionally set up a soldier to be killed in a combat situation, what would happen to the President? The case would be very difficult to prove, but what if the evidence was available to prove the President's guilt? First, the President would be immune from civil liability. The doctrine of sovereign immunity precludes bringing suit against the government without its consent. Sovereign immunity is founded on the ancient principle "that the King can do no wrong." Many states and the federal government waive sovereign immunity under certain circumstances, but not with the President or Congress as a result of combat injury or death.

Whether the President could be criminally prosecuted, provided there was any chance of such a charge being proved, is a more difficult question. No such accusation has ever arisen in the United States. Given the sheer improbability of such a circumstance coming about, it is very unlikely that it ever would. Even though they were never criminally prosecuted, the Watergate scandal of President Richard Nixon's administration and the Monica Lewinsky scandal of the Clinton administration show that the office of the Presidency does not guarantee against criminal prosecution. Even without criminal prosecution or the threat of civil liability, Congress could impeach a President and vote to remove him or her from office for committing the type of crime discussed in 2 Samuel 11.

The Lesson

Aesop wrote that passion is a good servant but a bad master.[6] The sins of 2 Samuel 11 have not disappeared with time. Adultery is an all-too-common behavior in modern American society, with one distressing difference. Society is more tolerant of adultery today than it was in David's lifetime. Even though public opinion polls reveal that the majority of Americans disapprove of adultery, it is not regarded with the seriousness that it once was. Throughout the 1990s, public opinion polls revealed that approximately one in six married adults admitted to engaging in extramarital relations.[7] What may have been an extreme rarity in the day of David is something engaged in by a substantial minority of American adults. The crimes that stem from adultery have not disappeared either. Most murders that stem from modern adultery are crimes of "passion" or crimes committed in anger, not the carefully contrived murder that David orchestrated.

John Bunyan wrote, "One leak will sink a ship, and one sin will destroy a sinner."[8] David's sin with Bathsheba set into motion a string of events that not only affected his life, but ruined the lives of others, starting with the first child born to Bathsheba, and including some tragedies that are explored in the next two chapters. As verse 10 states, the sword indeed never left David's house. David's sin with Bathsheba became known to all, including the members of his own family. As subsequent events would show, David lost his moral compass when it came to his family life, and this would manifest itself in a series of family tragedies. Although he gained Bathsheba, David lost his children. This incident was one of numerous tragedies that befell David's family.

Nevertheless, God forgave David for his sin. Although he would suffer the effects of this sin for the remainder of his life, David's repentance manifested itself in one of the most profound passages in the Old Testament, Psalm 51. Throughout the Middle Ages in Europe, this passage was commonly recited by condemned prisoners about to be executed. It was also recited by members of the church who committed crimes but wanted to escape criminal punishment in favor of having their case dealt with by church authorities, a practice called "benefit of clergy."[9] Psalm 51 would never have been written had David not committed these terrible sins. Without sin, there can be no forgiveness and redemption.

51:1 Have mercy upon me, O God, According to Your lovingkindness; According to the multitude of Your tender mercies, Blot out my transgressions. 2 Wash me thoroughly from my iniquity, And cleanse me from my sin.

3 For I acknowledge my transgressions, And my sin is always before me.4 Against You, You only, have I sinned, And done this evil in Your sight—That You may be found just when You speak, And blameless when You judge.

5 Behold, I was brought forth in iniquity, And in sin my mother conceived me. 6 Behold, You desire truth in the inward parts, And in the hidden part You will make me to know wisdom.

7 Purge me with hyssop, and I shall be clean; Wash me, and I shall be whiter than snow. 8 Make me hear joy and gladness, That the bones You have broken may rejoice. 9 Hide Your face from my sins, And blot out all my iniquities.

10 Create in me a clean heart, O God, And renew a steadfast spirit within me.11 Do not cast me away from Your presence, And do not take Your Holy Spirit from me.

12 Restore to me the joy of Your salvation, And uphold me by Your generous Spirit.13 Then I will teach transgressors Your ways, And sinners shall be converted to You.

14 Deliver me from the guilt of bloodshed, O God, The God of my salvation, And my tongue shall sing aloud of Your righteousness.15 O Lord, open my lips, And my mouth shall show forth Your praise.16 For You do not desire sacrifice, or else I would give it; You do not delight in burnt offering. 17 The sacrifices of God are a broken spirit, A broken and a contrite heart—These, O God, You will not despise.

18 Do good in Your good pleasure to Zion; Build the walls of Jerusalem. 19 Then You shall be pleased with the sacrifices of righteousness, With burnt offering and whole burnt offering; Then they shall offer bulls on Your altar. [NKJV]

12

Amnon | Rape

2 Samuel 13:1–29

13:1 In the course of time, Amnon son of David fell in love with Tamar, the beautiful sister of Absalom son of David.

2 Amnon became frustrated to the point of illness on account of his sister Tamar, for she was a virgin, and it seemed impossible for him to do anything to her.

3 Now Amnon had a friend named Jonadab son of Shimeah, David's brother. Jonadab was a very shrewd man. 4 He asked Amnon, "Why do you, the king's son, look so haggard morning after morning? Won't you tell me?"

Amnon said to him, "I'm in love with Tamar, my brother Absalom's sister."

5 "Go to bed and pretend to be ill," Jonadab said. "When your father comes to see you, say to him, 'I would like my sister Tamar to come and give me something to eat. Let her prepare the food in my sight so I may watch her and then eat it from her hand.'"

6 So Amnon lay down and pretended to be ill. When the king came to see him, Amnon said to him, "I would like my sister Tamar to come and make some special bread in my sight, so I may eat from her hand."

7 David sent word to Tamar at the palace: "Go to the house of your brother Amnon and prepare some food for him." 8 So Tamar went to the house of her brother Amnon, who was lying down. She took some dough, kneaded it, made the bread in his sight and baked it. 9 Then she took the pan and served him the bread, but he refused to eat.

"Send everyone out of here," Amnon said. So everyone left him. 10 Then Amnon said to Tamar, "Bring the food here into my bedroom so I may eat from your hand." And Tamar took the bread she had prepared and brought it to her brother Amnon in his bedroom.

11 But when she took it to him to eat, he grabbed her and said, "Come to bed with me, my sister."

12 "Don't, my brother!" she said to him. "Don't force me. Such a thing should not be done in Israel! Don't do this wicked thing. 13 What about me? Where could I get rid of my disgrace? And what about you? You would be like one of the wicked fools in Israel. Please speak to the king; he will not keep me from being married to you." 14 But he refused to listen to her, and since he was stronger than she, he raped her.

15 Then Amnon hated her with intense hatred. In fact, he hated her more than he had loved her. Amnon said to her, "Get up and get out!"

16 "No!" she said to him. "Sending me away would be a greater wrong than what you have already done to me."

But he refused to listen to her. 17 He called his personal servant and said, "Get this woman out of here and bolt the door after her." 18 So his servant put her out and bolted the door after her. She was wearing a richly ornamented robe, for this was the kind of garment the virgin daughters of the king wore. 19 Tamar put ashes on her head and tore the ornamented robe she was wearing. She put her hand on her head and went away, weeping aloud as she went.

20 Her brother Absalom said to her, "Has that Amnon, your brother, been with you? Be quiet now, my sister; he is your brother. Don't take this thing to heart." And Tamar lived in her brother Absalom's house, a desolate woman.

21 When King David heard all this, he was furious. 22 Absalom never said a word to Amnon, either good or bad; he hated Amnon because he had disgraced his sister Tamar.

23 Two years later, when Absalom's sheepshearers were at Baal Hazor near the border of Ephraim, he invited all the king's sons to come there. 24 Absalom went to the king and said, "Your servant has had shearers come. Will the king and his officials please join me?"

25 "No, my son," the king replied. "All of us should not go; we would only be a burden to you." Although Absalom urged him, he still refused to go, but gave him his blessing.

26 Then Absalom said, "If not, please let my brother Amnon come with us."

The king asked him, "Why should he go with you?" 27 But Absalom urged him, so he sent with him Amnon and the rest of the king's sons.

28 Absalom ordered his men, "Listen! When Amnon is in high spirits from drinking wine and I say to you, 'Strike Amnon down,' then kill him. Don't be afraid. Have not I given you this order? Be strong and brave." 29 So Absalom's men did to Amnon what Absalom had ordered. Then all the king's sons got up, mounted their mules and fled.

THE PRINCIPAL CHARACTERS

There are several principal characters in this story. The first is Amnon, the perpetrator of this crime. He was David's oldest son, and thus was in line to succeed him as king. The second is Tamar, David's (and his wife Ahinoam's) daughter and Amnon's half sister. Based on her statement in verse 13, we can assume that she was of marrying age, which was much younger than is considered the norm in today's culture. Still, even though she could have been married, she was probably very young, no older than fourteen or fifteen, when this occurred. The third is Absalom, Tamar's biological brother and another of David's sons, who will be discussed at greater length in the next chapter. The fourth is David, who figures prominently throughout much of the Old Testament, but here is depicted as a weak father.

THE CRIME

The first crime in this passage was the rape of Tamar. The second crime committed was the murder of Amnon. Most of the focus of this chapter will be on the rape of Tamar and on the crime of sexual assault. Under modern laws, Amnon would be guilty of incest. One Hebrew word to describe incest is *zimmah*, or refined immorality. Another is *tebhel*, or unnatural vice, which equates incest with bestiality. The word used to describe Amnon's act in 2 Samuel is *checedh*, reflecting a violation of the mores that should exist between siblings.[1]

The definition of incest, and whether it is considered taboo, varies between cultures. *Black's Law Dictionary* defines incest as, "The crime of sexual intercourse or cohabitation between a man and woman who are related to each other within the degrees wherein marriage is prohibited by law."[2] *Black's* definition extends to several biological relationships, including half-siblings.[3]

Under the laws of that day, Amnon was guilty of rape, but what about incest? Based on Tamar's plea that Amnon marry her, one might assume that marriage between half-siblings was allowed. Abraham, the founding patriarch of their descendants, was married to his half-sister Sarah. However, the Mosaic Law clearly condemns sexual relations between half-siblings (Deuteronomy 27:22 and Leviticus 18:9 & 11).[4] It is possible that marriage between half-siblings was either legal, or that violations of this prohibition were seldom enforced; such may have been the lax moral climate of David's household. If that is true, perhaps the social stigma attached to such marriages, while negative, was not as negative as the stigma attached to being an unmarried rape victim. The most likely possibility is that Tamar was merely trying to thwart Amnon's rape attempt by deceiving him with a false offer of marriage.[5]

In verse 17, Amnon refers to Tamar as "this woman." On January 26, 1998, President Bill Clinton, in a televised news conference, pointedly and slowly stated, "I did not have sexual relations with *that woman* (emphasis added), Miss (Monica) Lewinsky." Clinton, as subsequent events would show, was lying. Clinton's affair with Lewinsky and allegations of perjury in connection with those relations led to his impeachment. What is striking is that Lewinsky went from being the object of President Clinton's sexual obsession, to being referred to as "that woman," just as Tamar became "this woman" to Amnon. Such is often the case with illicit sex.

Amnon did not fear his father, and David did nothing more than get angry at his son's actions. Why should Amnon have felt shame or fear, and how could David stand in judgment of his son? This rape occurred on the heels of David's murderous affair with Bathsheba. Amnon knew that David had no moral standing on which to condemn him. Also, being the oldest son, he knew that David would not jeopardize his own legacy by preventing Amnon's rise to the throne.

Perhaps no sin is more difficult to forgive than sexual abuse, especially when it occurs within the family. Many people who have experienced sexual abuse within their household can relate to the characters in this story: the female victim who is powerless to fight back against her abuser and feels betrayed by her parents, the angry brother who cannot forgive the abuser or his parents, and the parents who watch their family fall apart because of the abuse.

The behaviors discussed in this book must be viewed in their proper cultural context. The perceptions and stigmas attached to some behaviors are not the same today as the day when this occurred. In this case, the pain inflicted on Tamar was magnified compared to what might occur today. Women, especially young women like Tamar, were not as empowered as women in modern Western society. Rape victim support groups were nonexistent, and women were second-class citizens, regarded as little more than the property of their father, brother, or husband. The shame of being sexually abused, which still lies beneath the surface today, was overt in Tamar's day. This incident made Tamar's marriage prospects extremely dim. All men within Tamar's community would know what had happened to her. In small communal settings, everyone knew everyone else's business, especially if it involved the king's family. Most Israelite men of the day would refuse to marry a woman who was not a virgin, let alone one who had been "soiled" by the crimes of rape and incest. Absalom knew this, and that is why he took Tamar under his care.

Of all crimes, child sexual abuse ranks as one of the most under-reported. Children, or young teenagers like Tamar probably was, often feel powerless to report abuse at the hands of a parent or older relative. At least one study claims that sibling sexual abuse is reported much less frequently than father-daughter sexual abuse.[6] Not surprisingly, some research also suggests that many cases of sibling sexual abuse go unreported to authorities because parents are reluctant to turn their sons over for prosecution, which shows that some things have not changed since the time of Amnon and Tamar.[7]

Some other things have not changed. The emotional pain experienced by Tamar, the callousness of the sexual deviant who would perpetrate such an act, and the seething rage that settled in the brother of the victim are mirror images of events that occur every day throughout the world. Sexual abuse at the hands of a sibling, usually at the hands of a brother at least five years older than the sister, is just as emotionally traumatizing as abuse committed by a father or stepfather.[8] One study reported that 47 percent of women who experience sibling sexual abuse never marry, compared to 27 percent of victims of other forms of familial sexual abuse. Women who experience sibling sexual abuse have also been reported as more likely to experience abuse at the hands of husbands, boyfriends, and other male authority figures.[9] Like David's family, households in which sibling sexual abuse occurs are described as dysfunctional in other ways. Poor parental role models like David, along with inconsistent and arbitrary discipline, also mark such households.[10]

The Lesson

Matthew Rogers wrote, "Lust never delivers what it promises."[11] We all know this, but, no matter how many lessons are available from history or from events around us, many people never internalize Rogers's words. Untold numbers of human beings allow themselves to be ruined by lust even though they know ahead of time that giving in to sexual lust, unless done within the confines of marriage, almost always leads to disaster.

This sad and sorry tale about rape and incest led to even more disasters, namely the murder of Amnon at the hands of his vengeful half brother Absalom. Years later, Absalom named a daughter Tamar, no doubt as a tribute to his sister, and a reminder of this crime to his father (2 Samuel 14:27). Unfortunately, neither the vendetta nor the tragedy ended with this story; it only began. The rest of the sad story is told in the story of Absalom, the subject of the next chapter.

13

Absalom | Treason

2 Samuel 15:1-6

15:1 In the course of time, Absalom provided himself with a chariot and horses and with fifty men to run ahead of him. 2 He would get up early and stand by the side of the road leading to the city gate. Whenever anyone came with a complaint to be placed before the king for a decision, Absalom would call out to him, "What town are you from?" He would answer, "Your servant is from one of the tribes of Israel." 3 Then Absalom would say to him, "Look, your claims are valid and proper, but there is no representative of the king to hear you." 4 And Absalom would add, "If only I were appointed judge in the land! Then everyone who has a complaint or case could come to me and I would see that he gets justice."

5 Also, whenever anyone approached him to bow down before him, Absalom would reach out his hand, take hold of him and kiss him. 6 Absalom behaved in this way toward all the Israelites who came to the king asking for justice, and so he stole the hearts of the men of Israel.

2 Samuel 17:11-14

11 "So I advise you (Absalom): Let all Israel, from Dan to Beersheba--as numerous as the sand on the seashore—be gathered to you, with you yourself leading them into battle. 12 Then we will attack him (David) wherever he may be found, and we will fall on him as dew settles on the ground. Neither he nor any of his men will be left alive. 13 If he withdraws into a city, then all Israel will bring ropes to that city, and we will drag it down to the valley until not even a piece of it can be found."

14 Absalom and all the men of Israel said, "The advice of Hushai the Arkite is better than that of Ahithophel." For the Lord had deter-

mined to frustrate the good advice of Ahithophel in order to bring disaster on Absalom.

2 Samuel 18: 1–17, 24, 31–33

1 David mustered the men who were with him and appointed over them commanders of thousands and commanders of hundreds. 2 David sent the troops out—a third under the command of Joab, a third under Joab's brother Abishai son of Zeruiah, and a third under Ittai the Gittite. The king told the troops, "I myself will surely march out with you."

3 But the men said, "You must not go out; if we are forced to flee, they won't care about us. Even if half of us die, they won't care; but you are worth ten thousand of us. It would be better now for you to give us support from the city."

4 The king answered, "I will do whatever seems best to you."

So the king stood beside the gate while all the men marched out in units of hundreds and of thousands. 5 The king commanded Joab, Abishai and Ittai, "Be gentle with the young man Absalom for my sake." And all the troops heard the king giving orders concerning Absalom to each of the commanders.

6 The army marched into the field to fight Israel, and the battle took place in the forest of Ephraim. 7 There the army of Israel was defeated by David's men, and the casualties that day were great— twenty thousand men. 8 The battle spread out over the whole countryside, and the forest claimed more lives that day than the sword.

9 Now Absalom happened to meet David's men. He was riding his mule, and as the mule went under the thick branches of a large oak, Absalom's head got caught in the tree. He was left hanging in midair, while the mule he was riding kept on going.

10 When one of the men saw this, he told Joab, "I just saw Absalom hanging in an oak tree."

11 Joab said to the man who had told him this, "What! You saw him? Why didn't you strike him to the ground right there? Then I would have had to give you ten shekels of silver and a warrior's belt."

12 But the man replied, "Even if a thousand shekels were weighed out into my hands, I would not lift my hand against the king's son. In our hearing the king commanded you and Abishai and Ittai, 'Protect the young man Absalom for my sake.' 13 And if I had put my

life in jeopardy—and nothing is hidden from the king—you would have kept your distance from me."

14 Joab said, "I'm not going to wait like this for you." So he took three javelins in his hand and plunged them into Absalom's heart while Absalom was still alive in the oak tree. 15 And ten of Joab's armor-bearers surrounded Absalom, struck him and killed him.

16 Then Joab sounded the trumpet, and the troops stopped pursuing Israel, for Joab halted them. 17 They took Absalom, threw him into a big pit in the forest and piled up a large heap of rocks over him. Meanwhile, all the Israelites fled to their homes.

24 While David was sitting between the inner and outer gates, the watchman went up to the roof of the gateway by the wall. As he looked out, he saw a man running alone.

31 Then the Cushite arrived and said, "My lord the king, hear the good news! The Lord has delivered you today from all who rose up against you."

32 The king asked the Cushite, "Is the young man Absalom safe?"

The Cushite replied, "May the enemies of my lord the king and all who rise up to harm you be like that young man."

33 The king was shaken. He went up to the room over the gateway and wept. As he went, he said: "O my son Absalom! My son, my son Absalom! If only I had died instead of you—O Absalom, my son, my son!"

THE PRINCIPAL CHARACTERS

The events in this chapter were set in motion by the events described in Chapter 12. Following the rape of his sister, Absalom lived the remainder of his life guided by one goal, exacting retribution against his father. Whatever faults he possessed, Absalom was not impulsive or hotheaded. He exercised great patience in taking his revenge. Absalom waited two years to exact his revenge against his half-brother Amnon for the rape of Tamar (2 Samuel 13:23, 28–29). Absalom lived in Geshur, beyond the reach of his father, for three years following Amnon's death (2 Samuel 13:38). After being recalled by David, he lived in Jerusalem for two years but never saw his father (2 Samuel 14:28). Absalom spent an additional two years, or maybe four years, in Jerusalem, during which time he had infrequent contact with David (2 Samuel 15:7).

Absalom spent between nine and eleven years coolly and methodically plotting against his father. Each step brought Absalom into closer contact with David, but rather than bringing the two of them closer to reconciliation, each move was one step closer to all-out rebellion.

The crime that Absalom committed was treason. Treason is, "The offense of attempting by overt acts to overthrow the government of the state to which the offender owes allegiance." There are five categories of treason, two of which may apply to Absalom. "Constructive treason" is "imputed to a person by law from his conduct or course of action, though his deeds taken severally do not amount to actual treason." This is a charitable interpretation of Absalom's initial actions, meeting citizens at the city gates and mediating their disputes, while subtly planting the idea in their minds that he was much more in touch with them than King David. His later actions—the more overt attempts to wrest the throne from his father—make Absalom guilty of "high treason," a term borrowed from English law, which is "treason against the king or sovereign."[1]

THE CRIME THEN AND NOW

The enforcement of treason laws is also fraught with danger. Treason laws are enacted by government leaders to insure they stay in power, as deterrents to those who oppose them. It is one of the most abused crimes in human history, primarily because the interpretation of treason has often rested with the governing authority. Treason by its nature puts the government in the roles of victim, judge, and jury. In a sense, a government that tries someone for treason is acting as judge and jury toward someone who stands accused of opposing it. Charges of treason were so often abused by the British during America's colonial period that the framers of the Constitution went to the effort of setting guidelines for accusations of treason. Treason is the only crime that is specifically addressed and controlled for in the Constitution. Article III Section 3 states,

> Treason against the United States, shall consist only in levying War against them, or in adhering to their Enemies, giving them Aid and Comfort. No Person shall be convicted of Treason unless on the Testimony of two Witnesses to the same overt Act,

or on Confession in open Court. The Congress shall have power to declare the Punishment of Treason, but no Attainder of Treason shall work Corruption of Blood, or Forfeiture except during the Life of the Person attainted.

The most infamous trial for treason in American history occurred in 1807, thirty-one years after the United States declared its independence. Aaron Burr was the grandson of Jonathan Edwards, one of America's first great evangelical ministers. Burr rose to the rank of Colonel during the American Revolution and practiced law in civilian life. Burr ran for President in 1800 and lost a highly contested election to Thomas Jefferson, but in an electoral setup that varies greatly from what Americans know today, Burr was awarded the office of Vice-President. During his term as Vice-President, Burr, after a long simmering feud, killed former Treasury Secretary Alexander Hamilton in a duel. Arrest warrants were issued, but Burr successfully evaded prosecution efforts.

What happened next is in question. Burr and a collaborator planned to organize an invasion of Mexico, hoping to wrest Mexico from Spanish control. When this plan fell through, Burr, according to prosecutors, sought to lead a secessionist movement on the United States' western frontier.

Burr was captured and put on trial for treason in Richmond, Virginia. Following a highly controversial, complex, and widely publicized trial, Burr was acquitted. Although prosecutors and Burr's political opponents, Thomas Jefferson among them, were outraged, the fact that Burr was acquitted was probably in the best long-term interests of the United States. The Burr case established that the rule of law was supreme to politics, even for discredited and disreputable politicians like Aaron Burr.[2] Had Burr been convicted, it may have cast the dye for subsequent prosecutions for treason in cases where the evidence was weak, against those who happen to be on the outs with the reigning political establishment.

Very few treason prosecutions have taken place in recent years in the United States. In fact, constructive treason is not recognized in the United States. Allegations of treason should not be made lightly, especially in a democracy. In a dictatorship or totalitarian government, treason can be defined and interpreted any way the government sees fit.

The words of 1 Samuel 18:33 are heart-wrenching, and any parent can feel David's anguish. No matter what Absalom had done to harm his father, David still could not help but love his son and grieve over his death. The problem of rebellious children aspiring to the throne of their father was not unique to David, or to Old Testament Israel. Whenever reading an Old Testament encounter with the king, one notices that no one could approach the king casually, not even the members of the king's family. In 1 Kings 1, it is apparent that Bathsheba could not approach King David without permission, and she showed him the same degree of reverence that ordinary subjects would. Kings of the ancient Middle East were so concerned about assassination, they could not afford to allow otherwise. They usually feared those closest to them, which usually was a son, brother, wife, daughter, or top aide. David's top aide was Joab, who refused the King's order not to harm Absalom. Joab knew that David's reign as king, and by extension his own position as David's top general, would never be secure as long as Absalom lived. Later, when Solomon assumed David's throne, one of his first acts was to have Joab killed, realizing that his kingdom would not be secure as long as Joab lived. Such is the nature of most dictatorships, past and present. It is hard for Americans to imagine a White House where the President had to live in constant fear of his own family.

Whenever a government is built around one person or a family monarchy, the risk of a violent or traumatic transfer of power, or the risk of passing on the mantle of leadership to a feckless family member, is ever present. Yugoslavia erupted into full-fledged war because of a power vacuum left by the death of Josip Tito in 1980. Dictatorial power in the Middle East (Syria, Jordan, Saudi Arabia) is passed from one family member to another with no input from the populace. Family members in these families engage in the same kinds of power struggles that the Old Testament experienced.

In contrast, American democracy, for all of its many flaws, shows its greatness during the transfer of power from one President to the next. Whereas most governments throughout history, and many governments today, have been thrown into turmoil when a leader is replaced, it is customary for Presidents leaving office to escort their successor to the inauguration platform, even in cases when the outgoing President was defeated by his successor, as was the case in 1992 (Bush/Clinton), 1980 (Carter/Reagan) and 1976 (Ford/Carter), or when elections were especially bitter or controversial, as with the 2000 election, when Albert Gore reluctantly, but peacefully, conceded to George W. Bush, and looked on from the platform as Bush was sworn in. The peaceful transfer of power on inauguration day is something that Americans should savor and never take for granted.

The Lesson

The force that drove Absalom to his death was hatred. He never forgave his father for the rape of his sister at the hands of their half-brother. In fact, his hatred and bitterness intensified as the years went on. Abraham Twerski wrote, "Harboring a resentment is letting someone you don't like live inside your head rent free."[3] Family grudges are probably the most intense because it means that someone we once loved has betrayed us.

Of all the biblical commands, the command to forgive wrongs done to us or our loved ones may be the most difficult to obey. A friend and former colleague of mine, Dr. Glenn Rohrer, is a respected and renowned professor of social work; he also has a Master of Divinity Degree in Pastoral Counseling. Glenn once told me that forgiveness is like grief in that it is not an event; it is a process. When a wound is deep and serious, true forgiveness seldom comes quickly; it takes time and great effort. The mere act of saying or thinking that we have forgiven someone is an important first step, but it is just that, a first step. Sometimes forgiveness is a process that takes a lifetime. On the other hand, sometimes grudges last a lifetime. For those who have suffered a grievous wrong, their choice is to spend a lifetime forgiving those who have wronged them or to spend a lifetime nursing a grudge. Forgiveness is much healthier.

14

Solomon | Polygamy

1 Kings 11:1–6

1 King Solomon, however, loved many foreign women besides Pharaoh's daughter--Moabites, Ammonites, Edomites, Sidonians and Hittites. 2 They were from nations about which the Lord had told the Israelites, "You must not intermarry with them, because they will surely turn your hearts after their gods." Nevertheless, Solomon held fast to them in love. 3 He had seven hundred wives of royal birth and three hundred concubines, and his wives led him astray. 4 As Solomon grew old, his wives turned his heart after other gods, and his heart was not fully devoted to the Lord his God, as the heart of David his father had been. 5 He followed Ashtoreth the goddess of the Sidonians, and Molech the detestable god of the Ammonites. 6 So Solomon did evil in the eyes of the Lord; he did not follow the LORD completely, as David his father had done.

THE PRINCIPAL CHARACTERS

When examining the complications that arose from polygamous marriages in the Bible, we see that some of the greatest men in the Old Testament are the subjects. The first mention of a polygamous marriage is of Lamech (Genesis 4:19), who married two women. The first polygamous relationship involving a noteworthy Old Testament figure was that of Abraham, his wife Sarai, and her handmaid Hagar. It also provides the first of numerous examples of the problems inherent in polygamous relationships. Unable to bear a child of her own, Sarai told Abraham to sleep with Hagar. Ishmael was the child of this union. The complications arose from Hagar's taunting Sarai for her inability to conceive, and from Abraham's lack of faithfulness in not waiting on the Lord's promise that his wife would conceive. Hagar and Ishmael were banished from Abraham's house.

Genesis 26:35 mentions the polygamous marriage of Esau and his two wives, and how they were a source of grief to Esau's parents, Isaac and Rebekah. Another well known polygamous relationship that led to many problems was Jacob's. The favoritism he showed toward the sons of Rachel led to his oldest son Reuben's having an affair with one of Jacob's concubines, and it culminated in Joseph's being sold into slavery.

There are other examples of dysfunctional polygamous marriages in the Old Testament, but the man who exemplifies polygamous excess at its grandest is Solomon. Solomon was the son of David and Bathsheba, born shortly after their first child died in infancy. Solomon was not the oldest of David's children, and therefore the unlikely successor to his father's throne. One of his first acts as king was to order the murder of his older half-brother Adonijah, a rival to the throne and for the affections of a woman in the kingdom.

Despite its violent beginning, the reign of Solomon held great promise. I Kings 3:6–15 tells how God appeared to Solomon in a dream and granted him whatever he would request. Solomon, much to the Lord's delight, asked for a discerning heart, or wisdom, to guide the people of Israel. God granted him that wisdom, and Solomon is known to history as one of the wisest men who ever lived. However, as Spanish-American philosopher George Santayana wrote, "The wisest man has something to learn."[1] Despite his intelligence, wisdom and his accomplishments, Solomon's legacy is mixed at best.

Solomon's biggest downfall was women, especially women from other countries and of other religious beliefs. Unable to contain his appetite for women of different nationalities, who he no doubt viewed as a novelty, Solomon embodied the stereotype of the sexually overindulgent monarch. Part of the reason he acquired so many wives and concubines was political. Swapping wives and concubines was a common method of insuring peace between kingdoms in the ancient Near East.

It is very unlikely that Solomon had 700 wives and 300 concubines. These numbers were in all likelihood a literary device meant to emphasize Solomon's excesses, and were not meant to be taken literally.

In polygamous relations, the number of concubines usually exceeded the number of wives. Some estimate that Solomon probably had about 70 wives.[2]

Today, Solomon's attitude toward his wives and concubines, and his tolerance of their religious practices, might graciously be characterized as inclusive. He allowed them to practice their pagan religion in his kingdom, almost to the point where the nation of God's chosen people lost its spiritual and moral bearings. He even engaged in some of their "detestable" religious practices himself. Throughout the Old Testament, one of the main arguments presented against polygamous marriage centers on the detrimental effect that pagan women from outside Israel would have on the Israelites' spiritual lives.

The Bible does not explicitly condemn polygamy, but Deuteronomy 17:17 warned a man against "taking many wives, lest his heart be led astray." *Nelson's Bible Dictionary* states that polygamy, like divorce, was tolerated because of the hardness of peoples' hearts.[3] The Mosaic Law even required a polygamous relationship in some instances; namely, if a man died and left a widow, the deceased man's brother was expected to take his widowed sister-in-law as his own wife, care for her, and have children with her.

The opening chapters of Genesis provide the blueprint for marital relations, one man and one woman. Paul states that deacons and overseers (bishops) should be the husband of one wife, believing that men who engaged in polygamous marriages should not assume positions of leadership within the church (1 Timothy 3:2; 1 Timothy 3:12; Titus 1:6).

THE CRIME

Polygamy is defined as having "more than one wife or husband at the same time."[4] There are other related offenses and behaviors. Bigamy means a second marriage distinguished from a first or other and, in bigamous situations, one spouse often is not aware of the other marriage. "Polyandry" is marriage to more than one man, a rarity, especially in the ancient Middle East. When we discuss "polygamy" we are usually talking about "polygyny," one man married to multiple wives. For the sake of simplicity, I use the more common term polygamy in this chapter.

THE CRIME TODAY Polygamy was not a crime during the Old Testament era. In fact it was common in the Middle East. It was also considered acceptable for wealthy men and monarchs to maintain a harem of wives and concubines. Polygamy is still practiced in parts of the Middle East and Africa. For example, Osama bin Laden, the Saudi Arabian founder and leader of the terrorist group Al Qaeda, is believed to be the son of a father who had ten wives, despite a Saudi law that limits a man to four wives.

The history and current status of polygamy in the United States is a different story. Polygamy is illegal in every state in the United States. According to *Black's Law Dictionary*, a person is guilty of polygamy if he or she marries or cohabits with more than one spouse at a time in purported exercise of the right of plural marriage.[5] In Utah, often the focal point of discussions about this topic, bigamy is a third-degree felony. Some other states punish bigamy less severely. In Missouri, bigamy is a Class A misdemeanor.[6]

No discussion about polygamy would be complete without a discussion of the Church of Jesus Christ of Latter Day Saints (LDS), commonly known as the Mormons. When the Mormon Church was founded in 1830, its founder, Joseph P. Smith, Jr. privately practiced polygamy, even though he publicly denounced it, and even though the *Book of Mormon*, which Smith himself claims to have discovered under "divine guidance," criticizes polygamy. Smith eventually openly advocated polygamy in accordance with the "ancient order of marriage" along the same lines of the marriages of Abraham, Isaac, and Jacob. Though they believed in the divinity of Jesus Christ, the early Mormons viewed their community through Old Testament lenses. The exact number of wives Smith had is not known and is the subject of controversy even today. Joseph Smith and his brother Hyrum were killed by a mob on June 27, 1844, in Carthage, Illinois.

Hoping to escape the pressure of local and state governments that detested their polygamous marriages along with their communal and clannish lifestyle, many remaining Mormons, led by Brigham Young, traveled west to establish the LDS church in Utah, which was not a state at the time. Young had more than fifty wives. Many Mormon founders and early pioneers practiced polygamous marriages, although

Smith and Young claimed that only 3–5 percent of the early Mormons practiced polygamy. At its height, polygamous marriage was practiced by 20–40 percent of nineteenth century Utah Mormons.[7] Some non-polygamous Mormons still viewed plural marriage as the ideal family setup, but, as might be expected, the basic human emotion of jealously often interfered with this ideology. In fact, one Utah Mormon, when asked by Brigham Young why he did not engage in plural marriage, replied that his wife had received her own revelation from God about plural marriage. She said that God had revealed to her that she should shoot any woman who became her husband's plural wife.[8] Such attitudes notwithstanding, the LDS Church formally sanctioned polygamy in 1852.

Over the remaining decades of the nineteenth century, the LDS church gradually distanced itself from polygamy, partly due to pressure from the United States government. In 1890, LDS President Wilford Woodruff urged Mormons not to create any more polygamous marriages. In 1904, LDS President Joseph F. Smith, the nephew of the LDS Church founder, authorized the excommunication of polygamous members, thus ending the mainstream LDS Church's formal ties to polygamy.

Ever since 1904, the mainstream LDS Church has disavowed any association with or endorsement of polygamy. However, isolated Mormon sects that still engage in polygamy remain, including the Apostolic United Brethren, the Church of Jesus Christ in Solemn Assembly, and Independent Mormon Fundamentalists, who view mainstream Mormons as being more interested in obeying the laws of man, which prohibit polygamy, than the law of God, which commands polygamy. The exact number of practicing LDS polygamists is the subject a great controversy, with some claims as high as 3–5 percent. Most who engage in polygamous marriage do so discreetly. Some Mormons have religious ceremonies performed for polygamous marriages, which are not officially recognized by the state in which they live. Some polygamous Mormons live in multifamily housing near the other members of the family, which allows them to live in close quarters but not under the same roof.

Prosecutions for polygamy are rare. Over the past several decades, the criminal justice system has grown increasingly reluctant to prosecute crimes involving sexual relations among consenting adults, including sodomy and polygamy. Another explanation for the paucity of polygamy prosecutions, at least in Utah, the historical home of many American Mormons, is that many current Utahans are the descendants of polygamous marriages. Although most Utah Mormons oppose polygamy, and some are even embarrassed by Mormonism's polygamous history, they are still reluctant to turn others over for criminal prosecution, cognizant of the bad experiences of their ancestors. Prosecutions usually come about as a result of other crimes that occur within such polygamous settings. In a bizarre and violent example, on June 5, 2002, Elizabeth Smart, a Salt Lake City teenager, was abducted from her home by a drifter and self-described Mormon prophet who had once done some work at the home. Smart was held captive for several months and forced to live in a polygamous "marriage" with her captor.

In another case, Arizona authorities prosecuted several adult male members of the Fundamentalist Latter Day Saints (FLDS) who engaged in polygamous marriage and sexual relations with teenaged women, some of whom were below the age of consent. The FLDS, which counts approximately 7,000 adherents, live primarily in Kingman, Arizona and nearby Hildale, Utah. Law enforcement authorities are aware of the polygamous lifestyle of the FLDS, and usually do not bother to pursue prosecution, but did so in this case because one of the parties was a minor at the time the "plural marriage" was consumated. The group's leader, Warren Jeffs, was on the FBI's Ten Most Wanted list until he was captured in August of 2006. Kelly Fischer, an FLDS adherent, was sentenced to (only) 45 days in jail for having sex with his 16-year-old partner, much to the consternation of local law enforcement, who feared that the light sentence would not serve as a deterrent for other polygamists who wanted teenaged brides. The young woman, who had turned 21 by the time Fischer was sentenced, refused to cooperate with authorities. In fact she wrote a letter to the judge on Fischer's behalf, which read, "We have a beautiful family together. I love my husband. He loves us and takes very good care of us. The children adore their father ... I don't need to explain my personal life to anyone." [9]

For the most part, those who engage in polygamous relationships prefer to keep a low profile, hoping to avoid criminal prosecution and public scrutiny. There are occasional challenges to antipolygamy laws, including in Utah. In 1982, a Murray, Utah police officer was fired when it was discovered he was living in violation of Utah's antipolygamy statute. The man claimed that Utah's antibigamy law violated his First Amendment rights, but Utah courts upheld the state's antipolygamy laws, and the United States Supreme Court refused to get involved.[10]

The practices of the early Mormons provide lessons in the potential evils of polygamy. In *Mormon Polygamy: A History*, R. S. Van Wagoner, a Mormon and a descendant of a polygamous marriage, states that LDS Church founder Joseph Smith created bitter enemies everywhere he went by repeatedly approaching women and telling them that they were his "spiritual wives" that God had commanded him to marry. Smith approached dozens or even hundreds of women with this lie, some of whom were married (in some cases to members of his church), and some of whom were very young. Needless to say, Smith made mortal enemies of many husbands, brothers, and fathers with this pickup line, which partly explains why he and his band of followers had to move constantly. In some cases, Smith imprisoned women in his home to coerce them into accepting his marriage proposal.[11]

Brigham Young, the other principle Mormon pioneer, also provides some lessons in the evils of polygamy, some of which are comparable to Old Testament stories. It is a rare woman indeed who is willing to share the affections and sexual relations of her husband with another woman. Therefore, Young kept some of his marriages a secret, even from his favorite wife (wives), or he at least kept some of his wives separate from his main household, often under very poor conditions, despite his enormous wealth. One such example was Chauncey Webb. In 1869 Webb was a 24-year-old divorced mother of two. She had been the object of Young's desires for several years, even before she was married. Against her wishes, but feeling the need to obey the dictates of Young, her "spiritual father," Webb married Young, becoming his nineteenth wife, even though he was sixty-eight years old, forty-four years her senior. She was forced to live with some of Young's other wives in virtual poverty until she mustered the courage to file for a high-profile and dangerous divorce. Fearing for her life, Webb fled Utah and began a crusade advocating monogamy and denouncing LDS polygamy.[12]

Polygamy is not viewed as disdainfully by some of its practitioners in the United States and other countries. Several years ago I read an article in *The Atlantic*, in which the American writer, visiting the Central African country The Congo, spoke with a local man who lived in a polygamous marriage. The two men had an exchange about freedom and democracy, with the American writer extolling the virtues of American democracy and explaining how a democratic government would better suit Africans than the dictatorships that currently dominate the continent. The Congolese man replied, "How can you say you are free, when your government only allows a man to have one wife? Here I can marry as many women as I choose, as long as I care for them."

When polygamy first came to the attention of the United States Supreme Court in 1879, it received a very hostile reception. In an opinion written a century before the advent of political correctness, appreciation of cultural diversity, and respect for diverse sexual practices, the Court wrote in condescension, "Polygamy has always been odious among the northern and western nations of Europe, and, until the establishment of the Mormon Church, was almost exclusively a feature of the life of Asiatic and of African people."[13]

Contrast the language of that ruling with the climate of today. Once thought to be a dead issue, the prospect of polygamy becoming legal, or at least socially tolerable, is not beyond the realm of possibility. In 1996, the United States Supreme Court, in *Romer v. Evans*, struck down a provision of Colorado's Constitution because it disallowed local governments from granting minority protection status to homosexuals. This ruling paved the way for *Lawrence v. Texas*, the case which struck down antisodomy laws. Granting protection to same-sex relations may open the door to legalizing other forms of sexual behavior that have traditionally been outlawed, provided the sexual behavior involves consenting adults. Among those who made this argument were three of the Court's Justices, who dissented from the majority in *Romer v. Evans*. Speaking for Justice Clarence Thomas and (former) Chief Justice William Rehnquist, Justice Antonin Scalia wrote, "The Court's disposition today suggests that (criminalizing polygamy is) unconstitutional, and that polygamy must be permitted in (Arizona, Idaho, Utah, New Mexico, and Oklahoma) on a state-legislated, or perhaps even local-option, basis—unless, of course, polygamists for some reason have fewer constitutional rights than homosexuals."[14] It is not unreasonable to expect polygamy to become legalized. Or it may go the route of many other laws pertaining to sexual relations—illegal, but never enforced.

The Lesson

Only a careful reading of the Bible can really give an idea of how dysfunctional and immoral polygamy is. The stories of Solomon and other Old Testament patriarchs tell us clearly that monogamy is the only way a marriage should exist. Although the Bible is full of stories of dysfunctional monogamous households, the examples of dysfunctional polygamous households are even more numerous, for several reasons. Polygamous marriages usually mean that one wife is favored over others, which itself is a usurpation of the original institution of marriage. Most polygamous marriages lead to jealousy and its highly undesirable outcomes.

The lesson from Solomon's life is not so much that polygamy is wrong in and of itself, but that polygamous excesses and indulgences ruined his relationship with God and stained his name for history. Only God knows the number of otherwise intelligent and wise men who have ruined their lives because of ill advised sexual misadventures. Solomon, history's "wisest man," is one of them.

Despite his overindulgence, polygamy, and sexual appetite gone amok, the story of Solomon and his many love interests contains lessons. First, the book of Ecclesiastes, a somber Old Testament book often assumed to be written by Solomon toward the end of his life, provides many sad, poignant lessons on the emotional and psychological consequences of living a life apart from God. On the positive side, the Song of Solomon is the Bible's greatest love poem. Even from the mire of a family life as immoral and dysfunctional as Solomon's came these words:

1 Behold, you are fair, my love!
Behold, you are fair!
You have dove's eyes behind your veil.
Your hair is like a flock of goats,
Going down from Mount Gilead.

2 Your teeth are like a flock of shorn sheep
Which have come up from the washing,
Every one of which bears twins,
And none is barren among them.
3 Your lips are like a strand of scarlet,
And your mouth is lovely.
Your temples behind your veil
Are like a piece of pomegranate.
4 Your neck is like the tower of David,
Built for an armory,
On which hang a thousand bucklers,
All shields of mighty men.
5 Your two breasts are like two fawns,
Twins of a gazelle,
Which feed among the lilies.
6 Until the day breaks
And the shadows flee away,
I will go my way to the mountain of myrrh
And to the hill of frankincense.
7 You are all fair, my love,
And there is no spot in you.
(Song of Solomon 4:1–7) [NKJV]

God used Solomon, a wise, great, but flawed man, to speak to married couples through the ages with words of divine poetry. The message is clear: Romantic love and the marriage between man and woman is a gift from God that we should cherish and protect.

15

Jezebel and Ahab | Subornation of Perjury

1 Kings 21:1-16

1 Some time later there was an incident involving a vineyard belonging to Naboth the Jezreelite. The vineyard was in Jezreel, close to the palace of Ahab king of Samaria. 2 Ahab said to Naboth, "Let me have your vineyard to use for a vegetable garden, since it is close to my palace. In exchange I will give you a better vineyard or, if you prefer, I will pay you whatever it is worth."

3 But Naboth replied, "The Lord forbid that I should give you the inheritance of my fathers."

4 So Ahab went home, sullen and angry because Naboth the Jezreelite had said, "I will not give you the inheritance of my fathers." He lay on his bed sulking and refused to eat.

5 His wife Jezebel came in and asked him, "Why are you so sullen? Why won't you eat?"

6 He answered her, "Because I said to Naboth the Jezreelite, 'Sell me your vineyard; or if you prefer, I will give you another vineyard in its place.' But he said, 'I will not give you my vineyard.'"

7 Jezebel his wife said, "Is this how you act as king over Israel? Get up and eat! Cheer up. I'll get you the vineyard of Naboth the Jezreelite."

8 So she wrote letters in Ahab's name, placed his seal on them, and sent them to the elders and nobles who lived in Naboth's city with him. 9 In those letters she wrote: "Proclaim a day of fasting and seat Naboth in a prominent place among the people. 10 But seat two scoundrels opposite him and have them testify that he has cursed both God and the king. Then take him out and stone him to death."

11 So the elders and nobles who lived in Naboth's city did as Jezebel directed in the letters she had written to them. 12 They proclaimed a fast and seated Naboth in a prominent place among the

people. 13 Then two scoundrels came and sat opposite him and brought charges against Naboth before the people, saying, "Naboth has cursed both God and the king." So they took him outside the city and stoned him to death. 14 Then they sent word to Jezebel: "Naboth has been stoned and is dead."

15 As soon as Jezebel heard that Naboth had been stoned to death, she said to Ahab, "Get up and take possession of the vineyard of Naboth the Jezreelite that he refused to sell you. He is no longer alive, but dead." 16 When Ahab heard that Naboth was dead, he got up and went down to take possession of Naboth's vineyard.

THE PRINCIPAL CHARACTERS

Ahab, the seventh king of the northern kingdom of Israel, ruled for more than twenty years, probably during the ninth century B.C. In some respects Ahab was one of Old Testament Israel's strongest kings, but in other respects he was one of its weakest. He possessed great political savvy, knowing that Israel was in a vulnerable position, surrounded by hostile neighbors, including the southern kingdom of Judah, and the Phoenicians, both of whom enjoyed considerable military superiority over Israel. He enjoyed some military successes, but met his own fate on the battlefield. His intelligence and political talents notwithstanding, Ahab was a poor spiritual role model for the Israelites, willingly compromising his religious principles to appease Baal worshippers, his wife prominent among them. I Kings 16:30 reads, "Ahab son of Omri did more evil in the eyes of the Lord than any of those before him."

Ahab's wife Jezebel is the more prominent character in this story, and she was a dominant figure in the kingdom of Israel both during her husband's reign and during the reigns of their sons. The name Jezebel is a modern synonym for a treacherous, immoral woman, which is ironic given that the name actually means "chaste, free from carnal connection."[1] Many have vilified her as the quintessential evil female and compare her to Shakespeare's Lady Macbeth, who taunted her husband for his perceived weakness.[2] Some feminists admire her for her strong independence in the midst of a male-dominated society. Gaines calls her a "fiery and determined person," who was "loyal to her husband," and lived life on her own terms.[3] However, the conventional view is much harsher. Liz Curtis Higgs, author of the bestselling *Bad Girls of the Bible*, calls her a leader, but a graceless and compassionless one.[4]

Jezebel became Queen of Israel through a political arrangement between Ahab and the Phoenician King. Giving the daughter of a monarch for marriage was a common method of insuring peace between kingdoms. Upon becoming Queen, Jezebel took the role of loyal wife to ruthless extremes. She clung to her practice of Baal worship and imparted it to the Israelites, much to the consternation of the prophet Elijah, with whom she was constantly at odds throughout her husband's reign, threatening to kill him on at least one occasion. Jezebel persecuted and ordered the killing of Yahweh worshippers and prophets (I Kings 18), while Ahab refused to intervene.

THE CRIME AND PUNISHMENT

The Mosaic Law, which governed Israelites under the reign of Ahab, expressly forbade swearing falsely, especially within the context of business disputes or judicial proceedings. In fact, bearing false witness, as was done in this passage, was a clear violation of the Ninth Commandment. Telling the truth when under oath was and still is the bedrock on which a judicial system rests. Actually, the modern definition of perjury does not apply to the Old Testament era, because people in Old Testament times were not required to take a formal oath as we do in judicial proceedings today. Nonetheless, the importance of telling the truth in legal contexts was well known and understood by ancient Israelites. If people in the Old Testament could not be depended on to tell the truth, especially in matters of life and death, their society could not function. Old Testament administrators of justice could not rely on scientific evidence such as DNA analysis, videotaping, radar detectors, and fingerprinting. For that matter, modern courts and police investigators still rely largely on the truthfulness of sworn witnesses. Contrary to popular perception, the testimony of witnesses, not sophisticated scientific technology, is still the bread and butter of criminal courts.

The importance of telling the truth in court was recognized long before the Ten Commandments were written. The very first law in the Babylon Code of Hammurabi, which was written more than 500 years before the Mosaic Law, addresses false testimony. The Code states, "If a man accused a man, and brought the charge of murder against him, but has not proved it, his accuser shall be put to death."[5]

The Mosaic Law recognized the importance of telling the truth under oath as well. Deuteronomy 19:16–19 reads:

16 If a malicious witness takes the stand to accuse a man of a crime, 17 the two men involved in the dispute must stand in the presence of the Lord before the priests and the judges who are in office at the time. 18 The judges must make a thorough investigation, and if the witness proves to be a liar, giving false testimony against his brother, 19 then do to him as he intended to do to his brother.

To modern readers, who, as Redman Biddy writes, see everything as having a price, Naboth's refusal to sell his vineyard and his being offended at the mere offer to buy the property may seem strange.[6] To understand Naboth's stance, one must understand what a family-owned piece of land meant to Old Testament Israelites. First, Naboth's vineyard had probably been passed down from several generations, maybe for as long as 300 years. To sell the family plot simply for the sake of a quick profit was abhorrent to most Israelites. Second, Naboth probably intended to pass the vineyard to his own children, so selling it would have deprived them of what was to become their rightful inheritance. Thirdly, and perhaps most importantly, selling the vineyard would have violated the Mosaic Law. Numbers 36:7 states, "The inheritance of the people of Israel shall not be transferred from one tribe to another; for every one of the people of Israel shall cleave to the inheritance of the tribe of his fathers."

Ahab's sullenness was overt and demonstrative. The customary mode of dining was to recline on a couch or a bed while eating. Upon assuming his usual position for dining, Ahab turned his back on the meal, refusing like a pouting child to eat his dinner.[7] So obvious was Ahab's distress that his servants notified Queen Jezebel, who came in to find out what was wrong with her husband. The idea that Naboth would refuse the request of the King and that Ahab would take such rejection so passively revolted Jezebel, who came from a kingdom where the monarch's authority was absolute and unquestioned, and where the rule of law was not as important as it was in Israel.

Jezebel's first crime was forgery, but her guilt of that crime is in doubt. Forgery is defined as "the creation or alteration of a written or printed document which, if validly executed, would constitute a record of a legally binding transaction, with the intent to defraud by affirming it to be the act of an unknowing second person."[8] Since we do not know whether Ahab was complicit in the forging of his name, we cannot be sure that Jezebel was guilty of forgery. In other words, is it illegal to forge someone's signature if they do not object? Ahab seems to be a passive co-conspirator in the plot. Jezebel wrote letters in the King's name and used his seal. *Barnes' Notes* (1997) states that the Hebrew mode of sealing seems to have been by attaching a lump of clay to the document, and impressing the seal thereupon. The order to bring Naboth before the people was not even a feigned honor, but a command to appear.[9]

The order to sit two "scoundrels" or "worthless persons" beside Naboth was given because the Mosaic Law dictated that two witnesses were necessary in order for a person to be condemned to suffer the death penalty. No matter how well intentioned a law, and how many safeguards are in place to ward off abuse, there is always a way around it. Jezebel compelled the two unnamed scoundrels to commit perjury, with deadly consequences, thus making her guilty of suborning perjury and conspiracy to commit murder, the primary motive being to rescue the broken pride of the King, and to send the message to all Israelites that disrespect for the monarchy would not be tolerated. Naboth was falsely accused of blasphemy, which was an open curse on God, and with blaspheming the King, which was tantamount to treason. Both offenses carried the death penalty. No doubt the trumped-up charge of blaspheming the king sent a message to all Israelites who dared oppose Ahab or Jezebel.

The false accusation of blasphemy resulted in the stoning of Naboth, which was administered immediately outside the city walls, in accordance with Levitical law (Leviticus 24:14–16). Naboth's sons were stoned along with him (II Kings 9:26) as it was common in Middle Eastern culture for children to suffer vicariously for their offending parents. Killing the sons was also part of the Queen's plot because, as rightful inheritors of Naboth's vineyard, they stood in the way of Jezebel's getting her way. There is little doubt that some of those who witnessed the proceedings and participated in the ritual stoning knew or strongly suspected that the charges against Naboth were false. However, so great was their fear of Jezebel and/or spiritual and moral depravity, that they carried out Jezebel's evil order.

When Jezebel instructs her husband to go and take possession of the vineyard, he does not question her, indicating that he was at least passively complicit in the scheme. Elijah had the courage to confront Ahab while the King was in route to take possession of the garden. Elijah stated that an ill fate awaited Ahab and Jezebel for their misdeed. He prophesied that dogs would lick up Ahab's blood in the same spot where they had licked the blood of Naboth and that an equally gruesome fate awaited Jezebel. However, Ahab, who appears genuinely chastened and contrite after the confrontation with Elijah, repents. As a demonstration of His never-ending forgiveness, God spared Ahab's life for the short term, but the prophecy was fulfilled and his kingly lineage came to an end shortly after his death. Ahab died in battle while in his chariot a couple of years later. The chariot was brought back to the site of Naboth's stoning; Ahab's blood was emptied and the dogs lapped it up (1 Kings 22:37–38).

Jezebel's reaction to Elijah's admonishment was much different. True to her basic character, she was unrepentant. She ruled indirectly through her sons for more than twenty years but met her fate in the manner prophesied by Elijah. Realizing that Jehu, who killed her son in a rebellion, was approaching her palace, Jezebel adorned herself, either in preparation for death or in a vain attempt to charm Jehu, and stepped out on her terrace to greet him. She was thrown from her balcony by three palace eunuchs and trampled; dogs ate her corpse.

THE CRIME NOW

Prior to the 1998 impeachment of President Bill Clinton, few Americans had ever heard the phrase "subornation of perjury." It is defined under federal law as the procurement of another person to commit perjury (lying under oath), but the perjury must have actually been committed in order for the procurer to be guilty.[10] Subornation of perjury is rarely prosecuted, largely because it is difficult to prove. In the Clinton case, prosecutors alleged that Clinton urged former intern White House Monica Lewinsky to lie to a grand jury about their illicit sexual relationship, but the urging was spoken rather than written. In the case of Jezebel, the crime was easy to prove because Jezebel, in her arrogance, put her scheme in writing.

I should offer my apologies to devoted fans of former President Bill Clinton. I do not intend to make this book a partisan discourse for or against any particular political persuasion, and anyone should acknowledge the fact that Clinton is a complex, highly intelligent man of many talents. But to those who asserted that Clinton's lying under oath to a grand jury was insignificant, I disagree. Being truthful in a judicial setting and in business dealings is one of the basic foundations on which our society rests. Even in recent years, untold numbers of lives have been ruined by people lying in court. Whether it be children who falsely accused school officials of child molestation, women who falsely accused men of rape, or police officers guilty of "testilying" (a phrase introduced courtesy of the O.J. Simpson trial), lying in judicial settings has grave implications. It resulted in the impeachment of the President of the United States; it has sent many innocent people to prison or to their death, and it usurps the justice system. The philosopher Samuel Johnson stated, "The devils themselves do not lie to one another, since the society of Hell could not subsist without truth any more than others."[11]

Another lesson from this story is the dangers of unchecked power. It has often been said that absolute power corrupts absolutely. Truer words were never spoken. Societies in which government authorities are not accountable for their actions are very unhealthy ones. This is one of the strengths of American government. The executive branch is held in check by the legislative branch, and both are held in check by the judicial branch of government. In courtroom proceedings, neither the prosecution nor the defense should always get its way. All people, no matter what their station in life, need to hear the word "no" occasionally. Unfortunately, Ahab and Jezebel, like many dictators, would not allow anyone near them who would dare utter the word.

Lessons for Individual Christians

The story of Jezebel and Ahab is a lesson to modern Christians in the dangers of covetousness and lying. Ahab was the most powerful person in his kingdom and maybe the wealthiest. He had everything a man could desire and wanted for nothing in the way of material possessions. He still was not satisfied. While his wife was guilty of breaking

135

the ninth commandment, Ahab was guilty of violating the tenth commandment, coveting his neighbor's possession. Governments cannot make laws against violating the tenth commandment unless we become able to perceive people's thoughts, as in George Orwell's novel *1984*, in which government officials accused people of "thought crimes." It seems Ahab is like many of us in at least one respect; we are never satisfied with what we have. While few among us would resort to approving the murder of someone whose property we covet, we are just as guilty as Ahab whenever we covet someone else's possession.

Unlike Ahab, Jezebel cared nothing about Naboth's vineyard; she cared about asserting her authority. She was consumed with the arrogance and egoism that come with unchecked power. Very often we find ourselves in disputes with coworkers, acquaintances, family members, and fellow church members over matters of at least some substance, but just as often we find ourselves caring less about the issue in dispute and instead become preoccupied with satisfying our own ego needs. As the father of two children who have been involved in athletics, I can attest to the fact that, with many parents, children's athletic contests become battles between mothers and fathers. Parents lose sight of the focus of athletics, namely the children, and instead become consumed with enhancing their own status. Again, such contests seldom lead to violence, although there are isolated cases to the contrary, but anytime we put our own egos ahead of the best interests of others, or ahead of the will of God, we are guilty of the same type of egoism as Jezebel. In this case, Jezebel put her own ego needs ahead of the people she was supposed to serve through leadership. One difference between Jezebel and us is that she, as queen, could have her way as she pleased; most of us do not have that sort of power. Distressing though it may seem, we must wonder if we would be just as ruthless as Jezebel if we were in a similar position.

Like several other jurisdictions in the United States, the federal court system has adopted structured sentencing. Structured sentencing is designed to make sentencing in criminal cases more uniform and consistent. Theoretically, any two people who commit the same crime and have a similar criminal history should receive the same sentence. However, judges are allowed to take other factors into account and may impose a harsher or more lenient sentence than what is called for in the guidelines. Aggravating factors justify a harsher sentence than what is called for in sentencing guidelines, and mitigating factors justify a lesser sentence. One of the mitigating factors is "acceptance of responsibility." If a judge believes that a defendant has accepted responsibility for a crime, that judge is justified in imposing a sentence that is more lenient than the sentence guidelines suggest. God also recognizes sincere repentance for our wrong deeds, no matter how vile they may seem, and stands ready to forgive, even with very imperfect people—like King Ahab, and all of us.

16

Jeremiah | Sedition

Jeremiah 37 & 38

37:1 Zedekiah son of Josiah was made king of Judah by Nebuchadnezzar king of Babylon; he reigned in place of Jehoiachin son of Jehoiakim. 2 Neither he nor his attendants nor the people of the land paid any attention to the words the Lord had spoken through Jeremiah the prophet.

3 King Zedekiah, however, sent Jehucal son of Shelemiah with the priest Zephaniah son of Maaseiah to Jeremiah the prophet with this message: "Please pray to the Lord our God for us."

4 Now Jeremiah was free to come and go among the people, for he had not yet been put in prison. 5 Pharaoh's army had marched out of Egypt, and when the Babylonians who were besieging Jerusalem heard the report about them, they withdrew from Jerusalem.

6 Then the word of the Lord came to Jeremiah the prophet: 7 "This is what the Lord, the God of Israel, says: Tell the king of Judah, who sent you to inquire of me, 'Pharaoh's army, which has marched out to support you, will go back to its own land, to Egypt. 8 Then the Babylonians will return and attack this city; they will capture it and burn it down.'

9 "This is what the Lord says: Do not deceive yourselves, thinking, 'The Babylonians will surely leave us.' They will not! 10 Even if you were to defeat the entire Babylonian army that is attacking you and only wounded men were left in their tents, they would come out and burn this city down."

11 After the Babylonian army had withdrawn from Jerusalem because of Pharaoh's army, 12 Jeremiah started to leave the city to go to the territory of Benjamin to get his share of the property among the people there. 13 But when he reached the Benjamin Gate, the captain of the guard, whose name was Irijah son of Shelemiah, the son of Hananiah, arrested him and said, "You are deserting to the Babylonians!"

14 "That's not true!" Jeremiah said. "I am not deserting to the Babylonians." But Irijah would not listen to him; instead, he arrested Jeremiah and brought him to the officials. 15 They were angry with Jeremiah and had him beaten and imprisoned in the house of Jonathan the secretary, which they had made into a prison.

16 Jeremiah was put into a vaulted cell in a dungeon, where he remained a long time. 17 Then King Zedekiah sent for him and had him brought to the palace, where he asked him privately, "Is there any word from the Lord?"

"Yes," Jeremiah replied, "you will be handed over to the king of Babylon."

18 Then Jeremiah said to King Zedekiah, "What crime have I committed against you or your officials or this people, that you have put me in prison? 19 Where are your prophets who prophesied to you, 'The king of Babylon will not attack you or this land'? 20 But now, my lord the king, please listen. Let me bring my petition before you: Do not send me back to the house of Jonathan the secretary, or I will die there."

21 King Zedekiah then gave orders for Jeremiah to be placed in the courtyard of the guard and given bread from the street of the bakers each day until all the bread in the city was gone. So Jeremiah remained in the courtyard of the guard.

38:1 Shephatiah son of Mattan, Gedaliah son of Pashhur, Jehucal son of Shelemiah, and Pashhur son of Malkijah heard what Jeremiah was telling all the people when he said, 2 "This is what the Lord says: 'Whoever stays in this city will die by the sword, famine or plague, but whoever goes over to the Babylonians will live. He will escape with his life; he will live.' 3 And this is what the Lord says: 'This city will certainly be handed over to the army of the king of Babylon, who will capture it.'"

4 Then the officials said to the king, "This man should be put to death. He is discouraging the soldiers who are left in this city, as well as all the people, by the things he is saying to them. This man is not seeking the good of these people but their ruin."

5 "He is in your hands," King Zedekiah answered. "The king can do nothing to oppose you."

6 So they took Jeremiah and put him into the cistern of Malkijah, the king's son, which was in the courtyard of the guard. They lowered Jeremiah by ropes into the cistern; it had no water in it, only mud, and Jeremiah sank down into the mud.

7 But Ebed-Melech, a Cushite, an official in the royal palace, heard that they had put Jeremiah into the cistern. While the king was sitting in the Benjamin Gate, 8 Ebed-Melech went out of the palace and said to him, 9 "My lord the king, these men have acted wickedly in all they have done to Jeremiah the prophet. They have thrown him into a cistern, where he will starve to death when there is no longer any bread in the city."

10 Then the king commanded Ebed-Melech the Cushite, "Take thirty men from here with you and lift Jeremiah the prophet out of the cistern before he dies."

11 So Ebed-Melech took the men with him and went to a room under the treasury in the palace. He took some old rags and worn-out clothes from there and let them down with ropes to Jeremiah in the cistern. 12 Ebed-Melech the Cushite said to Jeremiah, "Put these old rags and worn-out clothes under your arms to pad the ropes." Jeremiah did so, 13 and they pulled him up with the ropes and lifted him out of the cistern. And Jeremiah remained in the courtyard of the guard.

14 Then King Zedekiah sent for Jeremiah the prophet and had him brought to the third entrance to the temple of the Lord. "I am going to ask you something," the king said to Jeremiah. "Do not hide anything from me."

15 Jeremiah said to Zedekiah, "If I give you an answer, will you not kill me? Even if I did give you counsel, you would not listen to me."

16 But King Zedekiah swore this oath secretly to Jeremiah: "As surely as the Lord lives, who has given us breath, I will neither kill you nor hand you over to those who are seeking your life."

17 Then Jeremiah said to Zedekiah, "This is what the Lord God Almighty, the God of Israel, says: 'If you surrender to the officers of the king of Babylon, your life will be spared and this city will not be burned down; you and your family will live. 18 But if you will not surrender to the officers of the king of Babylon, this city will be handed over to the Babylonians and they will burn it down; you yourself will not escape from their hands.'"

19 King Zedekiah said to Jeremiah, "I am afraid of the Jews who have gone over to the Babylonians, for the Babylonians may hand me over to them and they will mistreat me."

20 "They will not hand you over," Jeremiah replied. "Obey the Lord by doing what I tell you. Then it will go well with you, and your life will be spared. 21 But if you refuse to surrender, this is what

the Lord has revealed to me: 22 All the women left in the palace of the king of Judah will be brought out to the officials of the king of Babylon. Those women will say to you:

"'They misled you and overcame you—those trusted friends of yours. Your feet are sunk in the mud; your friends have deserted you.'

23 "All your wives and children will be brought out to the Babylonians. You yourself will not escape from their hands but will be captured by the king of Babylon; and this city will be burned down."

24 Then Zedekiah said to Jeremiah, "Do not let anyone know about this conversation, or you may die. 25 If the officials hear that I talked with you, and they come to you and say, 'Tell us what you said to the king and what the king said to you; do not hide it from us or we will kill you,' 26 then tell them, 'I was pleading with the king not to send me back to Jonathan's house to die there.'"

27 All the officials did come to Jeremiah and question him, and he told them everything the king had ordered him to say. So they said no more to him, for no one had heard his conversation with the king.

28 And Jeremiah remained in the courtyard of the guard until the day Jerusalem was captured.

THE PRINCIPAL CHARACTERS

Who was Jeremiah? James Green describes Jeremiah this way: "Jeremiah was shy and sensitive, honest and human, somewhat impatient and impulsive, given to times of elation and dejection, courageous and confident, yet torn by a sense of inadequacy and an inner conflict."[1] He was called by God to prophesy as a youth, and he carried the burden and suffered persecution throughout his life because he was one of the few prophets among his contemporaries who would say what he believed to be God's words, rather than the words that government leaders wanted to hear.

"I guess I just wasn't made for these times." So wrote and sang The Beach Boys' Brian Wilson on the group's 1966 *Pet Sounds* album. Some Old Testament prophets, Jeremiah among them, must have shared Wilson's sentiments. Jeremiah is often referred to as the weeping prophet, so dire were his prophecies (Jeremiah 9). Redman Biddy refers specifically to Jeremiah when he calls Old Testament prophecy "the most dangerous profession."[2]

 Sedition is defined as "communication or agreement which has as its objective the stirring up of treason or certain lesser commotions, or the defamation of the government. An insurrectionary movement tending towards treason, but wanting an overt act; attempts made by meetings or speeches, or by publications, to disturb the tranquility of the state."[3]

According to J.A. Thompson, the two accounts of Jeremiah's arrest and imprisonment in Chapters 37 and 38 are probably two versions of one event. This retelling of an event happened in at least two other places in Jeremiah. His temple sermon is recounted in Chapters 7 and 26; his release by the Babylonians is told in Chapters 38, 39, and 40.[4] Green believes differently, noting some differences in the accounts.[5] Therefore, we do not know if this is an account of one "crime" with the accompanying persecution, or two separate events.

It is difficult for Americans to relate to this passage. We cannot fathom a person being imprisoned, especially under the conditions to which Jeremiah was exposed, simply for making unpopular predictions. This story should remind us of a freedom which we take for granted, freedom of speech. The freedom to openly criticize the government is a rarity, and is associated with modern democracies. Very few governments in world history have allowed their citizenry to openly criticize them, either by the spoken or the written word.

One of the most famous sedition trials in American history occurred in 1735 in New York, more than forty years before America declared its independence. John Peter Zenger, a German immigrant, published a politically partisan newspaper called the *New York Weekly Journal.* The paper often carried letters, stories, and advertisements that criticized New York's colonial governor, William Cosby. Cosby and his political allies had Zenger prosecuted for sedition on a bill of information prepared by the prosecutor, since no grand jury would indict him. Zenger's attorney, Andrew Hamilton, freely acknowledged that Zenger had broken the law, but he challenged the jury to disregard Zenger's guilt, and put the law of sedition on trial. Hamilton used the widely publicized case as a platform for advocating freedom to speak out against the government. The strategy worked and Zenger was acquitted.[6] It was a seminal moment in colonial America's history, and it laid the groundwork for the right to free speech, which we enjoy today.

"Inter arma silent leges," or "in times of war the law is silent," wrote former Chief Justice William Rehnquist in recounting examples from American history in which civil liberties and free speech have been suppressed during times of war. Some examples:

- The right to seek a writ of *habeas corpus* allows prisoners to challenge the legality of their incarceration. It is a basic Constitutional right guaranteed to all Americans. Section 9, Clause 2 of the U.S. Constitution prohibits the Congress from suspending the privilege of the writ of *habeas corpus* "unless when in Cases of Rebellion or Invasion the public Safety requires it." On April 27, 1861, at the outbreak of the Civil War, President Abraham Lincoln, fearing that Confederate spies and sympathizers would aid the Confederate military's attempts to capture Washington D.C., suspended *habeas corpus* privileges for anyone arrested between Washington and Philadelphia. Lincoln made this move over the objections of his cabinet and the Supreme Court. Dozens of people were arrested for activities viewed as seditious or pro-Confederate and were incarcerated without the right to challenge the legality of their imprisonment.

- Shortly after the United States' entry into World War I in 1917, Congress passed the Espionage Act, part of which held that anyone who "shall willfully cause or attempt to cause insubordination, disloyalty, mutiny, or refusal of duty, in the military or naval forces of the United States, or shall willfully obstruct the recruiting or enlistment service of the United States" was subject to a maximum 20-year prison term and a $10,000 fine. Charles Schenck was convicted of violating the law by printing and distributing leaflets urging draftees to resist the draft. The United States Supreme Court upheld his conviction.[7]

- In 1918, while the United States was still involved in World War I, the Sedition Act was used to punish those who encouraged opposition to American involvement in the War. Prosecutions under this act were part of the impetus for the creation of what later became known as the American Civil Liberties Union (ACLU).[8]

- During World War II, President Franklin Roosevelt ordered the internment of ethnic Japanese, none of whom had been implicated in seditious activities, in relocation centers on the West Coast. Their houses and businesses were sold, and most of these people never regained these possessions. In addition, curfews were imposed on ethnic Japanese in West Coast states.[9] These actions were taken despite the assertion by FBI Director J. Edgar Hoover that the United States had little to fear from the vast majority of ethnic Japanese on the West Coast.[10]

It is easy to judge these wartime actions with the benefit of 20/20 hindsight. What these actions teach us, as does the story of Jeremiah, is that Americans should be careful about rushing to prosecute those who speak against government action, whether they are opposing the country's involvement in war or anything else.

During the Vietnam War and subsequent military ventures, some U.S. citizens have been called unpatriotic when they predicted that the war would not end with a U.S. victory, if they said that the war effort was not going well, or if they criticized the decision to go to war. None of these people claimed to have instructions from God to make such statements, and we should not confuse partisan politics or human predictions with divinely inspired prophecy like that received by Jeremiah.

However, the story of Jeremiah raises a troubling question related to current war protests. Jeremiah was persecuted in part because he was accused of deflating the morale of the people and the soldiers by predicting that Judah's military endeavors would fail and that the kingdom would fall. Were he alive today, Jeremiah would be labeled "unpatriotic." While patriotism is an admirable trait, we must also remember the words of eighteenth-century English author Samuel Johnson, who said, "Patriotism is the last refuge of a scoundrel."[11] Slapping an unpatriotic label on someone is all too common in the United States, especially since September 11, 2001. An accusation of being unpatriotic is easy to make and difficult to refute. Once one has been labeled unpatriotic, it is hard for them to prove otherwise.

Should people who criticize government war efforts be labeled as unpatriotic or be accused of deflating troop morale for criticizing the war? During the Vietnam War, the vehement opposition to the war that was expressed in American streets and by government leaders was heard by soldiers in the field in Vietnam, and it had a negative impact on many soldiers' morale. It is impossible to discern human motives for making such statements; we cannot be sure if they are expressing their true feelings or if they have an ulterior motive, such as scoring political points, playing for the camera, venting rage against the military or the government, but—assuming that their feelings are genuine—should they be persecuted, either legally or by informal means? As difficult as it may be, Americans should be wary of trying to stifle dissent, even with, or especially with, issues that grab our emotions.

The Lesson

Jeremiah did not seek martyrdom, and he experienced very real and intense fear. In modern Western countries, seldom does obeying the will of God carry the risk of criminal punishment as it did with Jeremiah. However, many Christians in non-Western countries live every day with the fear of physical persecution and death at the hands of totalitarian governments. Examples include China, where many Christians must worship or study the Bible in secrecy, Saudi Arabia, where all citizens must be Muslims and no Bibles are allowed, and Sudan, where the Muslim government has engaged in a campaign of genocide against non-Muslims for several years.

Governmental persecution of outspoken people of God is far from extinct, and the list of martyrs for the Christian faith continues to grow. A recent example from Afghanistan illustrates. In late 2001, the United States ridded Afghanistan of the Taliban, the oppressive Islamic fascists that had ruled the country for several years and given refuge to Osama Bin Laden and Al Qaeda terrorists. Despite the overthrow of the Taliban, a recent event which made headlines around the world illustrates that Afghanistan, like many Muslim countries, is still in the business of persecuting people for their religious beliefs, or at least in cases where those beliefs conflict with that of the majority. In February of 2006, 41-year-old Abdul Rahman, an Afghan native, was arrested and imprisoned after his family accused him of converting to Christianity. Rahman had converted to Christianity sixteen years earlier while serving as a medical aid worker with an international Christian group that was helping Afghan refugees in Pakistan, where he lived for four years after his conversion. Rahman moved to Germany and lived for nine years, and returned to Afghanistan to claim custody of his children. In the course of a custody dispute, it was revealed that Rahman was a Christian and had been caught with a Bible. According to *shari-ah*, the law of Islam, any Muslim who commits apostasy (the renunciation of one's religion) in word or deed should suffer the death penalty. The prosecutor offered to drop the charges if Rahman would renounce his Christian faith and embrace the Islamic faith. The prosecutor said, "He would have been forgiven if he changed back. But he said he was a Christian and would always remain one. We are Muslims and becoming a Christian is against our laws. He must get the death penalty."[12] An international uproar forced Afghan officials to seek a face-saving way out (including an assertion that Rahman was mentally ill) of prosecuting Rahman, over the violent objections of Muslim clerics throughout Afghanistan, who clamored for Rahman's execution. Rahman had to be isolated from other prisoners to insure his safety.

Eighteenth-century French philosopher Voltaire said, "It is dangerous to be right when the government is wrong."[13] The story of Jeremiah reminds us that following the will of God seldom brings earthly rewards. Following God's will often makes those who do so unpopular, especially if it requires us to be outspoken. Jeremiah was not a masochist or a glutton for punishment, and he did not have a martyr complex, as evidenced in these passages. He dreaded and hated the persecution he faced for prophesying the truth, but his conscience and devotion to God would not permit him to do otherwise. While it is easy for us to say that we will do what we think is right no matter the consequences, we can only hope that we can have as much courage in the face of persecution as Jeremiah had. Only God knows how any of us would behave if placed in his situation.

17

Daniel | Civil Disobedience

Daniel 6:3-24

3 Now Daniel so distinguished himself among the administrators and the satraps by his exceptional qualities that the king planned to set him over the whole kingdom. 4 At this, the administrators and the satraps tried to find grounds for charges against Daniel in his conduct of government affairs, but they were unable to do so. They could find no corruption in him, because he was trustworthy and neither corrupt nor negligent. 5 Finally these men said, "We will never find any basis for charges against this man Daniel unless it has something to do with the law of his God."

6 So the administrators and the satraps went as a group to the king and said: "O King Darius, live forever! 7 The royal administrators, prefects, satraps, advisers and governors have all agreed that the king should issue an edict and enforce the decree that anyone who prays to any god or man during the next thirty days, except to you, O king, shall be thrown into the lions' den. 8 Now, O king, issue the decree and put it in writing so that it cannot be altered—in accordance with the laws of the Medes and Persians, which cannot be repealed." 9 So King Darius put the decree in writing.

10 Now when Daniel learned that the decree had been published, he went home to his upstairs room where the windows opened toward Jerusalem. Three times a day he got down on his knees and prayed, giving thanks to his God, just as he had done before. 11 Then these men went as a group and found Daniel praying and asking God for help. 12 So they went to the king and spoke to him about his royal decree: "Did you not publish a decree that during the next thirty days anyone who prays to any god or man except to you, O king, would be thrown into the lions' den?"

The king answered, "The decree stands—in accordance with the laws of the Medes and Persians, which cannot be repealed."

13 Then they said to the king, "Daniel, who is one of the exiles

from Judah, pays no attention to you, O king, or to the decree you put in writing. He still prays three times a day." 14 When the king heard this, he was greatly distressed; he was determined to rescue Daniel and made every effort until sundown to save him.

15 Then the men went as a group to the king and said to him, "Remember, O king, that according to the law of the Medes and Persians no decree or edict that the king issues can be changed."

16 So the king gave the order, and they brought Daniel and threw him into the lions' den. The king said to Daniel, "May your God, whom you serve continually, rescue you!"

17 A stone was brought and placed over the mouth of the den, and the king sealed it with his own signet ring and with the rings of his nobles, so that Daniel's situation might not be changed. 18 Then the king returned to his palace and spent the night without eating and without any entertainment being brought to him. And he could not sleep.

19 At the first light of dawn, the king got up and hurried to the lions' den. 20 When he came near the den, he called to Daniel in an anguished voice, "Daniel, servant of the living God, has your God, whom you serve continually, been able to rescue you from the lions?"

21 Daniel answered, "O king, live forever! 22 My God sent his angel, and he shut the mouths of the lions. They have not hurt me, because I was found innocent in his sight. Nor have I ever done any wrong before you, O king."

23 The king was overjoyed and gave orders to lift Daniel out of the den. And when Daniel was lifted from the den, no wound was found on him, because he had trusted in his God.

24 At the king's command, the men who had falsely accused Daniel were brought in and thrown into the lions' den, along with their wives and children. And before they reached the floor of the den, the lions overpowered them and crushed all their bones.

THE PRINCIPAL CHARACTERS

Who was Daniel? The name "Daniel" means "God has judged." Unlike most other Old Testament prophets, Daniel's identity is not tied to his father, whose name is not provided. A Jewish legend maintains that Daniel was descended from the Jewish King Zedekiah. Daniel was one of the Jews captured and sent into exile to Babylonia when King Nebuchadnezzar's army sacked Jerusalem, sometime around 605 B.C. Daniel, along with Shadrach, Meschach, and Abednego, was identified by the Babylonian king as among the smartest, wisest, and healthiest of the Jewish exiles. Because of his exceptional qualities, Daniel served in Nebuchadnezzar's palace. Daniel was given the Babylonian name Belteshazzar, but, unlike his three counterparts, he is remembered for his Hebrew name. Daniel accurately prophesied the untimely assassination of Nebuchadnezzar's successor Belshazzar at the hands of his own men. He also prophesied the downfall of the Babylonian empire at the hands of the Medes and the Persians.

Daniel was probably close to age seventy by the time Darius began his reign. Daniel found favor with the new Persian rulers just as he had with the Babylonians, so much so that he was on the eve of being appointed second only to the king in financial matters, or as W. H. Rule states "First Lord of the Treasury."[1] But Daniel's two fellow administrators (heads or premiers) and "satraps" (protectors of the realm) were jealous of Daniel's popularity and sought a way to ruin him. Failing to find him in violation of any existing law, they worked to create a law that they knew Daniel would violate.

 What was this law that Daniel violated? C.L. Seow states that Daniel was "caught acting normally."[2] Daniel's rivals petitioned the king to establish a law that would prohibit anyone from praying or making petition to any deity except the king. Was the king establishing himself as a deity? Probably not, as such a practice was not in keeping with that of other Persian kings of that era, most of whom were observers of Zoroastrianism. In addition, why would Darius have anointed himself a deity, but only for thirty days? Also, once Daniel was caught violating the law, could not the king, if he thought of himself in such vain terms, simply have declared the law void, or exempted Daniel from its consequences?

THE CRIME

The greater possibility is that the schemers convinced Darius that this law would unite the kingdom religiously, that the king, playing the role of a benevolent dictator, would petition any existing deity on their behalf. Darius was not assigning himself the position of God, but declared himself the only intermediary through which God could be reached for thirty days.[3]

Daniel almost surely knew that this law targeted him. Nevertheless he continued to pray openly as he always had. There are no specific provisions in the Old Testament for how often a person was supposed to pray. Praying three times each day, in front of open windows in his home, was Daniel's personal custom. Daniel's adversaries knew his routine and knew they would have no trouble building an airtight case against him. Whether Daniel's open prayer was an overt act of defiance or whether he was merely following his normal praying ritual, without regard for the consequences, we do not know.

We do know that Daniel refused to surreptitiously circumvent the law, which he could have done by closing his windows, or praying to himself, or merely waiting out the thirty days. More than likely Daniel simply went about his usual prayer routine, without trying to purposely antagonize Darius and without fearing the legal consequences. What Daniel was doing was engaging in an act of civil disobedience. Mohandas Gandhi, who led the fight for Indian independence in the 1940s through passive resistance, called Daniel one of the greatest passive resisters who ever lived.[4] The difference between Daniel and people like Gandhi is that Daniel was not trying to make a social statement or launch a revolution; he was simply engaging in worship the way he believed that God willed he should worship.

There is no mention of a trial, perhaps because Daniel's guilt was not in question. It seems that Darius agonized as long as possible, trying to figure some means of sparing Daniel while saving face, before handing down his sentence. Darius's attitude as Daniel enters the pit stands in marked contrast to Nebuchadnezzar's when Shadrach, Meschach, and Abednego were thrown into the fiery furnace (Daniel 3). Darius actually wishes—and seems to anxiously anticipate—that the sentence he imposed would be thwarted through divine intervention.

According to *Barnes' Notes*, the word "den" or *gowb* means pit or cistern, and it probably refers to an underground cave specially constructed for caging wild animals. The entrance was so narrow that it could be secured with a stone. The cave was probably walled on the sides, "enclosed within a wall through which a door led from the outer wall to the space lying between the walls," in which persons could "pass round and contemplate the wild beasts."[5] The signet that sealed the entrance to the den was an engraved emblem on a ring, which was dipped into hot wax and impressed on the rock in a way that would reveal any attempt to move the seal.[6]

Throwing condemned criminals into a den of lions was not a common form of capital punishment in ancient Persia, but *Barnes' Notes* states that there is evidence of such a mode of execution having been used in Babylon.[7] Execution by this method is not specifically mentioned anywhere in the Old Testament except for the story of Daniel. It may have been reserved for this one special occasion. Persians did not typically keep lions in a pit for executions; they were usually hunted and housed in zoos.

The scene after Daniel's rescue is ghastly, and it recalls the story of Achan in the book of Joshua. How many people were executed for contriving the scheme against Daniel? Some translations indicate that it was the other two administrators and their families, while other versions indicate that the execution extended to the two other administrators, all 120 satraps, and all of their families. The hope for a just ending to the story is dashed when we contemplate that innocent family members were executed for the sins of their husbands and fathers. The reader must bear in mind, however, that King Darius did not recognize the Mosaic Law; and, while he recognized the power of Yahweh, he could hardly be labeled a believer in the same manner as was Daniel. The Bible is silent on whether Daniel tried to intervene to save the lives of his rivals or their families.

THE CRIME NOW

The case of Daniel presents a perfect example of a criminal law motivated purely by politics. Governments sometimes create criminal laws that target an individual person or group of people. In this case, the other administrators, who could find no fault in Daniel, encouraged the king to create a law that they knew Daniel would violate.

It is difficult for modern Americans to imagine being prosecuted for simply exercising their right to pray while in their homes, but Americans do not have to search the history books very far to find unjust laws or examples of brave people who violated them. During America's slavery era, many states and cities in slave states enacted laws that prohibited blacks, both slave and free, from congregating in public places, in fear of slave rebellion. During the Jim Crow era, southern states enacted laws that relegated African-Americans to the status of second-class citizens. Other laws were only slightly subtler in their intent to discriminate. The Mann Act, enacted by Congress in 1911, prohibited the transportation of females across state lines for immoral purposes. Though the language of the Mann Act did not explicitly state that African-American males who dated Caucasian women were the targets, this was the case.

 Using the criminal law as a way to regulate religious practices is very common, as is using the criminal law for purely political purposes and targeting political or social enemies with specific criminal laws. The right to worship as we choose is a precious freedom that Americans unfortunately take for granted, but history is replete with examples to the contrary. Merely espousing a religious belief that contradicts that of religious or government authorities has led to the deaths of millions, and religious persecution in China, Sudan, Iran (modern day Persia, the scene of Daniel's ordeal), and Saudi Arabia demonstrate that the type of persecution suffered by Daniel is far from extinct.

One of the most important bedrocks of American government is supremacy of the rule of law. Daniel's story demonstrates that corrupt or evil government officials can usurp even something as noble as the rule of law. A law or legal system, no matter how well designed, is only as good as the people who administer it. Speaking of the actions taken by Daniel's fellow administrators, John Owens wrote, "There is a vast difference between being lawful and being right."[8] King Darius would not even allow himself to violate or summarily revoke a law he had set in place. He obviously regretted his decision, which may have been made without giving any thought to the ramifications, and it also was obvious that Darius knew he had been duped, as evidenced by the Draconian punishment given to the conspirators and their families.

Lesson for Individual Christians

One of the great difficulties Christians have with politics is compromise. Very often Christians view political matters in moral terms and feel that their morals should not be compromised. Daniel, by virtue of his exalted position under both Babylonian and Persian monarchs, was obviously very adept at politics; but he seemed to have the wisdom to know what battles were worth fighting. In Daniel's view, some battles were not worth fighting, but there were some that were worth dying for. Financial arguments, which Daniel was probably accustomed to, did not compare with spiritual matters.

One of the great difficulties in life is deciding which battles are worth fighting. Many people, including Christians, spend their lives focused on matters that are of no eternal significance, while glossing over those that are. Of the many lessons that can be taken from the story of Daniel, including courage in the face of danger and unfailing obedience to God, another lesson to be learned from examining the book of Daniel is that we should all desire the type of wisdom and discernment that Daniel possessed, knowing when it is essential to take a stand.

It is also worth noting that Daniel was an active participant in a government that many of his fellow countrymen viewed as oppressive. Many Jews, chafing under the dominion of the Babylonians and Persians, probably refused to serve those governments in any way. Daniel, unlike many of his countrymen, chose to work for the existing government, horribly imperfect though it was, rather than rebelling against a government despised by his fellow Jews. Even after being thrown into the lions' den and surviving the night, Daniel greeted the king who had put him there, not with haughtiness or arrogance, but with respect, as evidenced by his greeting, "Live forever," the normal salutation given to the king.

Many Christians adopt a very self-serving utilitarianism when deciding on a course of action; in other words, we will do right only when it seems to offer less resistance than doing wrong. Martin Luther King, Jr. wrote, "An individual who breaks a law that conscience tells him is unjust, and who willingly accepts the penalty ... is in reality expressing the highest respect for the law."[9]

The Hope

The best vignette I ever heard on the story of Daniel and the lions' den came from Charles Stanley, the Pastor of the First Baptist Church in Atlanta and the head of In Touch Ministries. Dr. Stanley related the story of when he was new to First Baptist and had acquired some powerful enemies in the church who were determined to get him fired. While he was engaged in one political battle after another with these church power brokers, a retired librarian extended several invitations to Stanley to visit her house for a chat and meal. Aware that this woman was not a power broker in the church, Stanley demurred for a while, thinking he had more powerful people with whom to partner. Undeterred, the woman continued to invite and, one night, Stanley finally accepted.

The woman directed Stanley's attention to a painting of Daniel in the lions' den, one that shows Daniel looking toward the sky. The woman kept asking Stanley what he saw in the picture. Every time he answered, the woman, aware of the battle that Stanley was facing with certain members of the church, would tell him that he was missing the most important part of the painting. Unable to ascertain her meaning, Stanley finally gave up and asked what he was missing. The woman replied, "Son, notice that Daniel isn't paying any attention to the lions." There will be lions in our lives that seek to devour us—some of our own making and some that are forced upon us. As long as our focus is fixed on God, those lions cannot harm us.

18

John the Baptist | Sedition

Matthew 14:1–12

14:1 At that time Herod the tetrarch heard the reports about Jesus, 2 and he said to his attendants, "This is John the Baptist; he has risen from the dead! That is why miraculous powers are at work in him."

3 Now Herod had arrested John and bound him and put him in prison because of Herodias, his brother Philip's wife, 4 for John had been saying to him: "It is not lawful for you to have her." 5 Herod wanted to kill John, but he was afraid of the people, because they considered him a prophet.

6 On Herod's birthday the daughter of Herodias danced for them and pleased Herod so much 7 that he promised with an oath to give her whatever she asked. 8 Prompted by her mother, she said, "Give me here on a platter the head of John the Baptist." 9 The king was distressed, but because of his oaths and his dinner guests, he ordered that her request be granted 10 and had John beheaded in the prison. 11 His head was brought in on a platter and given to the girl, who carried it to her mother. 12 John's disciples came and took his body and buried it. Then they went and told Jesus.

THE PRINCIPAL CHARACTERS Who was John the Baptist? In Matthew 11:11, Jesus Christ said, "I tell you the truth: Among those born of women there has not risen anyone greater than John the Baptist." No higher compliment was ever paid to a human being. John the Baptist, or John the Baptizer, was Jesus's relative, probably a distant cousin, although the Bible does not explain the exact nature of their kinship. We only know that Mary, the mother of Jesus, and Elizabeth, the mother of John the Baptist, were related, and that Elizabeth was much older than Mary.

John's father was a priest name Zacharias. John's birth, which occurred approximately six months before that of Jesus, was either a miracle or a biological improbability, since Luke 1 states that both of his parents were old and childless at the time John was conceived. Either way, Luke's Gospel makes it clear that John's life was to be special. From the moment of conception, John was set apart for ministry and prophesying.

John's personality, lifestyle, deportment, and ministry drew many comparisons to Elijah, the great Old Testament prophet. In fact, some of John's Jewish contemporaries thought he was Elijah returned to Earth. John is sometimes referred to as the last of the Old Testament-style prophets. Unfortunately, John is often depicted as an eccentric weirdo, even in churches, and such depictions do a disservice to him. More than likely John was better educated than many of his contemporaries, one of the benefits of being born into a priestly household.

John's lifestyle suggests that he was affiliated with a Jewish sect called the Essenes, but this is not explicitly stated in the New Testament.[1] The Essenes were characterized by a strict observance of Jewish law and ritual, but they were also distinguished by their communal and frugal lifestyle, sharing their possessions with those in their community and forsaking material wealth, living what today might be called the lifestyle of a group of collective minimalists. John commanded his hearers to share their material wealth (Luke 3:11), reflecting the Essene ideology. John's practice of baptizing believers was an extension of ceremonial purification, but it denoted a more thorough type of cleansing, a complete spiritual cleansing that was indicative of an attitude of repentance and making a complete about face in one's spiritual walk with God.

John's ministry attracted a huge following, as evidenced by the fact that Herod felt so threatened by him. It has been suggested that many of Jesus's twelve disciples were mentored by John. Jesus may have been a student of John's, which would explain why he chose John as his baptizer.[2] John's influence was also widespread. Acts 19, which records events twenty years after John's death, mentions that the great Ephesian preacher Apollos was one of John's disciples.

Another principal character in this story is Herod the Tetrarch or Herod Antipas. He was the son of Herod "the Great," the notorious tyrant who ruled at the time of Jesus's birth. Herod Antipas inherited one-fourth of his father's territory, all the while subject to Roman authority. He attracted John's criticism for having an immoral relationship with Herodias. There is some confusion over whether Herodias was Herod's sister-in-law, niece, or both. Herod's moral depravity is evidenced not only by his relationship with Herodias but by his sexual infatuation with her daughter. This girl's name is not mentioned in the New Testament, but she is identified by the historian Josephus as Salome.[3] Herod's weakness as a ruler, as a man, and as a husband, not to mention his savagery, is evidenced by the killing of John. Even putting John's murder aside, Herod Antipas was a feckless leader. In Luke 13:32 Jesus unflatteringly calls him a fox, denoting his sneaky, ambitious, and cowardly character.

A third character in this story is Herodias. Her cunning and evil make her comparable to Jezebel, the Old Testament queen whose name invokes the image of a wicked female (*see Chapter 15*). Herodias had previously been married to Herod's brother Philip, but she left Philip for Herod. Jerome, the fourth-century Christian Bible scholar, wrote that upon having John's head brought to her, Herodias spat on it and stuck a pin in the tongue.[4] Like Jezebel, Herodias was ambitious, and she used her weak husband to further her ambition, to the detriment of both. Josephus wrote that, years after John's death, Herodias, jealous of her brother Agrippa's power, demanded that the Roman Emperor Caligula hand Agrippa's authority over to Herod. The plan was thwarted, and both Herod and Herodias were banished.[5]

THE CRIME

If one had to label John's offense, the best label might be sedition. As mentioned in Chapter 16, sedition is a very slippery label. *Black's Law Dictionary* defines sedition as "communication or agreement which has as its objective the stirring up of treason or certain lesser commotions, or the defamation of the government."[6] The most famous or infamous use of such a law occurred during the early years of America's independence. In July of 1798, Congress passed the Alien and Sedition Acts, "which made it a criminal offense to utter or publish any false, scandalous and malicious writings against the government with intent to defame it, or bring it into contempt or disrepute or to excite hatred of people or stir up sedition against it."[7] The Acts, which were short lived, tightened residency requirements for citizenship, authorized the President (John Adams) to deport or jail illegal aliens, and criminalized anti-government speech.[8]

One must bear in mind that the late eighteenth century was a perilous time for the United States. At that time the United States was a new and militarily weak country, surrounded by territories held by aggressive European imperialist powers (France, Great Britain, and Spain) bent on increasing their own hegemony both in the United States and its surrounding territory. Much has changed since the eighteenth century. Even the most patriotic American cherishes the right to speak out against the government and criticize the actions of government leaders. The Monica Lewinsky scandal, which engulfed the Clinton Presidency in the 1990s, attracted vehement criticism from many quarters. Had Clinton—who, like Herod, was caught in an adulterous affair and who had a sexual infatuation with a woman young enough to be his daughter—attempted to do to his critics what Herod did with John the Baptist, even most Clinton supporters would have turned against him.

Unlike President Clinton, Herod did not need to concern himself with legal niceties or impeachment proceedings. However, Herod was concerned with the reaction of his subjects. He was afraid that his Jewish subjects, many of whom considered him a traitor to begin with for collaborating with the Romans, would rebel against him for imprisoning and executing the charismatic prophet and preacher. Plus, Herod was not totally devoid of wisdom, conscience, and the religious beliefs shared by his fellow Jews. For all of his materialism and shallowness, he still was able to recognize John for what he was—a true prophet of God who deserved his respect. Like many of his Old Testament predecessors, Herod found himself in a dilemma. He wrestled with doing the will of God by heeding the words of a true prophet, which he knew to be right, and pleasing those closest to him, which he knew to be wrong. While John was an unapologetic critic of Herod, a fellow Jew, there is no record of John criticizing the Roman occupiers of Palestine. Perhaps John saw Herod as someone who should have served as a role model for his fellow Jews, most of whom had no such lofty expectations of the pagan Romans.

Considerations for Christians Today

The story of John the Baptist raises a number of questions for the contemporary Christian. One of those questions is, "When should a Christian speak up?" Should Christians be outspoken about the actions of their government leaders, or should they stick to winning lost souls and nurturing those in their congregations? John the Baptist could have refrained from criticizing Herod and stuck to preaching to the common people, but he felt compelled to speak out.

During the Clinton-Lewinsky scandal, evangelist and missionary Franklin Graham said publicly that President Clinton had lost the moral authority to lead the country. While he was far from alone in his criticism of Clinton, Graham's criticism is especially noteworthy. The name Graham has opened the door to the White House many times over the past fifty years, as family patriarch Billy Graham had been a friend and adviser to almost every President since Dwight Eisenhower. Yet Franklin Graham, unlike his father, did not defend or mitigate Clinton's actions, and in doing so willingly placed himself outside President Clinton's sphere of influence. He chose to forgo the chance for a visit to the White House in favor of acting like John the Baptist, a voice crying in the wilderness. Not many American ministers would willfully forgo a White House visit for speaking what they believed to be the right thing. As Yale University law professor Stephen Carter writes, "Who wants to be a prophet without honor in his own land when White House breakfasts are available?"[9]

Contrast Franklin Graham's actions during the Clinton Presidency with those of his father Billy during the presidency of Richard Nixon. Reverend Graham and Richard Nixon had been close friends for more than fifteen years before Nixon was elected President in 1968. When the Watergate scandal, which eventually led to Nixon's resignation from the Presidency, broke in 1973, Graham fervently defended Nixon. Graham's defense of Nixon eventually turned to disappointment and heartbreak as Nixon's culpability came to light. Graham experienced further anguish when he listened to the secret White House tapes on which Nixon, who had never revealed his darker side to Graham, was heard using profanity and racially insensitive remarks while discussing myriad nefarious and illegal schemes. Through it all, Graham never joined the growing chorus of Nixon bashers. The two men remained friends until Nixon's death in 1994, and Graham presided over President Nixon's funeral. When asked by a reporter what he had to say to the President's numerous personal and political enemies, Graham said simply that he would urge them to forgive Nixon. Who was right, Franklin Graham, who publicly condemned President Clinton's sins, or Billy Graham, who did not condone President Nixon's sins, but who also never abandoned his close friend and political ally and called for forgiveness?

There are numerous other recent examples of Christians speaking out on social issues and criticizing government leaders. My personal observation is that, when a Christian advocates a point of view that is liberal or progressive, his or her actions are labeled "social activism." When a Christian advocates a point of view that is politically or socially conservative, that's called "meddling." Christian conservatives are warned against violating church-state separation and are accused of imposing their morality on others. One example of a prominent Christian liberal is Helen Prejean, a Roman Catholic nun who was portrayed by Susan Sarandon in the 1995 film *Dead Man Walking*. Prejean has been one of the most vocal advocates of the abolition of capital punishment in the United States for the past twenty years. She has never shied away from framing the death penalty in moralistic terms, yet she has never been accused of violating the church-state separation. (Less well known is Prejean's opposition to abortion, which places her outside liberalism.) Two other political liberals, Jesse Jackson and Al Sharpton, have never hesitated to deliver politically partisan messages in African-American churches, and have even solicited contributions for their Presidential campaigns via the church offering plate. Liberal Christians like Jackson and Sharpton do not hesitate to make many issues—such as government entitlement programs—into moral issues, with those who oppose such programs portrayed as morally bankrupt. Despite this infusion of religion and morals into politics, Sharpton and Jackson are seldom accused of violating church-state separation ideals.

Contrast the public and media treatment received by Christian conservatives Jerry Falwell, James Dobson, and Pat Robertson. Falwell, perhaps more than any Christian minister in recent decades, broke ground on mixing conservative political beliefs and Christianity when he founded an organization known as the Moral Majority, which, under his leadership, unapologetically endorsed political candidates who agreed with him on what he considered key moral issues. Falwell's moral agenda extended beyond traditional subjects such as abortion; it also encompassed issues related to fiscal responsibility and foreign policy. He made support for Israel a moral issue, and he was critical of South African anti-apartheid leaders such as Desmond Tutu, who Falwell called a phony. Falwell, who has assumed a lower public profile in recent years, is alternately blamed or credited with infusing conservative Christian ideals with politics, and equating political conservatism with conservative Christianity.

Dr. James Dobson, a psychologist and the founder of Focus on the Family, made his initial forays into public life as a child-rearing expert, but he has also been active in politics, especially with respect to abortion and education. To many, Dobson has become the face of the evangelical Christian right in the United States. Over the past three decades, Dobson has fused traditional, conservative family values with conservative politics. Dobson is an unapologetic conservative Republican, even though he has frequently criticized Republicans who deviate from what he sees as their core values of conservative Christian morals (including a staunch pro-life stand on abortion) and an allegiance to the traditional two-parent family. Many Christian liberals are critical of Dobson's implicit message that Christian values are synonymous with conservative stances on political and social issues.

Reverend Pat Robertson, the founder of the Christian Broadcasting Network and a former Republican Presidential candidate, has probably attracted the most criticism for making almost every political issue imaginable a moral issue as well. Controversial statements include his 2005 call for the "taking out" of Venezuelan President Hugo Chavez, and his 2006 statement that Israeli Prime Minister Ariel Sharon's crippling stroke was God's punishment for Sharon's territorial concessions to the Palestinians. (Robertson apologized to Sharon's son.) Falwell, Dobson, and Robertson, along with other people lumped under the label the "Christian right," always fend off accusations of excessively blending religion and politics.

Should Christians simply ignore the actions of their government? If the answer is yes, what does that say about the actions of John the Baptist? If the answer is no, when should Christians speak up and when should they remain silent and stick to winning souls and nurturing congregations? Those who believe that Christians should remain silent on social and political issues are ignoring some important events in American history when churches and religious leaders made immense contributions to America's social and moral fabric. One example is slavery. Although slavery had its opponents in the secular world, much of the opposition to slavery and the moves to abolish it originated in churches, and nineteenth-century Christians did not apologize for framing abolition arguments in biblical terms. Further, they had no hesitation in pushing the government to endorse biblical ideals, although the Bible never categorically condemns all forms of slavery. The same is true about the Civil Rights movement and anti-segregation efforts in the twentieth century.[10] Ironically, opponents to these efforts also justified their ideas on religious grounds. In any case, Christians did not sit on the sidelines or place themselves above the political fray when it came to speaking out against slavery and segregation.

Criminologist Samuel Walker writes, "Both liberals and conservatives are guilty of peddling nonsense about crime."[11] This is true about both liberal and conservative Christians and it applies to more issues than crime. It seems at times that both sides forget that the same Bible that inspires one political persuasion to action also inspires a different political persuasion to act as well. Christian liberals think that, if Jesus were alive today, he would be a liberal; Christian conservatives think Jesus would be a conservative. Both sides seem oblivious to the fact that liberal and conservative ideologies are manmade creations and that God cannot be reduced to either of these crude and inexact categorizations.

The Lesson

One criminal justice teaching tool that I learned and have passed on in some of my classes goes like this: I tell my students to write an essay, and summarize it to the rest of the class, with the following instructions:

> You have been appointed Attorney General of the United States. The Constitution has been abolished. There is no Congress, no judiciary, and no elections. In short, you have unlim-

ited power and are answerable to no one. In addition, you have been given an unlimited budget; there are no spending limits. Tell me what you would do to reduce or eliminate crime.

My students and I have fun with this little exercise, and it reminds students that attempts to reduce crime carry risks, especially to personal freedom and liberties. Some students say they would impose total martial law, have television monitors everywhere; and one student once simply said that he would shoot all first offenders. My favorite response was from a student who jokingly said, "The first thing I would do is pass a law that allowed me to kill anyone who ticks me off." Tragically, sedition laws have been interpreted and applied in that manner. Under some governments, a person is guilty of sedition if he or she simply criticizes a government official.

When reading the story of John the Baptist, we find much to admire in him, and Americans should also find much for which to be thankful. The people mentioned in this chapter—such as the Grahams, Jerry Falwell, Jesse Jackson, Al Sharpton, Pat Robertson, and James Dobson—would not be allowed to speak out under the rule of a petty tyrant like Herod. Of all the freedoms that Americans take for granted, the story of John the Baptist reminds us of one very important freedom guaranteed in the First Amendment to the Constitution of the United States, which reads:

> "Congress shall make no law respecting an establishment of religion, or prohibiting the free exercise thereof; or abridging the freedom of speech, or of the press; or the right of the people peaceably to assemble, and to petition the Government for a redress of grievances."

It took the sacrifice of many lives at the hands of many tyrants, both in biblical times and in subsequent eras, to teach us how precious and important this right is. Not only was John the Baptist one of the greatest preachers who ever lived, his life serves as a lesson in the importance of free speech in a democracy.

19

The Good Samaritan Robbers | Brigandage

Luke 10:25-37

25 On one occasion an expert in the law stood up to test Jesus. "Teacher," he asked, "what must I do to inherit eternal life?"

26 "What is written in the Law?" he replied. "How do you read it?"

27 He answered: "'Love the Lord your God with all your heart and with all your soul and with all your strength and with all your mind'; and, 'Love your neighbor as yourself.'"

28 "You have answered correctly," Jesus replied. "Do this and you will live."

29 But he wanted to justify himself, so he asked Jesus, "And who is my neighbor?"

30 In reply Jesus said: "A man was going down from Jerusalem to Jericho, when he fell into the hands of robbers. They stripped him of his clothes, beat him and went away, leaving him half dead. 31 A priest happened to be going down the same road, and when he saw the man, he passed by on the other side. 32 So too, a Levite, when he came to the place and saw him, passed by on the other side. 33 But a Samaritan, as he traveled, came where the man was; and when he saw him, he took pity on him. 34 He went to him and bandaged his wounds, pouring on oil and wine. Then he put the man on his own donkey, took him to an inn and took care of him. 35 The next day he took out two silver coins and gave them to the innkeeper. 'Look after him,' he said, 'and when I return, I will reimburse you for any extra expense you may have.'

36 "Which of these three do you think was a neighbor to the man who fell into the hands of robbers?"

37 The expert in the law replied, "The one who had mercy on him."

Jesus told him, "Go and do likewise."

THE PRINCIPAL CHARACTERS Who was the Good Samaritan? This passage of Luke's Gospel contains one of many parables told by Jesus. Parable, derived from the Greek word *parabolee*, is a teaching method in which earthly truths are used to relate a heavenly truth.[1] Jesus did not invent the parable as a teaching method; it was often used by rabbis during his earthly lifetime. As this passage is a parable, the people mentioned in this story are nameless, but are identified only by labels: a man, robbers, a priest, a Levite, and a Samaritan.

Even though the people in this parable have no names, the readers of the Gospel and those who first heard the parable can envision these people in their mind's eye. The "man" is completely anonymous. His ethnicity, religion, age, and social status are not mentioned. Perhaps Jesus referred to him simply as a man, realizing that most people hearing the story would imagine themselves or someone like them in his place.

A second character in the parable is the priest. The priest obtained his position by birth. All priests claimed to be descendants of Levi, one of Jacob's sons. Aaron, the brother of Moses and a descendant of Levi, was the first of the Israelite priests. The essential function of the ancient priest was that of mediator between the divine and human, by virtue of the priest's superior knowledge of, or power of communication with, the supernatural. The priest was the director, if not the actual performer, of sacrifices offered to a deity. Therefore, the priest in this instance was reluctant to touch the seemingly dead robbery victim, not so much because of callousness toward his plight, but perhaps because touching what he might have assumed was a dead body would make him unclean and thus unfit for his priestly duties. By Jesus's time, the priests had acquired a reputation of being unscrupulous, selfish, and ambitious, in part due to the politicization of the position by the Herodians.

A Levite was, as A.R. Faussett states, the witness and guard of the truth within Israel.[2] The Levite served as an assistant to the priest. Despite the title, most Levites were not descendants of Levi. Unlike the priests, most Levites did not work in the temple full time; they may have received some compensation for their temple work, which usually consisted of logistical and administrative duties, but they held other jobs and lived apart from the temple most of the time.[3] A close modern equivalent to the Levite would be a lay minister, deacon or church elder.

Then there is the central figure in the story, the Samaritan, whom Jesus never refers to as "good," but who he does call a "neighbor" in response to the original question posed by the "expert in the law." The Samaritans were a mixed ethnic group, composed of Jews that had intermarried with ethnic and religious groups after most of the Jews were carried away into exile, several centuries prior to the beginning of the New Testament period. The Samaritan history is shrouded in myth and propaganda.

The enmity between Israel and Samaria at the time of Jesus is traceable to the Old Testament. Ezra, Chapter 4, states that the Samaritans opposed resettlement of Jerusalem by the Jews who had been living in exile in Persia, even going so far as to write a malicious and untruthful letter about the Jews to the Persian king. The most virulent hostility between the Jews and Samaritans took root in the period between the Old and New Testaments. Jews charged that Samaritans intermarried with the non-Jews in the region, thus corrupting the purity of Jewish blood lines; they also held that Samaritans mixed Yahweh worship with the heathen practices of the pagans around them, thus corrupting the purity of Yahweh worship.

The Samaritan view of their history is far different. Many Samaritans blamed their negative image on Ezra's caustic writings; and the Samaritans claimed they held fast to Jewish worship and tradition, referring to themselves as *Shâmerîm* (the observant) rather than *Shômerônîm* (inhabitants of Samaria) as they were called by Jews returning from exile in Persia.[4]

In any case, the hatred between the Jews and Samaritans was overt, entrenched, and fierce. There was no such thing as modern political correctness, and no ethnic group felt obliged to make a false show of love toward those they did not like. In Matthew 10:4, Jesus tells his disciples to avoid Samaritan cities, probably realizing that the fledgling disciples would have their hands full ministering to fellow Jews, and also because he probably knew that their hatred of Samaritans was so intense that they could not overcome their prejudice and effectively minister to them. For the time being, Jesus ordered, leave ministering to the Samaritans to him alone. The Jews made no secret of their hatred toward the Samaritans, and the "expert in the law" to whom Jesus told this parable no doubt seethed with anger at Jesus's words. In fact, at the end of the passage, when asked to tell who the true "neighbor" was, the "expert" would not even utter the word Samaritan, so loathe were most Jews to use "Samaritan" in any way but a derogatory context.

The word used for robber in this parable is *leistes*. Some biblical translations refer to the men in this story as thieves, which suggest the mere taking of property. Robbers or brigands like the people described here not only deprived their victims of property, they often did so by violent means. Modern criminal statutes might label this behavior brigandage, common law robbery, or robbery by force. Aggravated assault or attempted murder might also be added to the list of charges. Brigandage is probably the most appropriate term in this case. Brigandage is defined as "robbery and plundering committed by armed bands, often associated with forests or mountain regions, especially if the area provides suitable hiding places for the brigands."[5]

The fear of brigandage resonated with the hearers of this parable, especially given the location. The road from Jerusalem to Jericho was well known as a haven for brigands, for several reasons. The region was rocky and mountainous, allowing robbers cover and hiding places. It was also sparsely inhabited in many places but frequently traveled, making it a natural spot for robbers to prey upon passersby. This road became even more hazardous as a result of Herod the Great firing 40,000 men who had been employed to work on the temple. Many of the out-of-work temple builders became brigands. Brigandage tends to thrive in times of social or political unrest, and the perpetrators sometimes claim to be waging a social and political battle against unjust conditions. As a result some brigands become folk heroes, including England's Robin Hood, and perhaps the New Testament figure Barabbas.

This route maintained its notorious reputation for many centuries after the telling of this parable. In 1852, a theology professor named Hackett made these remarks about the road from Jerusalem to Jericho after a visit there:

"No part of the traveler's journey is so dangerous as the expedition to Jericho and the Dead Sea. In spite of every precaution, hardly a season passes in which some luckless wayfarer is not killed or robbed in going down from Jerusalem to Jericho. The place derives its hostile character from its terrible wildness and desolation. If we might conceive of the ocean as being suddenly congealed and petrified when its waves are tossed mountain high, and dashing in wild confusion against each other, we should then have some idea of the aspect of the desert in which the Saviour has placed so truthfully the parable of the Good Samaritan. The ravines, the almost inaccessible cliffs, the caverns, furnish admirable lurking-places for robbers. They can rush forth unexpectedly upon their victims, and escape as soon almost beyond the possibility of pursuit." [6]

THE PUNISHMENT

Those who commited the assault received no punishment for this crime, at least in this account of the story, but the robbers are not the focus of this parable. The penalty for brigandage in ancient Rome was death. This may have been the crime for which the two men on either side of Jesus were crucified. Prescribing the death penalty for brigandage was not unique to Rome; in fact it was a common punishment for brigandage in the ancient world. Even today, in some Middle Eastern and African countries, where travelers are susceptible to such crimes, the penalty is death.

THE CRIME AND PUNISHMENT TODAY

This biblical story focuses not on the crime or the criminals, but on the reaction of the people who happened upon the victim. Many of the criminal justice system's harshest critics claim, with some justification, that the victim is often neglected in the administration of justice. The legal system is often criticized for focusing on the well-being of the accused. Even in instances in which the accused is targeted not for help, but for punishment, the restoration of the victim often takes a back seat to satisfying the public demand for vengeance.

There have been movements in recent years to address the plight of victims in criminal justice proceedings. In many jurisdictions, prosecutors employ victim assistance workers, who are tasked with keeping victims informed of the status of their cases. These same people may request that victims complete "victim impact statements," in which they provide accounts of the crimes, how the crimes affected them, both financially and personally, and what sanctions they would like to see imposed. It has long been common for courts to allow victims to testify or make oral statements during sentencing hearings, for a victim to provide a statement in a presentence report (a report written by probation officials to assist the judge in sentencing), or for a victim to receive financial restitution for expenses directly related to the crime, especially property crimes such as theft.

While many Christians bemoan the problem of crime, and many thirst for justice to be handed out to the offender, few Christian organizations actually reach out to crime victims in any concerted or organized fashion, perhaps assuming (wrongly) that such duties are best left to criminal justice professionals. This is unfortunate and tragic because many victims of crime, especially violent crimes such as rape or robbery, need spiritual healing and should be able to turn to the church for this healing. Many do turn to the church; some receive help and some do not. An Internet website, MarylandCrimeVictims.org, states that "faith communities are not prepared to address the needs of many crime victims, and victim services programs are not providing a full range of services that address the spiritual needs of victims." [7]

Lessons for Individual Christians

The archetypal example of apathy toward a crime victim occurred on March 13, 1964. Kitty Genovese of Queens, New York, was about to enter her apartment building at around 3:00 a.m., when she was attacked from behind by an assailant who was hiding behind the bushes. Genovese was stabbed, dragged to the bushes, and sexually assaulted. She screamed, and lights in nearby apartment buildings came on. The assailant left and Genovese crawled toward her building door, but the assailant returned and continued the assault. She screamed for help again, but no one came. At around 4:00 a.m., almost one hour after the assault started, the police received an anonymous phone call, but Genovese was already dead. During their investigation, which netted the culprit, the police interviewed the neighbors. Approximately thirty-eight neighbors reported seeing the attack but did not intervene nor call the police. The neighbors responded by saying that this was "not their problem" and that someone else should call. If only one witness had even bothered to call the moment the attack started, Genovese probably would have survived.[8]

On a far less profound level, I once heard a minister relate a similar occurrence in his life when discussing this parable. The day prior, he and several other ministers from other churches gathered together, and using our church van (but their own gas money) left for a golf outing. While en route to the golf course, the van, full of ministers, passed a middle-aged African-American woman and her children whose car was stalled on the side of the road. Rather than stopping to help, the ministers passed them by and went on to their golf game. Shortly after passing them by, the minister viewed himself in the same light as the priest and the Levite, even though this was not the life-and-death situation depicted in Luke.

This minister's story reminds us again of how easy it is to be callous and indifferent to the hurts of those around us. Every day, millions of people walk the streets of cities around the world (including America's big cities) and pass by people lying on the streets, giving scant thought to whether they are living or dead, let alone taking the time to personally attend to their well-being.

One thought that might have gone through the mind of the original hearers was, why would this man be traveling such a dangerous road alone? Wouldn't anyone with common sense know better than to do such a thing? This road was the quintessential "bad neighborhood" which people were advised to avoid while traveling alone or in small groups. The same might be said of a person who is victimized by a crime because he or she did not exercise good judgment, for example, a person who walks alone in a dark parking lot, someone who goes to an ATM alone late at night, a person who leaves his car or home unlocked, a woman who gets drunk and goes into a hotel room with several strange men. When people are victimized after making bad judgments, one might hear, "If that person had no more smarts than to put himself (or herself) in such a situation, he (or she) must share some of the blame for what happened."

There are actions we can take that can lessen our likelihood of becoming a crime victim, but to focus on whatever mistake the "certain man" in the parable might have made misses the point of this poignant and timeless lesson. People become crime victims, and, very often, crime victims—especially those who have been the victims of violent crimes such as the one discussed in this parable—need help. There is no mention of the Samaritan lecturing the man about being more cautious. Since the man had been stripped of his belongings, the Samaritan had no clue as to the man's social status. The Samaritan had no idea whether the man was rich or poor. The Samaritan had nothing to gain from helping the man; in fact he had much to lose, placing himself at physical risk by helping him, and he spent his own money to see that the man was cared for, never bothering to ask for reimbursement. The Samaritan, unlike many of us today who often stop at mailing a check to support someone in need, also invested his time to help the man, taking several hours out of his day to provide aid.

The Hope

State legal codes are replete with references to the term Good Samaritan. Most of these statutes address the degree of liability for medical professionals or ordinary citizens who aid accident victims. For instance, Wisconsin law states: "Any person who renders emergency care for a victim (or) … provides other reasonable assistance … is immune from civil liability for his or her acts or omissions in providing the assistance. This immunity does not apply if the person receives or expects to receive compensation for providing the assistance." Wisconsin law also states: "Any person who knows that a crime is being committed and that a victim is exposed to bodily harm shall summon law enforcement officers or other assistance or shall provide assistance to the victim." [9] The final episode of the popular 1990s situation comedy *Seinfeld* centered on the refusal of the four main characters to aid a man being robbed, thus violating a "Good Samaritan" law in a small Massachusetts town.

The term "Good Samaritan" is part of the English vocabulary, for Christians and non-Christians alike. The term has been used to the point where it has been trivialized, its poignancy and profundity lost on many of us. Lawmakers cannot make human beings love and care for one another the way the Samaritan did in Jesus's parable. Few biblical passages are as well known or touching as the parable of the Good Samaritan. Well known though it is, human beings need to be constantly reminded of how far we have to go in making its message part of the fabric of our being.

20

Simon the Zealot | Terrorism?

Matthew 10:2-4

2 These are the names of the twelve apostles: first, Simon (who is called Peter) and his brother Andrew; James son of Zebedee, and his brother John; 3 Philip and Bartholomew; Thomas and Matthew the tax collector; James son of Alphaeus, and Thaddaeus; 4 Simon the Zealot and Judas Iscariot, who betrayed him.

THE PRINCIPAL CHARACTERS

Who was Simon? Of all the chapters in this book, this one was the most problematic for me for a couple of reasons. One, to even suggest that one of Jesus's twelve disciples could be labeled a terrorist, especially in the post-9/11 world in which we live, provokes the ire of many Christians. Two, to suggest that Simon was affiliated with a terrorist group is also to engage in huge speculation, hence the question mark in the chapter title. The term Zealot has different applications, and we do not know which application applies to Simon. In any case, the Gospel writers saw fit to identify Simon by this title, or a close approximation of the title, both to distinguish him from Simon Peter and to insure that the reader knew about his political and religious affiliation. Even if Simon never engaged in any action that could be considered terrorism (under any definition), a discussion of terrorism and the Zealots is in order for a book such as this, even though this scant space does not do justice to such a weighty, complex, and emotion-laden topic.

As for Simon's identity, we know very little. He never speaks in the New Testament, and the only mention of him is in the listings of the twelve disciples. Jesus had a half-brother named Simon (Matthew

13:55), but it is probably not the same person, Simon being a common name at the time. Nathanael, a disciple often identified as being one and the same with Bartholomew, may actually have been Simon. Some biblical translations refer to Simon as a Cananaean or a Canaanite, but those labels refer to his ties to the Zealots rather than a specific geographical location.[1] One claim is that Mark's Gospel calls Simon a Cananaean because the term Zealot had an unsavory connotation at the time his Gospel was written. By the time Luke's Gospel was written a few years later the term Zealot was no longer impolitic.[2]

To most modern readers, the use of the word "Zealot" to identify Simon means little. However, to early Gospel readers, the term was loaded with connotations. The fact that one of Jesus's twelve disciples was identified as a Zealot has provoked great curiosity about this group. Zealot, from the word *zeloo*—meaning to like, admire, or be jealous—may simply refer to a group of Jews who were enthusiastic in their observance of the Jewish law.[3] If that definition applies to Simon, any further discussion of his political activities is moot.

It is the other definition of Zealot that makes Simon an intriguing and controversial character. The Zealots drew their inspiration from Elijah, an Old Testament prophet who was willing to fight against ruling religious and political authorities.[4] William Farmer notes another parallel between the Zealots of Jesus's time and Old Testament Israelite warriors. Based on the wartime successes of their Old Testament ancestors, many first century Zealots believed they were engaged in a holy war against the Roman Empire, just like Moses was against the Egyptians, like Joshua was against the nations living in Israel's Promised Land, and like David was against the Philistines. Based on Israel's glorious past, the Zealots believed that God would surely intervene on their behalf to defeat the Romans.[5]

According to the Jewish historian Josephus, there were four major philosophical sects of First Century Judaism, two of which, the Pharisees and the Sadducees, are well known to Bible readers. The third was the Essenes, which may have included John the Baptist (*see Chapter 18*) and the fourth was the Zealots. The Zealots were believed to have been founded by a man named Judas the Galilean. This Judas is not to be confused with Judas Iscariot, Jesus's disciple and infamous betrayer. However, the name Judas is noteworthy because Judas the Galilean became such a folk hero among patriotic Jews that many Jewish boys born about the same time as Jesus and Judas Iscariot were named after the Zealot founder.

Luke 2 states that Jesus was born while the Jews were being subjected to a harsh census that was imposed by the Roman government. To most Americans, a census is simply a minor inconvenience imposed on them every ten years. We are not cognizant of the differences between a modern census and the one imposed by ancient Middle Eastern dictatorships. The census of Luke 2 uprooted families, including the family of Jesus, and broke many Jewish communities, and it meant that the Jews were forced to pay taxes to an oppressive Roman government, which they despised. The Jews chafed under this hardship that was imposed by the hated Romans, who enacted the census in part to consolidate their rule over the region. The census also marked the physical arrival of Roman soldiers and governors in large numbers, meaning that Jews would come into close everyday contact with their foreign occupiers.

Most Jews complained about the census but, like Jesus's father Joseph, complied nonetheless; but for Judas the Galilean and others like him the census was the final straw. Judas the Galilean organized his like-minded confederates and rebelled. Most Zealots realized that an open revolt against the powerful Roman army was futile. They could not hope to defeat the Romans in a conventional battle. (This thinking would not last. Tragically, the Jews in Palestine, led by the Zealots, challenged the Romans around A.D. 65, and the city of Jerusalem was decimated.) Around A.D. 6, the Zealots began fighting what is now called asymmetrical warfare. Hit-and-run tactics against small contingents of Roman soldiers, as well as assassinations of Roman leaders and their Jewish collaborators, were trademark Zealot tactics. One of the first Zealot assassination targets was not a Roman, but a Jewish high priest named Jonathan. The Zealots would carry out assassinations in broad daylight, but in a crowded place so that they could quickly disappear into the crowd. This had the double effect of killing their adversary and making their adversaries fearful of public gatherings. A common Zealot instrument of assassination was a short *sica*, the Latin word for dagger. Their fondness for the *sica* or dagger led to their being nicknamed the Sicarii.[6]

The Zealots shared most of the philosophical and religious beliefs of the Pharisees, who rigidly adhered to Jewish customs and religious laws. The Zealots took their religiosity and nationalism to a different level. The Pharisees were nationalistic in their own right and resented Roman rule, but they took advantage of their position as leaders of oppressed Jewish minorities. For the Pharisees Roman rule was both odious and advantageous. Although they hated the Romans, they often used them as convenient targets for criticism. In the eyes of ordinary Jews, the Pharisees were patriotic and religious authorities who despised Roman rule as much as they did, but the Roman presence in Palestine rallied ordinary Jews behind the Pharisees, so the Pharisees fed off Roman unpopularity.

The Zealots did not attempt to maintain a symbiotic relationship with the Romans; they actively usurped Roman rule, by any means necessary. Josephus wrote, "They had an invincible love of liberty, for they hold God to be their only lord and master. They showed an indifference towards the tortures of their parents and friends, in their resolve to call no man master."[7]

Although there is no record of any of Jesus's other disciples being affiliated with radical political groups, the Gospels suggest that they did not fully understand his mission until after his ascension, as recorded in Acts 1. They constantly pressured Jesus to become a political leader who would restore Israel to its former greatness and rid them of Roman occupation. Jesus never caved into this pressure; rather, he taught his disciples that his ministry was for the entire world and for all of time, and that it transcended Jewish nationalism.

Jesus was aware of his fellow Jews' nationalistic desires, but where did his sympathies lie? What sort of relationship did he have with the Zealots? Jesus often had harsh words for the religious leaders, but nothing is recorded in the Gospels about anything Jesus may have said about the Zealots. Jesus never endorsed violent nationalism. It became clear that Jesus did not endorse violence to further his own ministry in the Garden of Gethsemane. His disciples were ready to fight for him, as evidenced by the assault on a temple servant (Luke 22:50). Jesus's refusal to fight disillusioned the disciples, who fled.

 The word "terrorist" did not exist in the first century. It is traceable to the French Revolution of the late eighteenth century, when the government executed more than 40,000 of its citizens. British philosopher Edmund Burke called this the "reign of terror," terror being a derivation of the French infinitive *terreur*, which means to frighten.[8] Most Americans see the terrorist stereotype embodied in an angry young Islamic male, Timothy McVeigh's 1995 bombing of Oklahoma City's Alfred Murrah Federal Building notwithstanding. This was not always the case with terrorist stereotypes. The mental image of a terrorist of the early twentieth century was of a hooded eastern or southern European anarchist, as typified by Gavrilo Princip, the young Serbian who triggered World War I by assassinating the heir to the Austrian throne in 1914; or by Sacco and Vanzetti, two Italian immigrants and members of the American anarchist movement who were executed in 1927 for armed robbery and murder in Massachusetts; or by Leon Czolgosz, a deranged anarchist who assassinated President William McKinley in 1901. The other major early twentieth-century terrorist acts in the United States were perpetrated by labor militants. The most notorious act was the October 1, 1910 bombing of the *Los Angeles Times*, which killed twenty-one people.[9] In the early twentieth century, terrorism at the hands of radical Muslims was not on America's radar screen. Terrorism is not new, and it did not begin with Islamic totalitarianism.

Three questions emerge when discussing terrorism:

1. Is violence a morally acceptable means of promoting a cause, such as political revolution, social change, or a religious belief?
2. Is one person's terrorist another person's freedom fighter?
3. Is the terrorist of today the statesman of tomorrow?

As for the first question, the establishment of most independent nations, including modern democracies such as Israel and the United States, were greatly aided by violence. America gained its independence through war, not negotiation.

As for the second question, Osama Bin Laden is one of the most reviled people in world history, if one is asking Americans. However, public opinion polls throughout the Muslim world paint a different portrait. Despite the cries of Muslims who claim that Bin Laden only reflects the views of a small minority of Muslims, a 2005 Pew Research Center poll revealed that 60 percent of Jordan's Muslims and 51 percent of Pakistan's Muslims have confidence in Bin Laden. His popularity in those two countries has increased since 2003. Bin Laden enjoys approval ratings of a substantial minority of Muslims in other countries, including Indonesia, Turkey, Lebanon, and Morocco.[10]

As for question 3, history is replete with examples of a "terrorist" or political rebel becoming one of the world's leading statesmen. Two examples are George Washington (and practically all of America's founding fathers); and South Africa's Nelson Mandela, who spent more than twenty-five years in prison for treason, was released in 1990, shared the Nobel Peace Prize in 1993, and served from 1994–1999 as Prime Minister of the country that had imprisoned him. Imagine how Americans might view George Washington or Thomas Jefferson if the British had suppressed the American Revolution. Conversely, how would we view Jefferson Davis, the President of the Confederacy during the 1860s, if the South had succeeded in its secession effort? Had the Confederacy won the Civil War, Davis might be viewed, at least by Southerners, as akin to George Washington.

The best example from recent history to illustrate the terrorist-turned-statesman is Menachem Begin. A Polish-born Jew who survived the Soviet-led persecution of Polish Jews and the Nazi-led Holocaust of Jews during the 1930s and 1940s, Begin left Europe toward the end of World War II to join the Zionist movement that was fighting for the creation of a Jewish state in Palestine. Begin led an organization called the Irgun Zvai Le'umi (National Military Organization). While many Zionists used diplomacy as their weapon, the Irgun used violence. Assassinating British soldiers who were occupying Palestine and terrorizing Palestinian Arabs were the Irgun's trademarks. Their most infamous action was blowing up the King David Hotel in July 1946, an act that killed ninety-one people. When the Irgun's fight against the British was at its height in the 1940s, British authorities in Palestine placed a £10,000 bounty on Begin. While many Jews denounced them, the Irgun claimed that violence succeeded in bringing the United Nations and Great Britain to the bargaining table to allow for the establishment of the nation of Israel.

What a difference time can make. In 1948, the British relinquished control over Palestine; and the nation of Israel was officially established and immediately recognized by the world's two superpowers, the United States and the Soviet Union. Three decades later, Begin was elected Prime Minister of Israel. Among his duties as Prime Minister was dealing and negotiating with the same British government which, thirty years earlier, placed a bounty on his head. In 1978, Begin, the former terrorist, shared the Nobel Peace Prize with Egypt's Anwar Sadat for the Camp David Accords, which ended the state of war between the two countries.

There is a thin line between terrorism and warfare. Terrorism is a form of asymmetrical warfare, a close cousin of guerilla warfare. The term guerilla warfare originated in the early nineteenth century during the French occupation of the Iberian Peninsula. Realizing they could not defeat the far superior French army in a conventional battle, Spanish and Portuguese resistance fighters or *guerrilleros* (irregulars) employed hit-and-run attacks and other sneak attack methods to keep the French off guard. Their strategy was to wear the opponent down rather than fight a huge open-field battle that they could not win. Guerilla warfare relies heavily on psychological strategies as well, with one side constantly trying to outguess and keep the other off guard.[11]

Whether a group of people are engaging in asymmetrical warfare or terrorism depends on one's perspective. One example is found in the Middle East between the Israelis and the Palestinians, the two groups whose rivalry is one of the most crucial and complicated problems facing all of the world's governments. The Israeli government labels attacks on its soldiers and citizens by Palestinians as terrorism. Palestinians who oppose what they view as Israeli oppression respond by saying that their only choice against the Israeli Army, the best equipped and trained in the Middle East, is to engage in surprise attacks and to constantly keep the Israelis off guard. Since they cannot possibly hope to defeat an army like Israel's using conventional means, they feel it necessary to resort to suicide bombings, car bombs, kidnapping, and other guerilla/terrorist methods.

An important distinction between the acts of the first-century Zealots and many modern Islamic terrorists, including the Palestinian terrorists who target Israel today, is that the Zealots did not target civilians, and they did not simply kill at random. Modern Palestinian terrorists, like most other Islamic terrorists, make no distinction between civilians and government officials or soldiers. In 1998, Osama Bin Laden, the leader of Al Qaeda, stated that anyone who paid taxes or participated in government was a fair target. He made no distinction between those in military and civilian clothing.[12] Indeed, terrorists often deliberately attack the most vulnerable targets they can find. Witness the 2004 incident in Russia, when Chechen terrorists took an entire school hostage, and 331 people, more than half of them school children, were murdered by the terrorists or died during rescue efforts. Likewise, the attacks of September 11, 2001 on the United States were, unlike the acts perpetrated by the First Century Zealots, acts of indiscriminate murder. Unlike the Zealots, most modern terrorists, including Islamic terrorist groups like Al Qaeda, Hamas, Hezbollah, and right-wing terrorists in the United States, purposely target the most vulnerable members of society, because they are easy targets, and doing so instills fear among ordinary citizens, not just political and military leaders. Therefore, although the actions of First Century Zealots can easily be condemned, they do not equate with the barbarous actions of many modern terrorists.

The Hope

Opinions on who Simon was and what he was like vary. If Simon was a hard-core, militant Zealot, the degree of change in him can only be matched by that of Paul. Simon's (possibly) radical transformation is well described by M. R.Vincent: "No name is more striking in the list [of disciples] than that of Simon the Zealot, for to none of the twelve could the contrast be so vivid between their former and their new position. What revolution of thought and heart could be greater than that which had thus changed into a follower of Jesus one of the fierce war party of the day, which looked on the presence of Rome in the Holy Land as treason against the majesty of Jehovah, a party who were fanatical in their Jewish strictures and exclusiveness?"[13]

Can God change the heart and mind of a terrorist? The obvious answer is yes. A much harder question for professing Christians (including me) to answer is whether we pray for a terrorist. Of all the statements that Jesus made in the Gospels, one of the most difficult to apply is Matthew 5:43–44, where Jesus says,

You have heard that it was said, "Love your neighbor and hate your enemy." But I tell you: Love your enemies and pray for those who persecute you."

I am not qualified to preach to my readers about this passage as it applies to people like Osama Bin Laden, and what I write here should not necessarily be translated into government policy. Governments cannot simply hope that terrorism will go away, so targeted killing of terrorists is a necessity for governments that are trying to protect their citizens. I will merely close this chapter with a message to the individual reader, an emphasis on one word in Matthew 5:44; that word is *tell*. Jesus did not make a request; he *commanded* his followers to pray for and love their enemies, even those who sought to kill them.

21

Barabbas | Insurrection

Matthew 27:15-26

15 Now it was the governor's custom at the Feast to release a prisoner chosen by the crowd. 16 At that time they had a notorious prisoner, called Barabbas. 17 So when the crowd had gathered, Pilate asked them, "Which one do you want me to release to you: Barabbas, or Jesus who is called Christ?" 18 For he knew it was out of envy that they had handed Jesus over to him.

19 While Pilate was sitting on the judge's seat, his wife sent him this message: "Don't have anything to do with that innocent man, for I have suffered a great deal today in a dream because of him."

20 But the chief priests and the elders persuaded the crowd to ask for Barabbas and to have Jesus executed.

21 "Which of the two do you want me to release to you?" asked the governor.

"Barabbas," they answered.

22 "What shall I do, then, with Jesus who is called Christ?" Pilate asked.

They all answered, "Crucify him!"

23 "Why? What crime has he committed?" asked Pilate.

But they shouted all the louder, "Crucify him!"

24 When Pilate saw that he was getting nowhere, but that instead an uproar was starting, he took water and washed his hands in front of the crowd. "I am innocent of this man's blood," he said. "It is your responsibility!"

25 All the people answered, "Let his blood be on us and on our children!"

26 Then he released Barabbas to them. But he had Jesus flogged, and handed him over to be crucified.

THE PRINCIPAL CHARACTERS

Who Was Barabbas? The name Barabbas or Bar-abba means "son of the father" or "son of their teacher," the latter definition suggesting that his father may have been a religious leader among the Jews of his region. Barabbas is mentioned in all four Gospels, but only in one setting, the final stage of Jesus's condemnation. His full name may have been Jesus Barabbas, the former being a common name at the time. Some early manuscripts did not include Barabbas's first name when mentioning him, feeling that such a person was not worthy to bear the same name as the Christ. If this is true, Pilate's question, according to Parker, may have been more poignantly worded, "Whom do you want me to release for you, Jesus Barabbas or Jesus who is called Christ?" Another possibility is that Barabbas was not this man's real name. "Son of the father" could mean son of any man's father, meaning that Barabbas's true identity was unknown to the Gospel writers.[1]

THE CRIME

Matthew's Gospel states that Barabbas was a "notable" or "notorious" prisoner, without mentioning his offense. Whether he was notable because of his crime or because of his possible rabbinical heritage is not known. The word used to describe his crime in John's Gospel is "*leistes*," or robber, the same word used to describe the brigands in the Good Samaritan parable. Here it refers to marauding bandits and political rebels who lived in the hills and conducted periodic raids against Roman occupation forces, mixing guerilla warfare tactics with common robbery and murder.[2] Mark and Luke state that Barabbas was imprisoned for insurrection and murder. Who or how many he robbed and/or killed is not known, nor are any of the particulars about his crime.

Barabbas may have been associated with the militant wing of the Zealots, a group that may have included Simon, one of Jesus's twelve disciples (see preceding chapter).[3] Whether or not Barabbas was a Zealot, the fact that he was charged with political insurrection accounts for his popularity with the masses, and why the Jews who so despised Roman oppression preferred his release to that of Jesus. In fact, it is possible that his associates or sympathizers were part of the crowd that condemned Jesus. Such a portrait runs counter to the image presented in the motion picture *The Passion of the Christ*, in which Barabbas is portrayed as a deranged savage. The practice of releasing a prisoner of the people's choice is not mentioned outside the Gospels, and the earliest versions of Luke make no mention of such a practice. Luke 23:17 is omitted in some versions of the New Testament.

Pilate

Another significant figure in this story is Pontius Pilate, the Roman governor who sentenced Jesus to death. Pilate found himself in a very difficult position. He knew Jesus was innocent of the crimes of which he was accused; his own conscience and that of his wife were pricked by the thought of condemning Jesus to death. His Jewish counterpart, King Herod, wanted no part of Jesus's trial, making Pilate directly responsible for the fair administration of justice and for keeping the masses, the Jewish religious leaders, and his Roman superiors happy. Gospel readers cannot know for sure what was in the mind of Pontius Pilate when he offered the crowd a choice of which prisoner to release. Since he knew that Jesus was innocent, and that Jesus was nonviolent, and also knowing that Barabbas was probably guilty of the crimes of which he was accused, Pilate likely figured that surely the crowd would see this, as well. Surely, Pilate may have thought, when the crowd saw Jesus standing alongside Barabbas, they would make the right choice and see both men as he saw them: one a murderer, the other the victim of trumped-up charges.

Pilate probably thought his idea to present Barabbas and Jesus to the crowd was a masterful political stroke. If the crowd did the right thing, if they could see the two men in contrast, as surely he thought they would, he could save face with the religious hierarchy that wanted Jesus dead without having to make the decision to free Jesus himself. He could merely pass the responsibility of freeing their enemy onto the crowd that the Jewish religious leaders were also trying to please. When the crowd cried for Jesus's crucifixion, Pilate performed what he must have thought was another act of political genius, publicly washing his hands of Jesus's guilt, an act now viewed as the epitome of cowardice.

If this was Pilate's thinking and strategy, it backfired, badly. He counted on the mob to be rational, which is usually a mistake. Clarence Darrow, one of the greatest American defense attorneys of the twentieth century, was renowned for taking on unpopular causes. He once wrote that he inherited his tendency to side with the minority and the underdog from his father, who usually distrusted majority opinion. Darrow's father was more sure of his cause precisely because most of the community were on the other side.[4] Although Darrow was not a Christian, his statement is a lesson in the dangers of mob justice and in siding with the opinion that has the loudest voice at that moment.

The idea of a modern judicial or political official deciding a criminal defendant's fate in the way Pilate did seems preposterous. However, using the justice system to further political aims still is very much a part of criminal justice today. Sheriffs, police chiefs, prosecutors, and judges are not above political grandstanding at the expense of justice. Pretrial publicity, a given in a country that prizes freedom of the press, can also be a detriment to a fair trial. It is one reason to be wary of news media polls that solicit public opinion about the guilt or innocence of a criminal defendant. An uninformed opinion is very dangerous when used to decide the fate of a human being, and one can never know how such opinion polls may affect the outcome of a case.

THE CRIME THEN AND NOW

The "outlaw as hero" is a recurring theme throughout human history and is the subject of folklore, literature, and musical ballads. One of the most famous examples of the outlaw-hero is Robin Hood, a part myth, part historic tale of a medieval Englishman who lived as a marauding forest outlaw after his property was unjustly taken from him by a local tyrant. Barabbas and his minions may have lived in the hills of that region, conducting periodic raids against Roman soldiers and authorities. The Gospels state that Barabbas led or participated in an insurrection, but this may have been a series of guerilla-style raids rather than an organized open rebellion against the mighty Roman army. Such guerilla warfare—or terrorism, depending on one's viewpoint—is a common tactic among groups who must fight a superior military force. Barabbas may have lived a Robin Hood sort of lifestyle, incurring the wrath of the Roman government while assuming a sort of folk hero status among fellow Jews who chafed under Roman rule.

The outlaw as hero has many modern parallels, and by the time the story has had a chance to mature, the outlaw's legend often becomes a far cry from the true story. Often such legends take centuries to develop, but not always. The 1967 film *Bonnie and Clyde* portrayed two ruthless Depression-era bank robbing murderers, Bonnie Parker and Clyde Barrow, as flawed yet sympathetic antiheroes or, as the movie's theme song, called them "pretty, loving people." Western outlaws such as William Bonney (Billy the Kid) and the James brothers have enjoyed similar folk hero status.

In some cases outlaw-heroes attain quasi-celebrity status during their lifetimes, thanks to media coverage or because their situations resonate with some element of the population. In 1984, Bernard Goetz, a slightly built Caucasian riding the New York City subway, was approached by several young African-American men who asked him for money. Goetz replied that he had something for each one of them, at which point he pulled out a pistol and shot the young men. Goetz, who was eventually prosecuted for the crimes, but convicted only of a weapons possession charge, became a hero to many Americans, including many New Yorkers who traveled on subways, who were angry at the actions of bullying toughs that accosted people in big cities. One bumper sticker read, "Goetz gets 'em since 1984."

Virtually every celebrated trial, from that of O.J. Simpson to Martha Stewart, makes the defendant a cause celebre for some political or social agenda, often without the consent of the defendant. Although he was never active in any sort of civil rights causes, O.J. Simpson, who was acquitted of killing his wife and an acquaintance in 1995 after the most media-saturated trial in U.S. history, became a hero to many African-Americans who distrusted police officers and the criminal justice system. Millionaire home diva Martha Stewart elicited sympathy from some women who identified with any woman being bullied by men.

Lest anyone think that hero worship of outlaws is new, witness the case of Richard Loeb. During the summer of 1924, Loeb and his friend, Nathan Leopold, kidnapped 14-year-old Bobby Franks and demanded $10,000 ransom for the boy's safe return. The ransom was paid, but rather than returning the boy as promised, Leopold and Loeb sexually abused, murdered, and mutilated Franks. Police investigation led to the arrests of Leopold and Loeb who, when questioned by police about their motive, simply stated that they wanted to devise and commit a perfect crime. Both young men were wealthy, educated, and highly intelligent, leading the murder to be dubbed a "thrill kill." Although the murder of Franks outraged Chicagoans and most Americans, many people were equally outraged at the marriage proposals that Loeb, the more handsome of the two defendants, received from female admirers.

Why do outlaws sometimes become heroes? The answers are myriad, but what many outlaw heroes have in common is opposition to an unpopular status quo (Martin Luther King, Jr.), or their followers view them as victims of an unfair justice system (O.J. Simpson). To many Americans, Rosa Parks is the ultimate heroic outlaw. Her willful refusal to give up her seat on a Montgomery, Alabama, city bus on December 1, 1955, was a seminal event in the American Civil Rights movement, and Americans of all races now revere her memory because of her courage to willfully violate an unjust law.

Some outlaws become heroes even though their crimes stem from no altruistic motive. In some cases the outlaw tries to ascribe a status unworthy of him or herself. During the late 1960s, Charles Manson, the leader of a small religious cult of hippie youths in Southern California, ordered the murders of at least seven people. He tried to portray himself as a Christ-like figure during his trial, once dramatically assuming the pose of a crucifixion victim in a packed courtroom.

Although the story of Barabbas is an object lesson in the dangers of using a mob to decide a person's guilt or innocence, the fact that Pilate was surprised by the crowd's call to free Barabbas over Jesus is also a lesson in the dangers of political and judicial officials being out of touch with the citizenry. Had Pilate been in touch with the crowd over whom he ruled, he would have known they would have preferred the release of Barabbas to that of Jesus. Such was the arrogance of many Roman authorities; they had no idea that the masses preferred those who violently opposed them to men of peace like Jesus Christ.

The Hope

Although Pilate's and Barabbas's actions were wrong, their actions were part of God's plan. Jesus had to die because it was necessary to fulfill God's plan. Pilate and Barabbas were unconscious players in the fulfillment of God's will. Sometimes, so are we. God's will will be done. The choice to go along is ours.

What became of Pilate is not certain, but some early Christian traditions hold that Pilate eventually became a strong believer in Christ.[5] The Gospels are not kind to Pilate, with good reason. Although he had the authority to free Jesus, which he knew was the right thing to do, he succumbed to the will of a mob and a group of religious elites to maintain his standing in the Roman government, and his name is synonymous with cowardice, immoral appeasement, and, worst of all, as the man who condemned the Son of God to death.

Pilate probably thought that sacrificing the life of one innocent man was a small price to pay for keeping the mob content. How wrong he was. The 1961 motion picture *Judgment at Nuremberg* was a fictionalized account of war crimes trials. It featured the trials of judicial officials who committed atrocities during the Nazi regime of the 1930s and 1940s. The movie concludes with a former German jurist and legal scholar, portrayed by Burt Lancaster, telling the leader of the American tribunal, portrayed by Spencer Tracy, of his sorrow for the Holocaust and the millions of deaths that stemmed partly from the actions of officials who used the law as a smokescreen for mass murder and genocide. Lancaster said to Tracy, "All those people dying, we didn't mean it to come to all that." Tracy replied, "It came to 'all that' the first time you condemned a man to death whom you knew to be innocent." [6] Intentionally condemning one innocent person to death is just as evil as murdering millions.

The story of the death and resurrection of Jesus Christ is not complete without Barabbas. Barabbas stands as a symbol for every human being who has lived since then. It seems fitting if we do not know Barabbas's true identity, because this "son of the father" represents all of us. Barabbas was the only one, however, who stood alongside Jesus on the day he died for everyone, so that we could have eternal life.

22

Jesus Christ | Blasphemy

Matthew 26:59-66

59 The chief priests and the whole Sanhedrin were looking for false evidence against Jesus so that they could put him to death. 60 But they did not find any, though many false witnesses came forward.

Finally two came forward 61 and declared, "This fellow said, 'I am able to destroy the temple of God and rebuild it in three days.'"

62 Then the high priest stood up and said to Jesus, "Are you not going to answer? What is this testimony that these men are bringing against you?" 63 But Jesus remained silent.

The high priest said to him, "I charge you under oath by the living God: Tell us if you are the Christ, the Son of God."

64 "Yes, it is as you say," Jesus replied. "But I say to all of you: In the future you will see the Son of Man sitting at the right hand of the Mighty One and coming on the clouds of heaven."

65 Then the high priest tore his clothes and said, "He has spoken blasphemy! Why do we need any more witnesses? Look, now you have heard the blasphemy. 66 What do you think?"

"He is worthy of death," they answered.

THE PRINCIPAL CHARACTERS

In addition to Jesus Christ, the other key figures in this passage are the men who presided over this event. They were the chief priests and the Sanhedrin. The Chief Priests are identified as Annas and Caiaphas in John's Gospel. The Sanhedrin was the highest ruling body and court of justice among the Jewish people in the time of Jesus.[1] The Romans allowed the Sanhedrin to retain authority and jurisdiction over religious crimes committed by their fellow Jews, but this authority had limits, one of which was that they could not impose capital punishment.

THE CRIME

Blasphemy is prohibited by Mosaic Law in Exodus 22:28. The word "blasphemy" is derived from the Greek word *blasphemia*, which means "defamation" or "evil speaking."[2] The prohibition of blasphemy stems from the Commandment to honor God's name. Old Testament Hebrews took this command so seriously that they considered it impious to even say God's name (YHWH, or Yahweh) aloud. Numbers 15:30 commands that a blasphemer be "cut off" from the people, but it does not specifically call for the death penalty for all blasphemers.

Leviticus 24:10–16 contains an account of death by stoning for the crime of blasphemy, a punishment which God directly commanded to be publicly administered by the entire community. The language of Leviticus 24:14 is noteworthy. God commands the Israelites to "lay their hands on his head." This is the same terminology used to describe a ritual animal sacrifice. As Leonard Levy states, "Laying on the hands acknowledged responsibility for the sacrifice and sought atonement for the community's sins."[3]

In contrast to blasphemy laws in other cultures and subsequent time periods, the definition of blasphemy as it was originally given under Mosaic Law was narrow. Under Mosaic Law, any act of blasphemy serious enough to warrant a death sentence required an overt, spoken slander against the name of God; it also required the testimony of at least two witnesses.[4] A person would have to openly curse God, and such a statement made in a state of extreme anger or duress could be forgiven.[5] Merely making a statement about God that was unpopular, or failing to perform a divinely commanded act, would not necessarily constitute blasphemy.

According to *New Unger's Bible Dictionary*, there are two general forms of blasphemy:

1. Attributing some evil to God, or denying him some good that we should attribute to Him (Leviticus 24:11 and Romans 2:24); or

2. Giving the attributes of God to a creature, which was the form of blasphemy the Jews charged Jesus with.[6]

From the Mosaic era, when blasphemy laws were narrow in scope and rarely prosecuted, to the time of Jesus, the definition of blasphemy had been broadened. To label Jesus's behavior as blasphemy was certainly a stretch of the original Mosaic definition of the term, since Jesus made no derogatory statements about God.

By Jesus's time, the definition of blasphemy was being interpreted in any manner which suited the agenda of the religious elite. The statement Jesus made in Matthew 26, even if it were false, would not have constituted blasphemy under Mosaic Law as written in Exodus and Numbers. This illustrates one of the many pitfalls associated with blasphemy laws.

The story of Jesus teaches that one of the biggest problems with blasphemy laws is that they are very subjective, and are subject to the interpretation of those who happen to be in power. Levy summarizes the relativity and lack of wisdom in many blasphemy laws: "The verdicts of time mock judgments and alter sensibilities. Socrates, Aristotle, Jesus ... William Penn, and Tom Paine (author of the Revolutionary War-era pamphlet *Common Sense*) were condemned for blasphemy. In the sixteenth century, Protestantism seemed blasphemous to the Roman Catholic Church; in the next century, Protestant countries punished Unitarians, Baptists, and Quakers as blasphemers."[7]

Blasphemy laws during the biblical era were not confined to Jewish culture. Besides the trial of Jesus Christ, the most famous blasphemy trial in Western civilization took place in 399 B.C. Socrates, the great master of Greek thought, was executed for blasphemy or impiety for creating doubts in the minds of youths about the truthfulness of Greek polytheism. More specifically, he was convicted of being "an evil-doer and a curious person, searching into things under the earth and above the heavens, making the worse appear the better cause, and teaching all this to others."[8]

THE TRIAL

Although what transpires in this passage is often referred to as a trial, it more closely resembled a hearing; but an even more descriptive term might be "inquisition." Jesus's initial hearing was conducted by some of his fellow Jews or, more specifically, a group of elite Jewish religious leaders. The conclusion of the hearing was foregone. Jesus would have been found guilty no matter what he or anyone else said.

Jesus did not put up a spirited defense to the charges against him. One reason was that he knew that the crucifixion must take place in order to fulfill his mission of salvation. Another reason was less profound and probably could have been deduced by even a mortal mind:

Jesus knew that it would be a waste of time to present heated denials of the charges. This was a kangaroo court. The decision of the council was made before Jesus entered the chamber. Plus, blasphemy in the culture of the New Testament era was practically impossible to refute. It is like charges of racism today. Once an accuser labels someone a racist, the accused can do nothing to change the mind of the accuser.

The acrimonious relationship between Jesus and many of the Jewish religious leaders of his day had been present throughout his ministry, as indicated by Jesus's stinging criticisms of the Pharisees, punctuated by his clearing of the temple. This animosity climaxed shortly after Jesus made what turned out to be his final trip to Jerusalem (Matthew 21).

The tearing of clothing upon hearing blasphemous words is traceable to 2 Kings 18 and 19, when Judah's King Hezekiah tore his clothes upon hearing that the Assyrian king had no regard for the God of Judah, and that God could not save Judah from the Assyrians; the Assyrian king was proven wrong.

Jesus was executed for treason, not blasphemy. The Roman authorities, who retained sole authority for ordering and administering executions, cared nothing for Jewish religious sensitivities or for their concerns over blasphemy. Therefore, blasphemy was not a capital offense under Roman law, unless it was equated with criticism of the Caesar. If a government leader assumes a position of deity, as some of the Roman Caesars did, sedition or treason is synonymous with blasphemy. Charges of treason were trumped up instead.

THE CRIME THEN AND NOW

The crime of blasphemy has a very long and complicated history, both before and after the time of Christ. Practically any society that engages in organized religious worship has prohibited actions that are seen as offensive to the deity that they worship. Leonard Levy, author of a comprehensive book on the subject, defines blasphemy simply as "speaking evil of sacred matters."[9] *Black's Law Dictionary* calls blasphemy, "Any oral or written reproach maliciously cast upon God, His name, attributes, or religion."[10]

Blasphemers are often persecuted by people of their own faith. Although blasphemy laws in the United States and most other Western countries are seldom if ever enforced today, they have been treated with much greater seriousness in prior eras. Thomas Aquinas, one of the principal thinkers of early Christianity, called blasphemy a worse crime than murder, because blasphemy was a crime against God, and murder was an offense against a fellow human being.[11] Just as Jesus was prosecuted for blasphemy by his fellow Jews, millions of Christians have been prosecuted for blasphemy by other Christians.

Throughout most of Christian history, blasphemy has had a close cousin, heresy. Many theologians, including John Calvin, did not differentiate between the two. During the Middle Ages, the Roman Catholic Church would typically condemn fellow Christians who criticized the Church or endorsed non-Catholic ideas as heretics, while accusations of blasphemy were reserved for Jews. The Catholic Church called Martin Luther, who led the Protestant Reformation, a blasphemer and a heretic. In turn, Luther applied the blasphemy label to the Catholic Church and to Jews. Medieval European Jews were frequent targets for persecution, since they denied the divinity of Christ. Blasphemy served as the pretext for denying European Jews basic civil rights, property ownership, and, in many cases, their lives.[12] In effect, anyone born a Jew was a blasphemer from birth.

As for blasphemy in the United States, many professing Christians and non-Christians have been prosecuted, though not nearly to the extent as in medieval Europe. Many colonial laws required citizens to attend church and to honor God, and some localities specifically outlawed blasphemy. The first legal code for the Virginia colony contained a law calling for the death penalty for anyone who maliciously spoke against the doctrine of the Trinity or any "person" in the Trinity, and for committing the crime of blasphemy. Mocking the Bible was viewed as blasphemy and carried the death penalty as well.[13]

The nineteenth century witnessed a revival of blasphemy persecution. One notable case, *People v. Ruggles*, was ruled on in 1811 by the New York Supreme Court of Judicature. The defendant was charged with blasphemy for publicly declaring that Jesus Christ was a bastard and Mary was a whore. He was sentenced to three months in jail and fined the enormous sum (for the time) of $500. His conviction was appealed, partly because New York did not even have a law against blasphemy. Ruggles's conviction was upheld. James Kent, an eminent nineteenth century jurist, wrote the opinion for the appellate court.

He wrote: "The free, equal, and undisturbed enjoyment of religious opinion, whatever it may be, and free and decent discussions on any religious subject, is granted and secured; but to revile, with malicious and blasphemous contempt, the religion professed by almost the whole community, is an abuse of that right."[14]

Blasphemy statutes are more common to states along the East Coast, as these states were in existence when the United States was in its infancy as a nation. The blasphemy statutes in Connecticut, Maryland, and Vermont were not repealed until 2006. Blasphemy statutes still exist in some states. Michigan's statute states, "Any person who shall willfully blaspheme the holy name of God, by cursing or contumeliously reproaching God, shall be guilty of a misdemeanor."[15] Massachusetts law states, "Whoever wilfully [sic] blasphemes the holy name of God by denying, cursing or contumeliously [insolently or abusively] reproaching God, his creation, government or final judging of the world, or by cursing or contumeliously reproaching Jesus Christ or the Holy Ghost, or by cursing or contumeliously reproaching or exposing to contempt and ridicule, the holy word of God contained in the holy scriptures shall be punished by imprisonment in jail for not more than one year or by a fine of not more than three hundred dollars, and may also be bound to good behavior."[16]

Laws against public profanity, which are more often enforced, stem from laws against blasphemy. Some states still tie blasphemy statutes to laws prohibiting obscenity in a public place. For example, Mississippi laws prohibit extreme profanity in a public place, and this law is grouped under the category "Blasphemy and Profanity."[17]

Leonard Levy posits that an argument can be made for criminal or at least civil blasphemy statutes, but they should not be directed at someone who merely disagrees with the prevailing religious or political establishment on a point of religion. Levy argues that hard-core blasphemy could be construed as hate speech directed against the adherents to a particular religious belief. As an example, he points to the "artwork" of Andres Serrano, who submerged a crucifix in a bottle of his own urine, and federally funded artwork depicting Lazarus and Jesus engaging in homosexual relations.

The world's most high profile blasphemy cases in recent years have centered on Islam, not Christianity. In 1988, Salman Rushdie, an English-educated novelist born to a Muslim family in India, published a novel titled *The Satanic Verses*. In the eyes of some Muslims, Rushdie blasphemed God by defaming the name of Mohammed, the principal prophet of Islam. His "crime" was aggravated by the perception that Rushdie was also guilty of apostasy, or renouncing his religion, which also calls for the death penalty under Islamic law. Ruhollah al-Khomeini, the fanatical leader or "Ayatollah" of Iran's totalitarian Islamic regime, issued a "fatwa," or a religious edict calling for Rushdie's assassination. Governments around the world condemned Khomeini, but Khomeini, who viewed anything that did not adhere to his own interpretation of Islam as satanic, did not care. Khomeini died in 1989, but the fatwa was never lifted. To date the assassination of Rushdie has not been carried out.

In 2006, many Muslims were whipped into frenzy over the publication of a cartoon—which appeared in a Danish newspaper and then was published in other European newspapers—showing Mohammad wearing a time bomb headdress. Muslims view any visual depiction of Mohammad as an attack on Islam, and the unflattering depiction was especially inflammatory. Muslims around the world attacked European embassies and called for the death of the Danish newspaper staff responsible for publishing the cartoon.

The Lesson

This chapter focuses on a relatively minor aspect of the much larger story of Christ's passion. Nevertheless, it serves as a lesson in the dangers of fanaticism, hatred in the name of religion, and the incalculable worth of freedom of speech. Christianity should comprise the faithful, not the fanatical. The religious authorities who opposed Jesus were so fanatical about their beliefs, so doggedly sure that someone who criticized or disagreed with them must be wrong, that they were willing and even eager to kill the person who disagreed with them. This was yet another example of hatred in the name of religion, using God as a justification to perpetuate their hatred.

Even though the concept of "freedom of speech" as we know it today was not part of the vocabulary of Jesus's day, this story illustrates why it is so important. The religious leaders who took part in Jesus's prosecution were positive that they were right and that he was wrong.

201

Such is nature of fanaticism. It is one thing for Christians to be firm in their beliefs and their faith, but it is something else to be so narrow-minded that we are not open to even hearing an opposing point of view. It was strange that these leaders who were so strong in their faith were so threatened by the teachings of Jesus and his followers that they felt he must be killed so that they could preserve their power. Christians should remember that our faith is strong enough to withstand the criticisms of non-Christians. Christianity is also strong enough to withstand disagreement among its adherents. If Christians are strong in their faith, they will combat anti-Christian ideas with the Gospel of Christ. No idea or argument is as potent and strong as that.

23

Jesus and the Thieves on the Cross | Cruel and Unusual Punishment

Luke 23:32–43

32 Two other men, both criminals, were also led out with him to be executed. 33 When they came to the place called the Skull, there they crucified him, along with the criminals—one on his right, the other on his left. 34 Jesus said, "Father, forgive them, for they do not know what they are doing." And they divided up his clothes by casting lots.

35 The people stood watching, and the rulers even sneered at him. They said, "He saved others; let him save himself if he is the Christ of God, the Chosen one."

36 The soldiers also came up and mocked him. They offered him wine vinegar 37 and said, "If you are the king of the Jews, save yourself."

38 There was a written notice above him, which read: THIS IS THE KING OF THE JEWS.

39 One of the criminals who hung there hurled insults at him: "Aren't you the Christ? Save yourself and us!"

40 But the other criminal rebuked him. "Don't you fear God," he said, "since you are under the same sentence? 41 We are punished justly, for we are getting what our deeds deserve. But this man has done nothing wrong."

42 Then he said, "Jesus, remember me when you come into your kingdom."

43 Jesus answered him, "I tell you the truth, today you will be with me in paradise."

THE PRINCIPAL CHARACTERS

Who were the thieves? No one knows the identity of these two men. No names are given in any of the Gospels. Although they are anonymous, one of them represents one of the most touching illustrations of divine love in human history. Matthew and Mark do not include the passage about the penitent thief, saying only that the two robbers joined the passersby in insulting Jesus, while John merely states that two men were crucified alongside Jesus. Based on Luke's account, all we know is that one of the men received forgiveness and salvation in his final moments of life. We can infer that the other remained unrepentant to the end.

Some translations call the men "malefactors," or "evil do-ers." This denotes a more aggressive type of crime than mere thievery.[1] Matthew and Mark's Gospels call them robbers. The word used by Matthew and Mark to describe them leads some to believe that the two men were affili-ated with the Zealots, the radical and violent group of Jewish nationalists that once included Simon, one of Jesus's disciples.[2] *Barnes' Notes* calls them "highwaymen."[3] They may have been brigands, like Barabbas, but less well known. They probably stole through use of force and maybe even murder.

The Eighth Amendment to the United States Constitution states: "Excessive bail shall not be required, nor excessive fines imposed, nor cruel and unusual punishments inflict-ed." Exactly how this Amendment should be interpreted and applied is an ongoing debate in American society and in its courts. Although the debate continues, there is no doubt that the writers of the Bill of Rights wanted to end torturous ex-ecutions and severe corporal punishments that had been practiced both in England and in the American colonies prior to America gaining its independence. The Eighth Amendment did not specifically banish capital punishment, and it did not spell an immediate end to physi-cal punishments. Whatever its proper application, the Eighth Amend-ment absolutely placed a ban on torturous punishments such as the long extinct practice of crucifixion.

One of the guiding principles that modern U.S. courts employ in deciding the legality of capital punishment was first articulated by the United States Supreme Court in 1958. In *Trop v. Dulles*, the Court wrote, "The [Eighth] Amendment must draw its meaning from the evolving standards of decency that mark the progress of a maturing society."[4] The *Trop* case did not concern capital punishment, but the evolving standard of decency has been applied to many death penalty cases, beginning with *Witherspoon v. Illinois* in 1968, when a court disallowed prospective jurors who voiced reservations about capital punishment from hearing a murder case.[5] The standard is also employed when dealing with methods of execution (many cases) and whether prisoners should be executed for murders committed before they reached adulthood (No longer can anyone be executed for a crime they committed before the age of 18).[6] Although most who are familiar with Christ's crucifixion are not familiar with the detailed application of this legal phrase, they can quickly recognize that crucifixion does not meet this test.

Crucifixion is one of the cruelest methods of execution ever devised. The Romans borrowed crucifixion from the Persians and Phoenicians.[7] Crucifixion was very humiliating and painful, both by design. Crucifixions were carried out on the main roads leading to and from town, in full view of those who would pass by. The ordeal to which Jesus had already been subjected, his physical and psychological agony in the Garden of Gethsemane, and the brutal scourging he endured, weakened him before he was crucified. Therefore, compared to many others who were crucified, Jesus spent a relatively short time—a few hours—hanging on the cross. It was not unusual for some condemned criminals to hang for days before dying.

The knowledge or perception of Jesus's crucifixion currently held by many is based on the 2004 film *The Passion of the Christ*, which presents a brutally graphic and somewhat accurate dramatization of Christ's life and death, at least to a greater extent than most prior films. *The Passion* is a great film, notwithstanding the unfounded cries of anti-Semitism and the predictable protests from Hollywood's politically correct establishment. *The Passion*, in addition to bringing great numbers of adults back to movie theaters for the first time in decades, accomplished what many churches have not done; it made moviegoers curious about Jesus Christ. However, there are some aspects of *The Passion* which, while not necessarily untrue, are not contained in Scripture, such as the scenes in which Jesus interacts with Mary, both as a child and as a young man, some of the scenes involving Judas Iscariot, and the scenes featuring Satan.

A far less dramatic, but equally informative, examination of Christ's crucifixion is Frederick Zugibe's *The Crucifixion of Jesus: A Forensic Inquiry*. It is the most comprehensive recent inquiry into the forensic aspects of Jesus's crucifixion in recent years, and it was published after *The Passion of the Christ* was released in theaters. Zugibe was disappointed in *The Passion*, but did not attack it on the same grounds as most of its other critics. Zugibe, a forensic pathologist who has spent more than fifty years studying the crucifixion, criticizes *The Passion* on scientific, not social or religious, grounds.

Of course, there are those who would strongly defend *The Passion* as an accurate portrayal of the crucifixion, as well. Since there is a good chance that many readers of this book have seen *The Passion of the Christ*, but that few have read Zugibe's book, I will not attempt to weigh in on which side is correct. Instead, what I will do is briefly present the eight aspects of the movie with which Zugibe takes issue:

1. *The Passion* did not accurately portray the extent of Jesus's suffering in the Garden. Zugibe interprets Luke 22:44 literally. Jesus may have experienced a condition called "hematidrosis," in which physical bleeding can result from extreme mental duress.

2. *The Passion* glossed over the physical trauma to the face due to trigeminal neuralgia that would have resulted from the crown of thorns.

3. Jesus could not have survived the scourging depicted in *The Passion*, especially given his already weakened state from hematidrosis, the injuries to his face, and given the fact that he had been subjected to incredible physical and emotional stress since his arrest and inquiries before the religious leaders, Pilate and Herod. The types of whips shown in *The Passion* would have caused death after several lashes.

4. If Jesus had survived the type of scourging shown in *The Passion*, he would have experienced extreme breathing difficulty, and he would have been much too weakened to support a 170–200-pound cross beam on his back, let alone survive for several hours after being nailed to the cross.

5. The trauma that was caused by the nailing of the hands and the feet was minimized. This condition, called causalgia, was much more painful and traumatic than was depicted in *The Passion*.

6. The foot rest, or suppadenum, was, according to Zugibe, something added to the crucifixion by subsequent artists. It was not a part of Roman crucifixion.

7. When Jesus's side was pierced, the blood and water should not have sprayed out as depicted in *The Passion*, but should have gently flowed out.

8. Given the types of injuries that Jesus suffered, the amount of blood that Mary Magdalene and Jesus's mother cleaned up would not have been present.[8]

Capital punishment as it was administered by the Romans in the New Testament is different in many respects from capital punishment in the modern United States. The differences lie not only in the methods and the mechanics but in philosophy and objectives. The Romans, like many other societies that have practiced capital punishment, tried to inflict as much pain and humiliation as possible on the condemned. Today, in the United States, the goal is to make death as painless and bloodless as possible, thanks to the Eighth Amendment. The Romans reserved the quick and relatively painless punishment of quick decapitation for Roman citizens. The degrading and torturous punishment of crucifixion was reserved for slaves and common criminals.

The Romans made capital punishment as public as possible, again in keeping with the practice of most other societies throughout history. The objective was to deter would-be offenders and to provide perverse amusement for bystanders. This has been the rule, rather than the exception, with capital punishment throughout human history. Even the Mosaic Law sometimes commanded that capital punishment be administered publicly, as a message to others, and as a sort of purifying ceremony, ridding sin from their midst.

Until the late nineteenth century, many, in fact most, executions in the United States were administered in public. In fact, executions in colonial America and during the first half of the nineteenth century were public spectacles. The crowd at an 1827 public hanging in

Cooperstown, New York, was so dense that a viewing stand gave way, killing two spectators. In Albany, New York, another 1827 hanging drew a crowd of 30–40,000. Realizing that the deterrent value of public executions was negligible at best, and that many middle class and affluent residents found them repulsive, New York officially banned public executions in 1835, but they continued nonetheless for several decades.[9]

Sometimes public hangings, which were designed to deter criminal behavior, broke out in riots. They were sometimes characterized as carnival-like, with drunken brawls, pickpocketing, and outright rioting in some cases. One of the worst examples occurred in Maine in 1835, where a crowd of between 10,000 and 12,000 people rioted. The riots, crime, general public revulsion at public executions, and the emergence of large penitentiaries in all states led to most executions being carried out in prison yards, and later behind prison walls. The last known government-sponsored public execution took place on May 21, 1937, in Galena, Missouri, before a crowd of 500.[10]

In many American towns and cities, public hangings were carried out on Sundays. The reason was that this allowed people who spent the week working to view the hanging on the one day they were most likely to come to town, Sunday, when they went to church. In some towns, it was nothing unusual for a family to take the Sabbath day off, go into town to attend church, and enjoy a picnic in town after church while viewing a public hanging.

Gradually, capital punishment was moved out of public view. Only a select few are allowed to witness an execution today. Advocates of making capital punishment as painless as possible and isolating it from public view argue that to do otherwise violates societal norms of decency. Some opponents of capital punishment argue that making capital punishment painless and isolated from the public is a hypocritical attempt to sanitize the barbaric practice of state-sponsored killing.

The Hope

In this terrible story lies humankind's greatest hope. Jesus Christ suffered and died for the sins of all people. Lost in such a grandiose statement is a simpler truth. Jesus would have willingly died for any one person, so great is God's love for each and every human being that has ever lived. The first person to experience this indescribable love and mercy, the thief on the cross, is anonymous to history. This passage suggests that the man did not live a good life. He was a thief, a robber, and maybe a murderer, but he is in paradise.

Would God forgive a vile murderer and accept him into his kingdom today? Theodore Robert Bundy was one of the most infamous serial killers in American history. His total murder toll will never be known, but he is believed to have killed at least twenty-eight women and girls in several states over a period of years. On January 24, 1989, he was executed by the state of Florida for murdering a 12-year-old girl; he was also convicted of murdering two Florida State University students. Hours before his execution, Bundy granted a taped interview to Dr. James Dobson, the head of Focus on the Family. Here is an excerpt from that interview:

Dobson: I'm not sure there's anything you could say that people would believe, yet you told me ... that you have accepted the forgiveness of Jesus Christ and are a follower and believer in Him. Do you draw strength from that as you approach these final hours?

Bundy: I do. I can't say that being in the Valley of the Shadow of Death is something I've become all that accustomed to, and that I'm strong and nothing's bothering me. It's no fun. It gets kind of lonely, yet I have to remind myself that every one of us will go through this someday in one way or another.[11]

Is Ted Bundy, the quintessential embodiment of earthly evil, in heaven with the penitent robber who was executed alongside Jesus Christ? Only God knows.

24

Stephen and the Mob | Lynching

Acts 6:8-15; 7:1-2, 51-60

6:8 Now Stephen, a man full of God's grace and power, did great wonders and miraculous signs among the people. 9 Opposition arose, however, from members of the Synagogue of the Freedmen (as it was called)—Jews of Cyrene and Alexandria as well as the provinces of Cilicia and Asia. These men began to argue with Stephen, 10 but they could not stand up against his wisdom or the Spirit by whom he spoke.

11 Then they secretly persuaded some men to say, "We have heard Stephen speak words of blasphemy against Moses and against God."

12 So they stirred up the people and the elders and the teachers of the law. They seized Stephen and brought him before the Sanhedrin. 13 They produced false witnesses, who testified, "This fellow never stops speaking against this holy place and against the law. 14 For we have heard him say that this Jesus of Nazareth will destroy this place and change the customs Moses handed down to us."

15 All who were sitting in the Sanhedrin looked intently at Stephen, and they saw that his face was like the face of an angel.

7:1 Then the high priest asked him, "Are these charges true?"

2 To this he replied: "Brothers and fathers, listen to me!

51 "You stiff-necked people, with uncircumcised hearts and ears! You are just like your fathers: You always resist the Holy Spirit! 52 Was there ever a prophet your fathers did not persecute? They even killed those who predicted the coming of the Righteous One. And now you have betrayed and murdered him—53 you who have received the law that was put into effect through angels but have not obeyed it."

54 When they heard this, they were furious and gnashed their teeth at him. 55 But Stephen, full of the Holy Spirit, looked up to heaven and saw the glory of God, and Jesus standing at the right hand of God. 56 "Look," he said, "I see heaven open and the Son of Man standing at the right hand of God."

57 At this they covered their ears and, yelling at the top of their voices, they all rushed at him, 58 dragged him out of the city and began to stone him. Meanwhile, the witnesses laid their clothes at the feet of a young man named Saul.

59 While they were stoning him, Stephen prayed, "Lord Jesus, receive my spirit." 60 Then he fell on his knees and cried out, "Lord, do not hold this sin against them." When he had said this, he fell asleep.

THE PRINCIPAL CHARACTERS

Who was Stephen? Stephen bears the distinction of being Christianity's first martyr, or at least the first person whose martyrdom is recorded in the New Testament. Stephen was also among the church's first deacons, men who were charged with insuring that Grecian Jewish widows were given the same care as other Jewish widows. He was probably a Hellenistic (Greek) Jew himself, based on the tone of his speech in Acts 7.[1]

The "Freedmen" in Acts 6:8 were Jews of Italian extraction that had settled in Jerusalem, and they stirred the Jewish religious hierarchy into a state of agitation.[2] In Jesus's case, Italians (Romans), agitated by a group of Jews, killed Jesus. In Stephen's case, a group of Jewish religious leaders killed him after being agitated by a group of Italians.

THE CRIME(S)

By some reckonings, there were two crimes committed in this passage. One, according to the accusers, was Stephen's "blasphemy." Stephen referred to Jesus as the "Righteous One"; some translations use the term "Just One." Stephen was referring to the fact that Jesus was innocent of the crimes of which the religious leaders had accused him. Some of the same religious leaders may have participated in both trials. In fact, the chief priest in Acts 7:1 may have been Caiphas, who presided over Jesus's nighttime trial. Stephen accused the leaders of abandoning their true faith by having Jesus killed. Stephen was no guiltier of blasphemy than Jesus was, but, like Jesus he stood no chance of getting a fair inquiry before this group of fanatics. Like Jesus, Stephen did not shrink in fear even though he knew his life was in danger. Unlike Jesus, he defended himself by seeking to persuade his accusers that they were wrong and that Jesus was the fulfillment of the Old Testament.

Whether or not there was a second crime committed, at least in the literal sense, is not clear. This organized, ritualized lynching of Stephen creates confusion. The Gospels indicate that Jewish authorities did not have the authority to administer capital punishment, especially for religious offenses. It was left to the Romans to condemn Jesus to death and carry out his execution. How does this explain the killing of Stephen? There are at least three possible explanations. One explanation is that the period between Jesus's crucifixion and Stephen's death witnessed a change in government in that area. Pontius Pilate's authority, already somewhat tenuous during Jesus's ministry, may have experienced a breakdown during that period. Shortly after the crucifixion of Christ, Pilate authorized a military crackdown in Samaria to suppress a phony messianic movement. The Jews in the area protested to Pilate's superiors, and Pilate was removed from office. Therefore it is possible that this region had no Roman procurator at the time, which would have allowed the Jewish authorities freer reign in criminal matters.[3] Even if this was the case, the killing of Stephen was the result of mob justice. He was executed without trial; more emotion than logic was involved here.

Another explanation is that the mob was so frenzied that they did not care if the execution was legal. While Acts indicates that the mob that killed Stephen was angered because of his speech, we do not know if this anger exploded in murder. Based on the fact that the men who stoned Stephen went through the ritual of laying their coats at Saul's feet, obviously they were calm enough to adhere to the usual methodical rituals that were part and parcel of a stoning.

The third possibility is that the religious leaders were acting as a mob outside the authority of the law. If this is true, this was an act of angry but ritualized murder. The modern term that would be used to describe such an act would be "lynching." The terms "lynching" and "lynch mob" did not exist during the New Testament era, but the term is descriptive of the mob that killed Stephen. There are two explanations for the origin of the word lynching. One centers on Charles

Lynch, an eighteenth century Virginia patriot, planter, militia colonel, and politician who participated in the violent and hastily organized suppression of an uprising by colonial loyalists, English agents, former slaves and Indians. Another explanation for the term's origin is that another Virginian named William Lynch, a contemporary of Charles Lynch, organized a group of men to illegally track down a group of outlaws who had fled Virginia for North Carolina.[4]

Lynching is loosely defined as executing or punishing an accused criminal offender outside legal authority. Although there are differences between the type of lynching that killed Stephen and the lynchings that have occurred in the United States, there is at least one commonality. Lynching, by its very nature, is administered in public view, but illegally. One of the rationales for a lynching is general deterrence, sending a message to would-be offenders about what might happen to them if they commit the same crime. The public aspect of lynching in the United States is evidenced by many lynchings that were reported by newspapers in the latter part of the nineteenth century and the first few decades of the twentieth.

Lynch mobs often lack confidence in the official legal mechanisms that are supposed to deal with lawbreakers. In the case of Stephen, the mob knew that Roman authorities would disregard their anger over Stephen's statements, as they would view the dispute as a religious difference among Jews.

Those who participate in lynch mobs usually possess a strong sense of self-righteousness, assuming the moral high ground and sincerely believing that they are doing the right thing, in cases where the law either cannot or will not do the job for them. In some cases, a lynch mob sees itself as merely expediting the legal process. For example, an 1875 lynch mob in Maryland issued a resolution that stated, "In the event of a trial he (the alleged offender) shall be hanged. There is no moral difference in the means of destroying him," be it by legal or illegal means of execution.[5]

Lynching has a long history throughout the United States, especially in the South and the West. Fortunately lynching has experienced a precipitous decrease in the United States in recent decades. The years from the1880s to the 1920s have been sardonically labeled the "golden age of lynching" in the United States.[6] Lynching accounted for more than 6,000 deaths between 1880 and the 1930s, with an average of 100 African Americans lynched each year between 1889 and 1918.[7]

For several decades, the Ku Klux Klan (KKK) was one of the few organized lynch mobs in the United States. The KKK was founded in Tennessee in 1865, at the end of the Civil War, in part because its founders lacked confidence or trust in the new government, which was empowering and giving rights to free blacks, something the racist KKK could not stand. The KKK had to operate underground during its first few years of existence, but by the late nineteenth century it had emerged as a very public and politically powerful organization. It is no coincidence that the heyday of the KKK was the same period as the golden age of lynching.[8]

Most, though not all, of the targets during the golden age of lynching were African-Americans. The lynchings were designed to do more than simply punish a lawbreaker, and they were designed to do more than simply deter other would-be offenders. The intention behind many lynchings in the American South was to terrorize its black population. Even if an African-American was innocent of charges, especially the killing of a white person or the sexual assault of a white woman, the message had to be sent to other blacks that even the appearance of such an act would not go unpunished. Lynchings of this sort, like the killing of Stephen, were meant to do more than punish the offender. They were designed to uphold the social order and buttress those in authority.

African-Americans have not been the only targets of lynch mobs in American history. One of the most notorious lynchings in American history was that of Leo Frank, who was killed by a Georgia mob in 1913. Frank, a Jew, managed a pencil factory in Atlanta. On April 27, 1913, Mary Phagan, a 12-year-old employee of Frank's, was found murdered in the factory. Frank was charged with Phagan's murder. His trial was a fiasco. The media and the public grabbed hold of the Frank case, and Frank became the target of long-simmering antagonisms that less affluent Southerners and a resurgent Ku Klux Klan harbored toward Atlanta's relatively wealthy Jewish population.

Frank, by any standard, was not given a fair trial. The climate of the time would not allow it, nor would Frank's politically ambitious prosecutor. Frank was convicted and sentenced to death. Realizing that

Frank's trial had been a farce and that there was considerable evidence linking another factory employee to Phagan's murder, Georgia Governor John Slaton commuted Frank's sentence to life imprisonment. The Governor's mansion was attacked by mobs, and Slaton was forced to flee to California for three months. Worst of all, a group of men calling themselves the Knights of Mary Phagan stormed the prison where Frank was housed, and drove him 150 miles to Marietta, Georgia. They hung Frank and had their photo taken alongside his corpse. The lynch mob included a former governor, a former sheriff, and other prominent Georgia citizens. None was prosecuted.[9] Lynch mobs seldom fear prosecution because they know that local law enforcement will either support or ignore their efforts.

A different kind of lynch mob mentality has emerged in recent years. Unlike lynch mobs of the past, these groups do not break into jails and string up accused criminals. However, they use fear, intimidation, threats of violence, and actual violence against innocents to terrorize. For example, there is the Rodney King case in Los Angeles. On March 4, 1991, a private citizen taped several Los Angeles police officers administering a severe beating to King, a small-time criminal. King, an African American, led the officers on a high speed chase and refused to obey their instructions when he exited his car. King was struck fifty-six times. It was clear to experts and casual observers alike that the force used against King was excessive. The officers, all of whom were white, were fired and prosecuted for the King beating.

In 1992, four officers were tried and acquitted on virtually all of the charges stemming from the King beating. The acquittals astounded most observers, including the President of the United States, George H.W. Bush, and outraged others. On April 29, the day of the acquittal, Los Angeles erupted in riots, and the violence spread to other cities in the United States and Canada. Sixty people died and 2,100 were injured in Los Angeles alone. In this case, the victims of the lynching were not the perpetrators of the original crime, but innocent bystanders, and the lynch mobs were not organized or methodical. Unlike many previous lynch mobs, there was no clear objective other than to inflict as much violence and mayhem as possible on whoever crossed their path. Although the rioters had a few high-profile apologists, including Jesse Jackson and California Congresswoman Maxine Waters, the vast majority of African Americans condemned the violence, even though they were angered by the officers' acquittal. When the officers were retried a year later on federal civil rights charges, few had any doubt they would be convicted, and they were.

Today's lynch mobs also come in the form of the news media. The news media, especially the 24-hour news networks, are often relentless in their badgering of people involved in high profile criminal cases. Sometimes the media's target is an alleged victim leveling charges against a popular public figure, as with singer Michael Jackson's child molestation case or the rape charge leveled against basketball star Kobe Bryant. In other cases, the media's target is the accused, who is found guilty in the court of public opinion even though no criminal charges are ever filed. Witness the case against Gary Condit. Condit was a United States Congressman from California. In 2001, Chandra Levy, a young woman who had once interned in Condit's office, was reported missing. Rumors circulated that Condit and Levy had been engaged in an illicit affair, and that Condit had played a role in Levy's disappearance. Even though no charges were ever filed against Condit, and no evidence was produced linking him to Levy's disappearance, his reputation was ruined by the media attention, and he was defeated in his reelection bid. Levy's remains were eventually discovered. Her death was ruled a homicide, but no charges were ever filed.

Similar examples include the members of Duke University's lacrosse team, who were tried and convicted in the court of public opinion before any charges were filed for the alleged rape of an "exotic dancer" at a party they threw on March 13, 2006; and Joran van der Sloot, a 17-year-old Dutch citizen accused by the media, but never formally charged by authorities, of the murder of Natalee Holloway, an American teenager who disappeared on May 30, 2005 while vacationing in Aruba. Although all of these cases may ultimately result in the arrest and conviction of some of the people who have been scrutinized by the media, what is being done to them by the cable news outlets and Internet bloggers is shameful, and is a high tech version of the same type of mob that stirred up passions against Stephen. Such irresponsible coverage is the price we must pay for the right to freedom of speech and freedom of the press.

The Lesson

The cause for which Stephen was martyred is greater than any other. Unlike some lynching victims, Stephen was innocent of the charges leveled against him. There is much to learn about the story of Stephen, the most prominent lesson being about courage, faith in Jesus Christ, and the willingness to give one's life for the Gospel. There are also lessons to be learned about the dangers of rushing to judgment and letting our emotions take control of our actions when it comes to life-and-death matters like criminal justice. God gave human beings emotions with which to feel, but he also gave us minds with which to reason and think. Lynching and mob justice of the sort that killed Stephen are examples of the triumph of emotion and rage over reason and patience.

The killing of Stephen signaled the beginning of a great wave of persecution of the early Christian church, led by Saul, the subject of the next chapter. What the mob who killed Stephen did not know was that this persecution was exactly what the early church needed. Because this persecution forced the Jerusalem Christians to disperse, it also led to the dispersion and spreading of the Gospel in a way that would not have happened otherwise. The story of Stephen's murder was not complete without the second part of Acts 8:1. It is no coincidence that Acts 8 follows with the story of Phillip, one of the Jerusalem Christians selected as deacon at the same time as Stephen, preaching and sharing the Gospel to Jews and non-Jews in areas far from his home.

I watched an interview conducted by Steve Croft of CBS's *60 Minutes* with comedian and television star Jerry Seinfeld. Among the questions Croft asked was, "In your opinion, what is the most underrated human emotion?" Seinfeld said "irritation." Human beings accomplish the most when they are irritated, dissatisfied with things as they exist. According to Seinfeld, that is one reason that so many great comedians, most of whom are chronic malcontents, come from New York City. The environment and fast-paced lifestyle of that great, noisy, crowded, yet strangely endearing, metropolis keep its populace in a constant state of irritation and dissatisfaction. Irritation is what motivates people to make changes and to try and improve their lives. Another question Croft posed was, "What is the most overrated human emotion?" Seinfeld said "contentment." Contentment breeds laziness, and people don't strive to improve themselves or conditions around them when they are content. According to Jerry Seinfeld, this is the reason so few comedians come from the tropical island paradise of Hawaii.

To label the violent persecution of the early church at Jerusalem "irritation" both oversimplifies the complex problems and understates the violent persecution it faced. However, the example from the Seinfeld interview illustrates the fact that God did not create us or implant Christians with the Gospel so that we could be merely content. The Christian life was never intended to be easy.

25

Paul | Letters from Prison

Acts 8:1-3

8:1 And Saul was there, giving approval to his (Stephen's) death.

On that day a great persecution broke out against the church at Jerusalem, and all except the apostles were scattered throughout Judea and Samaria. 2 Godly men buried Stephen and mourned deeply for him. 3 But Saul began to destroy the church. Going from house to house, he dragged off men and women and put them in prison.

Acts 20:22-24 (Paul speaking)

22 "And now, compelled by the Spirit, I am going to Jerusalem, not knowing what will happen to me there. 23 I only know that in every city the Holy Spirit warns me that prison and hardships are facing me. 24 However, I consider my life worth nothing to me, if only I may finish the race and complete the task the Lord Jesus has given me—the task of testifying to the gospel of God's grace.

THE PRINCIPAL CHARACTERS Who was Paul? These verses demonstrate the remarkable transformation that Paul experienced. He was transformed by the Holy Spirit from a fanatical persecutor of Christians into one of Christianity's boldest voices. He went from working tirelessly to imprison Christians to becoming a tireless worker—and prisoner himself—for the cause of Christ. With the exception of Jesus Christ, and perhaps Peter, Paul is without question the most influential human being in Christian history. Paul authored approximately 25 percent of the New Testament, which were actually letters to churches or individuals. Paul was also a prominent figure throughout the book of Acts. He was Christianity's first great thinker, one of its most prolific writers, and one of the faith's greatest preachers. T.L. Donaldson states, "Paul's letters represent a window into nascent Christianity of inestimable value."[1] Even with all of his worldly wisdom and knowledge, Paul probably could not estimate the profound impact of his letters, which were written during a time when the government and the existing religious order were doing everything possible to silence and persecute him.

Saul (Sha'ul), Paul's Hebrew name, was born in Tarsus, a Cilician city renowned as a center of commerce and education during the Roman Empire. Saul's birthplace was indicative of the direction his life would take. Being raised in Tarsus was akin to growing up in a university town of today, such as Chapel Hill, North Carolina, Athens, Georgia, or Ann Arbor, Michigan. The product of an excellent education, Saul became a Pharisee. The word Pharisee, which is derived from the Aramaic word "*perashiym*," means, "separated." While "separated" originally meant that these men were set apart for studying the Scriptures, the meaning of the title changed over time in the minds of many Pharisees.[2] "Separated" came to mean superior to those around them, especially Jews who were less educated, and practically all non-Jews.

Pharisees believed in strict observance of Old Testament laws and rituals. They were devoted Israelite nationalists, which put them at odds with the Roman rulers of the day. Although the Pharisees were not known for material wealth, they exercised considerable influence over the religious and social thought among first-century Jews. Jesus reserved his harshest criticisms for these religious and intellectual elitists (Matthew 23). Although some Pharisees—Nicodemus and Joseph of Arimathea prominent among them—became followers of Christ, most Pharisees were rigid, elitist, self-righteous, and uncompromising in their beliefs; and some Pharisees played a crucial role in Jesus's crucifixion.

After Saul's miraculous encounter with Jesus Christ on the Damascus road (Acts 9), he is referred to as Paul, the Greek version of his name, which indicates that his life and thought were influenced by Greek (or Hellenistic) thinking and culture. It also was an indication that Paul, while not abandoning his Jewish heritage, was embracing a faith that was meant to be spread to all people. In fact, one chasm that

Paul never bridged with some of his fellow Christians was his belief that the Gospel was for everyone, not just the Jews. One of Paul's most significant accomplishments was his ability to blend early Christianity, which was the product of Hebrew thought, with Greek thought, which greatly influenced the Western thought we know today.

As evidenced by his dogged persecution of early Christians—Stephen among them (Acts 6:8–8:1)—Saul certainly embodied this stereotype of the Pharisee, but this same dogged determination and iron will served him well in his Christian walk. After his conversion, Paul's outlook and spiritual values changed, but it seems his personality traits stayed intact. God turned Paul's personal flaws into his greatest assets. Paul had a very strong and forceful personality, and never shied away from offering his opinion to anyone who would listen, and to many who did not want to hear him. Even some of the early Christian pioneers, including Peter (Galatians 2), Mark, and Barnabas (Acts 15:37–40), had their personal and philosophical differences with Paul.

Fortunately, Paul's intellectual capacity and outspoken nature were greatly exceeded by his genuine love for Christ and his love for his fellow human beings, even those who brutally persecuted him. The word love is mentioned more than 100 times in Paul's letters, and more than thirty times in his prison letters. Even more notable is 1 Corinthians 13, commonly called "the love chapter," which stands as one of the most moving pieces of prose ever written on the subject of love.

THE CRIME

Paul was imprisoned so often that, in Ephesians 4:1, he referred to himself as a prisoner of the Lord. Like many New Testament martyrs, Paul was accused of anything that seemed to satisfy the arresting authorities at that moment and time, be it blasphemy, for stating that Jesus was the son of God or for speaking against the polytheistic views held by many Greeks and Romans; or for treason, by stating that a God was higher than Caesar; or for inciting a riot, which sometimes followed his fiery encounters with both Jewish and Greek religious and political leaders.

THE PUNISHMENT

The focus of this chapter is on what Paul did while undergoing one of the numerous punishments he suffered for his outspoken devotion to Jesus Christ. That is why I have subtitled this chapter "Letters from Prison."

Of the thirteen letters authored by Paul, five of them—Ephesians, Philippians, Colossians, 2 Timothy, and Philemon—were written from prison. Paul experienced several forms of imprisonment. His death is not recorded in the New Testament, but most traditions hold that he was executed in Rome.

Even the most dedicated Christian may be tempted to view imprisonment as a setback. Despite his blind and devoted faith to Jesus Christ, Paul may have thought that his work for the cause of Christ would be better served if he put his considerable oratory skills to work by preaching or teaching in public, where he was sure his message would be heard.

Prisons have changed across time and cultures. Prisons were not used as long-term, standalone punishments in the United States until the 1830s. In New Testament times, prisons were primarily used as holding facilities for people awaiting trial or execution. However, they were sometimes used as a standalone punishment. Most forms of imprisonment, including that experienced by Paul on some occasions, were very unpleasant even by ancient standards, let alone the standards of today. The vast majority of prisoners had no right to clean living conditions or decent care. Inmate lawsuits and correctional accreditation bodies were nonexistent. Conditions in jails were not meant to be comfortable, so they seldom were.

During what is thought to be his last imprisonment, Paul, as a Roman citizen, was afforded a prison life more akin to modern house arrest than total incarceration. Any prisoner awaiting trial before the emperor was afforded such accommodations, setting them apart from most other accused criminals. Paul was chained day and night to a Roman bodyguard and was not allowed to roam about in the community. He was allowed to receive visitors, which allowed his letters to reach their destination.[3] Apparently, Luke was at Paul's side throughout most of his imprisonment. Paul dictated, rather than actually wrote, some of his letters, and Luke may have served as his recorder on some occasions. Tychius, unknown to most Christians, bears the distinction of being the man who delivered some of Paul's letters, and he was Paul's frequent visitor and companion.

There are a few commonalities among prisons, without regard to the time period or location. One is that prison life, for most people, is boring. For many people, time spent in prison is simply time wasted. The flip side of this coin is that this boredom often forces or allows a person to be alone with his or her thoughts. In fact, the term "penitentiary," coined by American penal reformers in the nineteenth century, reflected the hope that prison life would provide a chance for inmates to be alone, to realize the errors of their ways, and repent or offer *penitence* to God for their misdeeds. How well this idea has worked is a separate debate, but one fact is clear: Many Christians and non-Christians throughout the centuries have used prison life as a chance to experience spiritual rebirth or renewal, or as an opportunity to put some of their most sincere and innermost thoughts on paper for others to read. There are hundreds of examples; presented below are a few.

1. The book of Revelation, written by John, who was living in exile on the island of Patmos, is another example of New Testament prison literature. Even though John's punishment and his writings were different from Paul's, it is a demonstration of the power of God to use human beings even when they are in seemingly unpleasant circumstances.

2. John Bunyan (1628-1688) was one of the greatest Christian writers of the last millennium. Bunyan's *The Pilgrim's Progress* was published in two parts, the first in 1678 and the second in 1684. It is the allegorical story of a man named "Christian," who travels throughout the land on a spiritual journey, searching for God and for wisdom, encountering all sorts of temptations and tribulations along the way, in the form of characters with names such as "Talkative," "Envy," "Hopeful," and "Atheist." Standard reading for most ministry and theology students even today, *The Pilgrim's Progress* stands as one of the most important and influential writings in the history of the Christian faith.

Because of his refusal to preach the gospel in accordance with the dictates of the official Church of England, Bunyan was imprisoned in England's Bedford County jail in 1660, where he remained for twelve years, although he was occasionally allowed to visit friends and family. During his imprisonment, unable to preach in public and having little else to occupy his time, Bunyan, who possessed little formal education, began writing. He was released from prison in 1672 and resumed preaching, only to be imprisoned again six years later, whereupon he resumed his writing, penning the second portion of *Pilgrim's Progress*.[4] Had Bunyan not been imprisoned, the world would never have known *The Pilgrim's Progress*.

3. Before he was assassinated in 1968, Martin Luther King, Jr. was jailed many times for his civil rights activities. He was arrested for conducting a nonviolent civil rights protest in Birmingham, Alabama, during Easter weekend 1963. While assigned to solitary confinement in the Birmingham city jail, King, responding to a request from local clergy to call off his public demonstrations for civil rights, penned one of the most famous documents ever written by an American on the subject of civil disobedience. Among other things, he wrote: "Just as the Apostle Paul left his village of Tarsus and carried the gospel of Jesus Christ to the far corners of the Greco-Roman world, so am I compelled to carry the gospel of freedom beyond my own hometown. Like Paul, I must constantly respond to the Macedonian call for aid."[5]

4. Another type of prison letter is what might be called "letters from death row." Paul wrote some letters, Philemon among them, while he was optimistic about his chances of being released from prison and regaining his freedom. However, other writings were penned when he knew that death was imminent. Paul's "letter from death row" is 2 Timothy. Although Paul and Timothy were not related, Paul's writings indicate that the two men enjoyed a sort of father-son relationship. Paul speaks in disappointed terms of several people who have abandoned him in his loneliest moments, but he also speaks longingly and optimistically of a better life in heaven that awaits him. Paul also states that he has done his best for the work of the Gospel. As Paul senses that he is approaching the end of his earthly life, he writes in 2 Timothy 4:6–8:

> As for me, I am already being poured out as a libation, and the time of my departure has come. I have fought the good fight, I have finished the race; I have kept the faith. From now on there is reserved for me the crown of righteousness, which the Lord, the righteous judge, will give me on that day, and not only to me but also to all who have longed for his appearing.

5. Maeyken Wens was the wife of a sixteenth-century Anabaptist minister and mason. She was imprisoned by church authorities in Antwerp for reading the Bible. Wens was interrogated and tortured but still would not renounce her Anabaptist beliefs. She was eventually sentenced to death by burning; and, shortly before her execution, Wens wrote a letter to her teenaged son. Thieleman Van Bragt includes the letter in *Bloody Theater*:

> O dear son, though I am taken from you here, strive from your youth to fear God, and you shall have your mother again up yonder in the New Jerusalem, where parting will be no more. My dear son, do not be afraid of this suffering; it is nothing compared to that which shall endure forever. Cease not to fear God because of this temporal death."[6]

Wens's letter was reprinted in a daily devotional book titled *The One Year Book of Christian History* by E. Michael and Sharon Rusten. The Rustens titled the devotional, "What Would You Say in a Last Letter to Your Children?"[7] What is the last message *you* would like to leave on Earth?

Another question is whether we can say, as did Paul, that we did our best and fought the good fight for the Gospel. An interesting aspect of prison letters is that the writers, left with little sense of earthly pride or pretension, bare their souls and seem to see the world in different ways from how they perceived it when outside prison walls.

6. The prison experience may lead a writer to examine his/her innermost emotions and lay them bare for the reader, but by no means are such emotions always positive, let alone spiritually inspirational. Paul's letters and many great religious works stemmed from imprisonment, but so did Adolph Hitler's *Mein Kampf*, the odious, hateful tome that inspired Nazism, the European Holocaust of the 1930s and 1940s, and German involvement in World War II.

The Hope

One does not have to search very far for a message of hope in the story of Paul. Despite his hardship, he speaks of that hope himself. Paul exhorted his readers to pray for him. Amazingly, he did not exhort his fellow believers to work or pray for his release, but instead he prayed for the courage to continue to carry on the mission of spreading the Gospel. Ephesians 6:19–20 reads,

> Pray also for me, that whenever I open my mouth, words may be given me so that I will fearlessly make known the mystery of the gospel, for which I am an ambassador in chains. Pray that I may declare it fearlessly, as I should.

While reading Paul's prison letters, we easily forget the circumstances under which they were written, such is Paul's exuberance for the Gospel. Even though he was imprisoned and unable to move about freely, Paul referred to himself in Ephesians 6:20 as an ambassador for Christ, ambassador being a term usually ascribed to someone who travels to deliver a message. Paul even faced death with a sense of optimism because of what awaited him in the next life. His letters of encouragement from prison still offer hope to Christians no matter how dire the circumstances may seem. The hope that Paul embraced is the hope available for everyone, the hope of redemption.

End Notes

Introduction

[1] The Quotations Page Internet Web site, www.quotationspage.com, January 10, 2006.

[2] 5 U.S. 137, (1803).

[3] I. Drapkin, *Crime and Punishment in the Ancient World* (Lexington, MA: Lexington Books, 1989).

[4] Ibid.

[5] W.R. Farmer, *Maccabees, Zealots, and Josephus: An Inquiry into Jewish Nationalism in the Greco-Roman Period* (New York: Columbia University Press, 1956).

Chapter 1

[1] C.T. Francisco, "Commentary on Genesis," in *The Broadman Bible Commentary, Volume 1*, ed. C. J. Allen (Nashville, TN: Broadman Press, 1973), pp. 101–288.

[2] L. Hicks, "Cain." *The Interpreter's Dictionary of the Bible* (Nashville, TN: Abindgon Press, 1962), *New Interpreter's Study Bible* (CD ROM Abingdon Press, 2003).

[3] 356 U.S. 86, 1958.

[4] A. Clarke, *Clarke's Commentary* (Nashville, TN: Abingdon Press, 1996. Ages and Biblesoft Electronic Database, 2002 PC Study Bible CD-ROM).

[5] J. Braithwate, *Restorative Justice and Responsive Regulation* (New York: Oxford University Press, 2002), p. 15.

[6] F. K. Farr, "Cain." In the *International Standard Bible Encyclopaedia*, ed. J. Orr (Biblesoft: Electronic Database, PC Study Bible on CD-ROM, 1995), original publication date 1915, Chicago: Howard-Severance Company.

[7] D. J. Champion, *The Roxbury Dictionary of Criminal Justice* (Los Angeles: Roxbury Publishing, 1997).

[8] D. R. Biddy, *Crime Stories from the Bible* (Bloomington, IN: First Books, 2002), p. 4.

[9] J. S. Exell, *The Biblical Illustrator* (Ages and Biblesoft, 2002, PC Study Bible CD-ROM), original publication date 1887, London.

[10] *Matthew Henry's Commentary on the Whole Bible: New Modern Edition*, Electronic Database (Boston: Hendrickson Publishers, 1991, PC Study Bible, CD-ROM).

[11] Francisco, op. cit.

[12] Francisco, op. cit.

Chapter 2

[1] C.T. Francisco, "Commentary on Genesis," in *The Broadman Bible Commentary, Volume 1*, ed. C. J. Allen (Nashville, TN: Broadman Press, 1973), pp. 101–288.

[2] A. Barnes, *Barnes' Notes*, (Electronic Database 1997 Biblesoft, PC Study Bible CD-ROM) original publication date 1847, London: Blackie and Son.

[3] W. Ewing, "Sodomite." In the *International Standard Bible Encyclopaedia*, ed. J. Orr (Biblesoft: Electronic Database, PC Study Bible on CD-ROM, 1995), original publication date 1915, Chicago: Howard-Severance Company.

[4] Ibid.

[5] *Lawrence v. Texas*, 539 U.S. 558, 2003.

[6] 478 U.S. 186 (1986).

[7] 539 U.S. 558 (2003).

[8] M. Davies, "Male Sexual Assault Victims: A Selective Review of the Literature and Implications for Social Services," *Aggression and Violent Behavior*, 7, no. 3 (2002): 203–214.

[9] Francisco, supra.

Chapter 3

[1] B. K. Waltke with C. J. Fredricks, *Genesis: A Commentary* (Grand Rapids, MI: Zondervan, 2001), p. 462.

[2] Ibid.

[3] A. M. Dershowitz, *The Genesis of Justice: Ten Stories of Biblical Injustice that Led to the Ten Commandments and Modern Law* (New York: Warner Books, 2000).

Chapter 4

[1] H. Lockyer, Sr. (ed). *Nelson's Illustrated Bible Dictionary* (Thomas Nelson Publishers, 1986, Biblesoft, 2002, PC Study Bible CD-ROM).

[2] S. Stevenson, "Freedom to and Freedom from: Prevention of Trafficking in Eastern Europe," *Social Justice in Context*, 1, no. 1: 83–92.

[3] U. S. State Department Internet Web site, www.state.gov, November 13, 2005; S. Stevenson, "Freedom to and Freedom from: Prevention of Trafficking in Eastern Europe," *Social Justice in Context*, 1, no. 1: 83–92.

[4] A. C. Marek, "Border Wars." *U.S. News and World Report*, 139 (no. 20): 46–56, November 28, 2005.

[5] J. A. Lozano, "Jury Convicts Three in Deadly Smuggling Case." *The Associated Press*, February 9, 2006.

[6] U. S. State Department Internet Web site, www.state.gov, November 13, 2005.

[7] Ibid., January 5, 2006.

[8] Ibid.

[9] Ibid., January 9, 2006.

Chapter 5

[1] M. F. Unger, R. K. Harrison (ed.), *The New Unger's Bible Dictionary* (PC Study Bible CD ROM), original publication date 1957, Chicago: Moody Press.

[2] G.B. Eager, "Harlot." In the *International Standard Bible Encyclopaedia*, ed. J. Orr (Biblesoft: Electronic Database, PC Study Bible on CD-ROM, 1995), original publication date 1915, Chicago: Howard-Severance Company.

[3] L. F. Friedman, *Crime and Punishment in American History* (New York: Basic Books, 1992).

[4] Nev. Rev. Stat. Ann. § 269.175 (2005).

[5] Nev. Rev. Stat. Ann. § 41.1397 (2005).

[6] T. H. Leale, "The Lessons of Judah's History," J. S. Exell, *The Biblical Illustrator* (Ages and Biblesoft, 2002, PC Study Bible CD-ROM), original publication date 1887, London.

Chapter 6

[1] A.R. Fausset, *Fausset's Bible Dictionary* (Biblesoft, 1998 PC Study Bible CD-ROM); M. F. Unger, R.K. Harrison (ed.), *The New Unger's Bible Dictionary* (PC Study Bible CD ROM), original publication date 1957, Chicago: Moody Press.

[2] *Nelson's Illustrated Bible Dictionary* (Hendrickson Publishers, 1996, Biblesoft, PC Study Bible CD-ROM, 2002).

[3] A. Barnes, *Barnes' Notes* (Electronic Database 1997 Biblesoft, PC Study Bible CD-ROM) original publication date 1847, London: Blackie and Son.

[4] I. W. Charny, ed. *Encyclopedia of Genocide, Volume 1* (Santa Barbara, CA: ABC-CLIO, 1999).

[5] J. Hagan, W. Rymond-Richmond, and P. Parker, "The Criminology of Genocide: The Death and Rape of Darfur." *Criminology* 43 no. 3 (2005): 525–562.

[6] "Nürnberg trials." *Encyclopædia Britannica* from Encyclopædia Britannica Online. http://search.eb.com/eb/article-9056532, March 9, 2006.

[7] R. J. Rummel, "Power Kills, Absolute Power Kills Absolutely." *Encyclopedia of Genocide, Volume 1*, I.W. Charney ed. (Santa Barbara, CA: ABC-CLIO, 1999), pp. 23–34.

[8] R. J. Rummel, "The New Concept of Genocide." *Encyclopedia of Genocide, Volume 1* (Santa Barbara, CA: ABC-CLIO, 1999), pp. 18–23.

[9] F. Graham, *Rebel with a Cause* (Nashville: Thomas Nelson Publishers, 1995), pp. 276–277.

[10] L. Morrow, *Evil: An Investigation* (New York: Basic Books, 2003), p. 59.

[11] Rwanda. (2006). *Encyclopædia Britannica*. March 13, 2006, from *Encyclopædia Britannica*.

[12] Online http://search.eb.com/eb/article-214507

[13] J. M. Pollock, *Ethics in Crime and Justice*, 3rd edition. (Belmont, CA: West/Wadsworth, 1998), p. 18.

[14] "Darfur." In *Encyclopædia Britannica*. July 7, 2006, from Encyclopædia Britannica Online: http://search.eb.com/eb/article-9028769.

Chapter 7

[1] *Black's Law Dictionary*, 6th Ed., (St. Paul, MN: West Publishing, 1990).

[2] L. F. Friedman, *Crime and Punishment in American History* (New York: Basic Books, 1992).

[3] *Black's Law Dictionary*, op. cit.

[4] *Black's Law Dictionary*, op. cit.

[5] *Black's Law Dictionary*, op. cit.

[6] R.R.S. Neb. § 28-1302 (2005); R.R.S. Neb. § 28-106 (2005).

[7] O.C.G.A. § 16-10-31 (2005).

[8] G. E. Rush, *The Dictionary of Criminal Justice*, 6th ed., (New York: Dushkin/Mc-Graw Hill, 2003).

[9] *Black's Law Dictionary*, op. cit.

[10] *Jewish News Weekly Internet Website*, http://www.jewishsf.com, October 27, 2005.

[11] H. Chapin, *W.O.L.D.*, Story Songs, Ltd, 1973.

Chapter 8

[1] W. H. Morton, "Commentary on Joshua," in *The Broadman Bible Commentary*, Volume 2, C. J. Allen ed. (Nashville: Broadman Press, 1970), pp. 297–376.

[2] G. McConville, "Joshua," in *The Oxford Bible Commentary*, J. Barton and J. Muddiman eds. (New York: Oxford University Press, 2001), pp. 158–176.

[3] A. Barnes, *Barnes' Notes* (Electronic Database 1997 Biblesoft, PC Study Bible CD-ROM) original publication date 1847, London: Blackie and Son.

[4] G. E. Rush, *The Dictionary of Criminal Justice*, 6th ed. (New York: Dushkin/Mc-Graw Hill, 2003).

[5] J. Mackay, *Allan Pinkerton: The First Private Eye* (New York: James Wiley and Sons, 1996).

[6] Nathan Hale. *Encyclopædia Britannica*. March 23, 2006, from Encyclopædia Britannica Online http://search.eb.com/eb/article-9038867.

[7] M. Teague, "Double Bind: The Untold Story of How British Intelligence Infiltrated and Undermined the IRA." *The Atlantic Monthly* 297 no. 3: 53–62 (2006), p. 53.

[8] Ibid., p. 56.

[9] J. D. Pistone and R. Woodley, *Donnie Brasco: My Undercover Life in the Mafia* (New York: Signet, 1996).

[10] W. Queen, *Under and Alone: The True Story of the Undercover Agent Who Infiltrated America's Most Violent Outlaw Motorcycle Gang* (New York: Random House, 2005).

[11] J. M. Pollock, *Ethics in Crime and Justice*, 3rd edition. (Belmont, CA: West/Wadsworth, 1998), p. 189.

[12] S.S. Souryal, *Ethics in Criminal Justice: In Search of the Truth*, 3rd ed. (Cincinnati: Anderson Publishing, 2003).

[13] M. Jones, *Criminal Justice Pioneers in U.S. History* (Boston: Allyn and Bacon, 2004).

[14] S. Bok, *Lying: Moral Choice in Public and Private Life* (New York: Random House, 1979).

[15] Ibid.

Chapter 9

[1] A. M. Dershowitz, *The Genesis of Justice: Ten Stories of Biblical Injustice that Led to the Ten Commandments and Modern Law* (New York: Warner Books, 2000), p. 74.

[2] A. Barnes, *Barnes' Notes*, (Electronic Database 1997 Biblesoft, PC Study Bible CD-ROM), original publication date 1847, London: Blackie and Son.

[3] W. H. Morton, "Commentary on Joshua." *The Broadman Bible Commentary*, Volume 2, C.J. Allen ed. (Nashville, TN: Broadman Press, 1970) pp. 297–376.

[4] A. Ritchie, "The Troubling of Achan." J. S. Exell ed. *The Biblical Illustrator* (Biblesoft, 2002), original publication date 1887, PC Study Bible CD-ROM.

[5] *Black's Law Dictionary*, 6th Ed. (St. Paul, MN: West Publishing, 1990), p.1566.

[6] Ibid., p14.

[7] Ibid.

[8] Ibid., p. 1566; M. Jones, *Criminal Justice Pioneers in U.S. History* (Boston: Allyn & Bacon, 2005).

[9] M. Jones, *Community Corrections* (Prospect Heights, IL: Waveland, 2004).

[10] A. Barnes, *Barnes' Notes* (Electronic Database 1997 Biblesoft, PC Study Bible CD-ROM), original publication date 1847, London: Blackie and Son.

[11] A. Clarke, *Clarke's Commentary* (Nashville, TN: Abingdon Press, 1996. Ages and Biblesoft Electronic Database, 2002 PC Study Bible CD-ROM).

Chapter 10

[1] The Internet Movie Database Web site, http://www.imdb.com/title/tt0078788/ quotes, October 28, 2005.

[2] *Black's Law Dictionary*, 6th Ed. (St. Paul, MN: West Publishing, 1990).

[3] J. R. White, *Defending the Homeland: Domestic Intelligence, Law Enforcement, and Security* (Belmont, CA: Wadsworth Publishing, 2004).

[4] C. L. Van Doren, *A History of Knowledge: Past, Present and Future* (New York: Ballantine Books, 1992.)

[5] "Andersonville." *Encyclopædia Britannica*. 2006. Encyclopædia Britannica Online. 22 July 2006, http://search.eb.com/eb/article-9007449.

[6] *Black's Law Dictionary*, op. cit.

[7] E. M. Rusten and S. Rusten, *The One Year Book of Christian History* (Wheaton, IL: Tyndale, 2003).

Chapter 11

[1] L. Morrow, *Evil: An Investigation* (New York: Basic Books, 2003), p. 17.

[2] The Quotations Page Internet Website, http://www.quotationspage.com, November 6, 2005.

[3] O.C.G.A. § 16-6-19 (2005).

[4] "Experts: Cohabitation Ruling Not N.C.-Wide," *The Associated Press*, July 22, 2006.

[5] *Black's Law Dictionary*, 6th Ed. (St. Paul, MN: West Publishing, 1990), p. 309.

[6] The Quotations Page Internet Website, http://www.quotationspage.com, November 8, 2005.

[7] General Social Survey Internet Website, http://webapp.icpsr.umich.edu/GSS/, April 2, 2006.

[8] J. Bunyan, *The Pilgrim's Progress* (New Kensington, PA: Whitaker House, 1981), original publication date 1684, p. 240.

[9] M. Jones, *Community Corrections* (Prospect Heights, IL: Waveland Press, 2004).

Chapter 12

[1] F. E. Hirsch, "Crime." In the *International Standard Bible Encyclopaedia*, ed. J. Orr (Biblesoft: Electronic Database, PC Study Bible on CD-ROM, 1995), original publication date 1915, Chicago: Howard-Severance Company.

[2] *Black's Law Dictionary*, 6th Ed., (St. Paul, MN: West Publishing, 1990), p. 761.

[3] Ibid.

[4] B. F. Philbeck, Jr., "1 and 2 Samuel." In *The Broadman Bible Commentary, Volume 3* (Nashville, TN: Broadman Press, 1970), pp. 1–145; G. H. Jones, "1 and 2 Samuel." In J. Barton and J. Muddiman (eds.) *The Oxford Bible Commentary* (New York: Oxford University Press, 2001), pp. 196–232.

[5] A. Clarke, *Clarke's Commentary* (Nashville, TN: Abingdon Press, 1996. Ages and Biblesoft Electronic Database, 2002 PC Study Bible CD-ROM). C. F. Keil and F. Delitzsch, (Boston: Hendrickson Publishers, 1996, Electronic Database, PC Study Bible CD-ROM), original publication date, 1866.

[6] R. T. Francoeur, *Becoming a Sexual Person* (New York: Macmillan, 1982).

[7] E. Cole, "Sibling Incest: The Myth of Benign Sibling Incest." *Women & Therapy*, Vol. 1 (1982), pp. 79–89.

[8] M. J. Cyr, P. Wright, McDuff, and A. Perron, "Intrafamilial Sexual Abuse: Brother-Sister Incest Does Not Differ from Father-Daughter and Stepfather-Stepdaughter Incest." *Child Abuse and Neglect, Vol. 26* (2002), pp. 957–973.

[9] D. E. H. Russell, *The Secret Trauma: Incest in the Lives of Girls and Women* (New York: Basic Books, 1986).

[10] M. Laviola, "Effects of Older Brother-Younger Sister Incest: A Study of the Dynamics of 17 Cases." *Child Abuse & Neglect, Vol. 16* (1992), pp. 409–421; J. M. Rudd and S. D. Herzberger, "Brother-Sister Incest/Father-Daughter Incest: A Comparison of Characteristics and Consequences." *Child Abuse & Neglect, Vol. 23* (1999), pp. 915–928.

[11] Sermon Central Internet Website, www.sermoncentral.com, February 18, 2006.

Chapter 13

[1] *Black's Law Dictionary*, 6th Ed. (St. Paul, MN: West Publishing, 1990), p. 1501.

[2] J. Barker, "The Treason Trial of Aaron Burr: America's Would-be Caesar." *Famous American Crimes and Trials: Volume 1: 1607–1859*, F. Y. Bailey and S. Charmak (eds.) (Westport, CN: Praeger Press, 2004), pp. 141–160.

[3] A. J. Twerski, *Addictive Thinking: Understanding Self-Deception*, 2nd ed. (Center City, MN: Hazelden Foundation, 1997), p. 85.

Chapter 14

[1] The Quotations Page Internet Website, http://www.quotationspage.com, January 21, 2006.

[2] M. P. Matheney, Jr., "Commentary on 1 Kings." In *The Broadman Bible Commentary, Volume 3* (Nashville, TN: Broadman Press, 1970), pp. 156–225; W. Dietrich, "1 and 2 Kings." In *The Oxford Bible Commentary* (New York: Oxford University Press, 2001), pp. 232–266.

[3] *Nelson's Illustrated Bible Dictionary* (Hendrickson Publishers, 1996, Biblesoft, PC Study Bible CD-ROM, 2002).

[4] *Black's Law Dictionary*, 6th Ed. (St. Paul, MN: West Publishing, 1990), p. 1159.

[5] Ibid.

[6] *Utah Code Ann.* § 76-7-101 (2005); 568.010 R.S.MO. (2006).

[7] R. S. Van Wagoner, *Mormon Polygamy: A History* (Salt Lake City, UT: Signature Books, 1986).

[8] Ibid.

[9] H. Ryan, "Polygamist Gets 45 Days for Sex with Teen Bride," Cable News Network Internet Website, http://www.cnn.com/2006/LAW/08/03/polygamist.sentenced/index.html, August 3, 2006.

[10] R. S. Van Wagoner, *Mormon Polygamy: A History* (Salt Lake City, UT: Signature Books, 1986

[11] Ibid.

[12] Rusten, E. M. and S. Rusten. *The One Year Book of Christian History* (Wheaton, IL: Tyndale House Publishers, 2003).

[13] *Reynolds v. United States*, 98 U.S. 145, 1879.

[14] *Romer v. Evans*, 517 U.S. 620, 1996.

Chapter 15

[1] A. R. Fausset, *Fausset's Bible Dictionary* (Biblesoft, 1998 PC Study Bible CD-ROM).

[2] Ibid.

[3] J. H. Gaines, "How Bad was Jezebel?" *Bible Review* 16, no. 5, (2000): 13–23.

[4] L. C. Higgs, *Bad Girls of the Bible* (Colorado Springs, CO: Waterbrook Press, 1999).

[5] D. N. Freedman, *The Nine Commandments: Uncovering a Hidden Pattern of Crime and Punishment in the Hebrew Bible* (New York: Doubleday, 2000), p. 140.

[6] D. R. Biddy, *Crime Stories from the Bible* (Indianapolis, IN: First Books, 2002).

[7] D. F. Roberts. "Jezebel." In the *International Standard Bible Encyclopaedia,* ed. J. Orr (Biblesoft: Electronic Database, PC Study Bible on CD-ROM, 1995), original publication date 1915, Chicago: Howard-Severance Company.

[8] G. E. Rush, *The Dictionary of Criminal Justice,* 5th ed. (Guilford, CT: Dushkin/McGraw Hill, 2000).

[9] A. Barnes, *Barnes' Notes* (Electronic Database 1997 Biblesoft, PC Study Bible CD-ROM), original publication date 1847, London: Blackie and Son.

[10] 18 USCS § 1622, 2003.

[11] S. S. Souryal, *Ethics in Criminal Justice: In Search of the Truth,* 2nd ed. (Cincinnati: Anderson Publishing, 1998), p. 221.

Chapter 16

[1] J.L. Green, "Commentary on Jeremiah." C. J. Allen (ed.) *The Broadman Bible Commentary, Volume 6* (Nashville, TN: Broadman Press, 1971), pp. 1–202.

[2] D. R. Biddy, *Crime Stories from the Bible* (Indianapolis: 1st Books, 2002).

[3] *Black's Law Dictionary,* 6th Ed. (St. Paul, MN: West Publishing, 1990), p. 1357.

[4] J. A. Thompson, *The New International Commentary on the Old Testament: The Book of Jeremiah* (Grand Rapids, MI: William B. Eerdmans Publishing, 1980).

[5] Green, op. cit.

[6] E. Gillespie, "The Sedition Trial of John Peter Zenger: The Power of the Printed Word," F. Y. Bailey and S. Chermak (eds.) *Famous American Crimes and Trials* (Westport, CN: Prager Publishers, 2004), pp. 63–82.

[7] W. H. Rehnquist, *All the Laws but One: Civil Liberties during Wartime* (New York: Alfred A. Knopf, 1998).

[8] S. Walker, *Popular Justice: A History of American Criminal Justice,* 2nd ed. (New York: Oxford University Press, 1998).

[9] Rehnquist, op. cit.

[10] M. Jones, *Criminal Justice Pioneers in U.S. History* (Boston: Allyn & Bacon, 2005).

[11] The Quotations Page Internet Website, http://www.quotationspage.com, January 21, 2006.

[12] D. Cooney, "Afghan Man Prosecuted for Converting from Islam to Christianity." *The Associated Press,* March 20, 2006.

[13] The Quotations Page Internet Website, http://www.quotationspage.com, November 8, 2005.

Chapter 17

[1] W. H. Rule, "Daniel and His Enemies." J.S. Exell ed. *The Biblical Illustrator,* Biblesoft, 2002, (original publication date 1887) PC Study Bible CD-ROM.

[2] C. L. Seow, *Daniel* (Louisville, KY: Westminster John Knox Press, 2003).

[3] J. J. Owens, "Commentary on Daniel," C. J. Allen (ed.) *The Broadman Bible Commentary, Volume 6* (Nashville: Broadman Press, 1970), pp. 373–460.

[4] P. L. Redditt, *Daniel: The New Century Bible Commentary* (Sheffield, England: Sheffield Academic Press, 1999).

[5] A. Barnes, *Barnes' Notes* (Electronic Database 1997 Biblesoft, PC Study Bible CD-ROM) original publication date 1847, London: Blackie and Son.

[6] Ibid.

[7] Ibid.

[8] Owens, op. cit. p. 416.

[9] The Quotations Page Internet Website, http://www.quotationspage.com, November 8, 2005.

Chapter 18

[1] R. B. Miller, "John the Baptist," In the *International Standard Bible Encyclopaedia*, ed. J. Orr (Biblesoft: Electronic Database, PC Study Bible on CD-ROM, 1995), original publication date 1915, Chicago: Howard-Severance Company.

[2] M. Grant, *Saint Peter: A Biography* (New York, Scribner, 1994).

[3] C. M. Kerr, "Herodias." In the *International Standard Bible Encyclopaedia*, ed. J. Orr (Biblesoft: Electronic Database, PC Study Bible on CD-ROM, 1995), original publication date 1915, Chicago: Howard-Severance Company.

[4] D. Erickson, Sermon Central.com Internet Website, www.sermoncentral.com, February 19, 2006.

[5] Kerr, op. cit.

[6] *Black's Law Dictionary*, 6th Ed., (St. Paul, MN: West Publishing, 1990), p. 1357.

[7] Ibid.

[8] Ibid.

[9] S. L. Carter, *God's Name in Vain: The Wrongs and Rights of Religion in Politics* (New York: Basic Books, 2000), p 19.

[10] Ibid.

[11] S. Walker, *Sense and Nonsense about Crime and Drugs: A Policy Guide*, 6th ed. (Belmont, CA: Thomson Publishing, 2004), p. 21.

Chapter 19

[1] A. R. Fausset, *Fausset's Bible Dictionary* (Biblesoft, 1998 PC Study Bible CD-ROM).

[2] Ibid.

[3] *Nelson's Illustrated Bible Dictionary* (Hendrickson Publishers, 1996, Biblesoft, PC Study Bible CD-ROM, 2002).

[4] T. H. Gaster, "Samaritans." *Interpreter's Dictionary of the Bible* (Nashville, TN: Abindgon Press, 1962), *New Interpreter's Study Bible* (CD ROM, Abingdon Press, 2003).

[5] High Beam Encyclopedia Web Site, www.encyclopedia.com, March 20, 2005.

[6] A. Barnes, *Barnes' Notes* (Electronic Database 1997 Biblesoft, PC Study Bible CD-ROM), original publication date 1847, London: Blackie and Son.

[7] Maryland Crime Victims Resource Center Internet Web Site, www.mdcrimevictimes.org, March 20, 2005.

[8] A. M. Rosenthal, *Thirty-Eight Witnesses* (New York: McGraw Hill, 1964); W. M. Oliver and J. F. Higenberg, Jr. *A History of Crime and Criminal Justice in America* (Boston: Allyn & Bacon, 2006).

[9] Wis. Stat. § 940.34 (2004).

Chapter 20

[1] C. M. Kerr, "Simon the Canaanite, or Simon the Cananean, or Zealot." In the *International Standard Bible Encyclopaedia,* ed. J. Orr (Biblesoft: Electronic Database, PC Study Bible on CD-ROM, 1995), original publication date 1915, Chicago: Howard-Severance Company.

[2] G. F. Brandon, *Jesus and the Zealots* (New York: Charles Scribner and Sons, 1967).

[3] W. A. Heidel, "Zealot, Zealots." In the *International Standard Bible Encyclopaedia,* ed. J. Orr (Biblesoft: Electronic Database, PC Study Bible on CD-ROM, 1995), original publication date 1915, Chicago: Howard-Severance Company.

[4] *Nelson's Illustrated Bible Dictionary* (Hendrickson Publishers, 1996, Biblesoft, PC Study Bible CD-ROM, 2002).

[5] W. R. Farmer, *Maccabees, Zealots, and Josephus* (New York: Columbia University Press, 1956).

[6] S. F. Hunter, "Assassins." In the *International Standard Bible Encyclopaedia,* ed. J. Orr (Biblesoft: Electronic Database, PC Study Bible on CD-ROM, 1995), original publication date 1915, Chicago: Howard-Severance Company.

[7] S. G. F. Brandon, *Jesus and the Zealots: A Study of the Political Factor in Primitive Christianity* (New York: Charles Scribner's Sons, 1967), p. 34.

[8] J. R. White, *Terrorism and Homeland Security,* 5th ed. (Belmont, CA: Thomson Wadsworth, 2006).

[9] M. Jones, *Criminal Justice Pioneers in U.S. History* (Boston: Allyn & Bacon, 2005).

[10] Pew Global Attitudes Project Internet Web Site, http://pewglobal.org, February 12, 2006.

[11] P. Medhurst, *Global Terrorism* (New York: United Nations Institute for Training and Research, 2002).

[12] National Commission on Terrorist Attacks Upon the United States, *The 9/11 Commission Report* (New York: W.W. Norton and Company, 2004).

[13] M. R. Vincent, *Vincent's Word Studies in the New Testament* (Electronic Database, 1997 Biblesoft, PC Study Bible CD ROM), originally published by Charles Scribner and Sons, New York, 1887.

Chapter 21

[1] *Life Application Bible: New International Version* (Wheaton, IL: Tyndale House Publishers and Grand Rapids, MI: Zondervan Publishing, 1991), p. 1716.

[2] T. Rees, "Barabbas." In the *International Standard Bible Encyclopaedia,* ed. J. Orr (Biblesoft: Electronic Database, PC Study Bible on CD-ROM, 1995), original publication date 1915, Chicago: Howard-Severance Company.

[3] P. Parker, "Barabbas." *Interpreter's Dictionary of the Bible* (Nashville, TN: Abindgon Press, 1962), *New Interpreter's Study Bible* (CD ROM, Abingdon Press, 2003).

[4] C. Darrow, *The Story of My Life* (New York: Grosset and Dunlap, 1932).

[5] F. Stagg, "Commentary on Matthew." C. J. Allen (ed.) *The Broadman Bible Commentary, Volume 6* (Nashville: Broadman Press, 1970), pp. 61–253.

[6] S. Kramer, Director *Judgment at Nuremberg,* MGM Studios, 1961.

Chapter 22

[1] *Nelson's Illustrated Bible Dictionary* (Hendrickson Publishers, 1996, Biblesoft, PC Study Bible CD-ROM, 2002).

[2] T. Rees, "Blasphemy." In the *International Standard Bible Encyclopaedia,* ed. J. Orr (Biblesoft: Electronic Database, PC Study Bible on CD-ROM, 1995), original publication date 1915, Chicago: Howard-Severance Company.

[3] L. W. Levy, *Blasphemy: Verbal Offenses against the Sacred, from Moses to Salman Rushdie* (New York: Alfred A. Knopf, 1993), p. 8.

[4] M. F. Unger, R. K. Harrison (ed.), *The New Unger's Bible Dictionary* (PC Study Bible CD ROM), original publication date 1957, Chicago: Moody Press.

[5] Ibid.

[6] Ibid.

[7] Levy, op. cit., p. 568.

[8] S. S. Souryal, *Ethics in Criminal Justice: In Search of the Truth,* 2nd ed. (Cincinnati: Anderson Publishing, 1998), p. 8.

[9] Levy, op. cit., p. 1.

[10] *Black's Law Dictionary,* 6th Ed. (St. Paul, MN: West Publishing, 1990).

[11] Levy, op. cit.

[12] Ibid.

[13] L. F. Friedman, *Crime and Punishment in American History* (New York, Basic Books, 1992).

[14] *People v. Ruggles,* 1811 N.Y. 124.

[15] MCLS § 750.102 (2006).

[16] ALM GL ch. 272, § 36, (2004).

[17] Miss. Code Ann. § 97-29-45 (2006).

Chapter 23

[1] B. S. Easton, "Thief." In the *International Standard Bible Encyclopaedia,* ed. J. Orr (Biblesoft: Electronic Database, PC Study Bible on CD-ROM, 1995), original publication date 1915, Chicago: Howard-Severance Company.

[2] S. G. F. Brandon, *Jesus and the Zealots: A Study of the Political Factor in Primitive Christianity* (New York: Scribner and Sons, 1967).

[3] A. Barnes, *Barnes' Notes* (Electronic Database 1997 Biblesoft, PC Study Bible CD-ROM), original publication date 1847, London: Blackie and Son.

[4] 356 U.S. 86, 1958.

[5] 391 U.S. 510, 1968.

[6] *Roper v. Simmons,* 543 U.S. 551, 2005.

[7] M. O. Tolbert, "Commentary on Luke,"C. J. Allen (ed.) *The Broadman Bible Commentary, Volume 9* (Nashville: Broadman Press, 1970), pp. 1–188.

[8] F. T. Zugibe, *The Crucifixion of Jesus: A Forensic Inquiry* (New York: M. Evans and Company, 2005).

[9] L. M. Friedman, *Crime and Punishment in American History* (New York: Basic Books, 1992).

[10] S. Walker, *Popular Justice: A History of American Criminal Justice,* 2nd ed. (New York: Oxford University Press, 1998).

[11] Focus on the Family, Pure Intimacy Internet Website, http://www.pureintimacy.org, October 29, 2005.

Chapter 24

[1] A. R. Fausset, *Fausset's Bible Dictionary* (Biblesoft, 1998 PC Study Bible CD-ROM).

[2] L. Alexander, "Acts." Eds. J. Barton and J. Muddiman *The Oxford Bible Commentary* (New York: Oxford University Press, 2001), p. 1028, 1061.

[3] T. C. Smith, "Commentary on Acts." Ed. C. J. Allen *The Broadman Bible Commentary, Volume 10* (Nashville: Broadman Press, 1970), pp. 1–152.

[4] American National Biography Internet Website, www.anb.org, October 29, 2005.

[5] C. D. Phillips, "Exploring Relations Among Forms of Social Control: The Lynching and Execution of Blacks in North Carolina, 1889–1918." *Law and Society Review* 21 no. 3 (1987): 361–374.

[6] L. M. Friedman, *Crime and Punishment in American History* (New York: Basic Books, 1992).

[7] J. L. Massey and M. A. Myers, "Patterns of Repressive Social Control in Post-Reconstruction Georgia, 1882–1935." *Social Forces* 68 no. 2 (1989): 458–488; L. M. Friedman, op. cit.

[8] L. M. Friedman, op. cit.

[9] L. Dinnerstein, *The Leo Frank Case* (Athens, GA: University of Georgia Press, 1999).

Chapter 25

[1] T. L. Donaldson, "Introduction to the Pauline Corpus." Eds. J. Barton and J. Muddiman *The Oxford Bible Commentary* (New York: Oxford University), p. 1062.

[2] E. Rivkin, "Pharisees." *Interpreter's Dictionary of the Bible* (Nashville, TN: Abindgon Press, 1962), *New Interpreter's Study Bible* (CD ROM, Abingdon Press, 2003).

[3] M. Greenberg, "Prison." *Interpreter's Dictionary of the Bible* (Nashville, TN: Abindgon Press, 1962), *New Interpreter's Study Bible* (CD ROM, Abingdon Press, 2003).

[4] J. Bunyan, *The Pilgrim's Progress* (New Kensington, PA: Whitaker House, 1981), original publication date 1684.

[5] M. L. King, Jr., "Letter from Birmingham City Jail." W. J. Bennett, Ed., *The Book of Virtues: A Treasury of Great Moral Stories* (New York: Simon and Schuster, 1993), p. 258.

[6] E. Michael Rusten and S. Rusten, *One Year Book of Christian History* (Wheaton, IL: Tyndale House Publishers, 2003.

[7] Ibid.

About the Author

Mark Jones has been a professor of criminal justice at East Carolina University in Greenville, North Carolina since 1993. He teaches undergraduate and graduate courses on numerous criminal justice topics, including organized crime, probation and parole, terrorism, and criminal justice history.

In 2006 Jones traveled to Israel, where he participated as an academic fellow in the Foundation of Defense of Democracies' program on terrorism. Jones regularly conducts training sessions for correctional professionals and police officers, primarily on ethics. He has authored dozens of articles, book chapters, and book reviews in academic journals and magazines for criminal justice practitioners, made hundreds of presentations at academic conferences, and written two college textbooks: a comprehensive text on probation and parole entitled *Community Corrections*, and *Criminal Justice Pioneers in U.S. History*, a one-of-a-kind compilation of short biographies of important criminal justice figures in American history.

In *Criminals of the Bible: Twenty-Five Case Studies of Biblical Outlaws*, Jones blends his expertise in the field of criminal justice, honed by more than twenty years of study and teaching, with his lifelong love and devotion to the Bible

A native of Griffin, Georgia, Jones received a B.S. in Recreation and Leisure Studies from the University of Georgia in 1982, which led to his employment as a Recreation Supervisor at Lee Correctional Institute, a men's prison, in Leesburg, Georgia. In 1983, he took a job as an adult probation officer for the Georgia Department of Corrections and began studying for his M.S. degree in Criminal Justice from Georgia State University. He began teaching college courses in 1987 as an adjunct instructor for Mercer University. In 1989, Mark and wife Donna, along with their 1-year-old son, Sam, moved to Huntsville, Texas so that Mark could work toward his Ph.D. degree in criminal justice from Sam Houston State University. While a student and part-time instructor at Sam Houston State, daughter Beth was born. Now he and his family live in Winterville, North Carolina. They are members of The Memorial Baptist Church in Greenville.